Praise for *Glow Kids*

"Read this book. Save our children's brains, now. *Glow Kids* is not a Chicken Little, 'The sky is falling' squawk of senseless panic. It is a clearly stated, brain science- and valid study–packed, well-reasoned call to action against one of the most destructive threats to our children—and society—of all time. Every parent, educator, therapist, doctor, caregiver, and legislator needs to read it and follow Dr. Kardaras's marching orders before we do any further damage to the brains of an entire generation."

—Paula Poundstone, comedian, author,
social commentator, Screen-Free Kids activist

"Kardaras reminds us that technology can insidiously and unpredictably turn against us. *Glow Kids* is a paradigm-shifting, mind-bending account of excess and tragedy that should serve as a clarion call to rethink our ever evolving relationship with advancing technology."

—Dr. Howard J. Shaffer, associate professor of psychiatry
at Harvard Medical School, director of the Division
of Addiction at Cambridge Health Alliance

"Every parent and teacher and those who work with youth should read this book to be informed about the downside of what many of us have seen as a tremendous advancement in civilization." —*New York Journal of Books*

"Details how compulsive technology usage and reliance on screens can neurologically damage the developing brain of a child the same way that drug addiction can." —*Vice*

"*Glow Kids* is a must-read for parents, prospective parents, educators, and anyone interested in learning about how the screens we look at every day affect us." —Dan's Papers

"Groundbreaking . . . Examines the detrimental effects of technology addiction on the developing brains of young children." —*The Fix*

"Kardaras's eye-opening study is sure to spark discussions among parents and educators."
—*Booklist*

"In this important new book, Nick Kardaras draws our attention to a growing problem—the addiction many children are developing to digital media. Drawing on extensive research and his experience as a therapist, Kardaras warns us of the dangers we are exposing many of our children to, and what can be done to address it. For parents, educators, and anyone who wants to ensure that this generation of children will have the opportunity to grow up to become healthy adults, this book is an invaluable resource and a wake-up call about the risks they face when we allow unfettered access to 'screen time.'"
—Pedro A. Noguera, Ph.D., Distinguished Professor of Education at UCLA, former tenured professor at Harvard's School of Education and NYU's Steinhardt School of Education, author of *City Schools and the American Dream,* and a regular commentator on educational issues on CNN, MSNBC, and NPR

"I love this book! It lays out for us the uncomfortable truth about the ways in which the economic interests of the tech industry are often at odds with the needs of our children. This is a must-read for everyone."
—Hilarie Cash, Ph.D., cofounder and executive director of reSTART (first tech-addiction rehab in the United States), coauthor of *Video Games & Your Kids: How Parents Stay in Control*

"In *Glow Kids,* Dr. Kardaras makes a compelling case that screens are the drug of the new millennium and that kids are being manipulated by companies that care more about profit than about our kids' minds."
—Touré, cultural critic, author, and former cohost of MSNBC's *The Cycle*

"*Glow Kids* uncovers the various players—both the obvious and not so obvious—contributing to the growing problem of tech addiction and screen-related mental health issues. With the rigor of an investigative journalist and the insight of an addiction specialist, Kardaras manages to make a complex and uncomfortable topic both palatable and accessible. A highly recommended read." —Victoria Dunckley, M.D., integrative child psychiatrist and author of *Reset Your Child's Brain*

"The horrifying truth of digital media addictions . . . Dr. Nicholas Kardaras combines his clinical experience working with patients addicted to digital media, peer-reviewed research, and clinical acumen to compile a critical book all must read. The mental health of the current generation depends on what society does with this information in regards to digital media addictions and the ramifications to neurological development in children. The developmental trajectory of digital media–addicted kids are dismal and affects millions of kids in the United States. We can no longer sit idle and must take action!" —Commander Dr. Andrew Doan, M.D., Ph.D., head of the Department of Mental Health Addictions & Resilience Research, Department of the Navy/U.S. Pentagon, and author of *Hooked on Games*

GLOW KIDS

GLOW KIDS

HOW SCREEN ADDICTION
IS HIJACKING OUR KIDS—
AND HOW TO BREAK THE TRANCE

NICHOLAS KARDARAS, PH.D.

St. Martin's Griffin
New York

www.stmartins.com

Design by Letra Libre, Inc.

The Library of Congress has cataloged the hardcover edition as follows:

Kardaras, Nicholas, 1964– author.
   Glow kids : how screen addiction is hijacking our kids—and how to break the trance / Nicholas Kardaras, Ph.D.—First edition.
         p. cm.
   Includes bibliographical references and index.
   ISBN 978-1-250-09799-6 (hardcover)
   ISBN 978-1-250-09800-9 (ebook)
1. Internet addiction in adolescence.   2. Internet and teenagers.   I. Title.
   RJ506.I58 K37 2016
   616.85'8400835   2016018420

ISBN 978-1-250-14655-7 (trade paperback)

Our books may be purchased in bulk for promotional, educational, or business use. Please contact your local bookseller or the Macmillan Corporate and Premium Sales Department at 1-800-221-7945, extension 5442, or by email at MacmillanSpecial Markets@macmillan.com.

First St. Martin's Griffin Edition: September 2017

13

In almost every house we've been,

We've watched them gaping at the screen.

They sit and stare and stare and sit

. . .

Until they're hypnotized by it,

But did you ever stop to think,

(What) This does to your beloved tot?

IT ROTS THE SENSES IN THE HEAD!

IT KILLS IMAGINATION DEAD!

. . .

IT MAKES A CHILD SO DULL AND BLIND

HE CANNOT THINK HE ONLY SEES!

—Roald Dahl

Excerpt from the Mike Teavee poem from

Charlie and the Chocolate Factory

as sung by the Oompa-Loompas

CONTENTS

ACKNOWLEDGMENTS

THIS BOOK WAS THE CULMINATION OF MANY YEARS OF CLINICAL work, research and cultural insights. None of which happened in a vacuum. Throughout the process, I had the love and wisdom of my wonderful wife, Luz, an elementary schoolteacher who was not only an invaluable resource on this topic but my constant supporter, friend and inspiration.

I began to realize how important this topic was, first as a result of my clinical work with kids, then in my role as a father to two young, amazing boys, Ari and Alexi. I can't say that I'm always a perfect parent, but I have tried my best to teach them the important things in life: love, a sense of awe about the world, compassion for others and a sense of self-reliance. I have also tried my best to let them know that kids with glowing faces tend to lose some of those things.

My son came into my office late one night as I was in front of my computer working on the book and asked me what I was writing about. "I'm writing about how glowing screens can be bad for you." He then wisely said: "Then why are you in front of one writing your book?"

The irony was not lost on me.

But writing this book has felt, I admit, like a very important mission. I feel that it's critical to get all of the important information and research out there so that we can at least stem the tide of the Glow Kids epidemic.

I am grateful to my literary agent, Adam Chromy, who saw the vision for this book and helped me to shape it in a way that my editor, Karen Wolny, found compelling. Karen "got it" from our first call together, and I'm honored to work with such a great team. I also need to thank my parents; although not a Glow Kid, I wasn't the easiest son in the world. Their resilient and unconditional love has profoundly shaped who I am. Finally, a sincere thanks to everyone who is not mentioned here but who also helped me along the way to fight the good fight. Thank you all.

PREFACE TO THE PAPERBACK EDITION

MOLLY RINGWALD, THE BELOVED TEEN MOVIE QUEEN OF THE '80s, recently told Manhattan's York Prep graduating seniors during their commencement that any remake of her iconic high school film *The Breakfast Club* would "just be teens on their phones for two and a half hours."

A sign of the times, many might say; just the way things are these days with these darn kids! But what we are seeing is that the screen revolution—social media, video games, iPads, apps, smartphones—is more than just "the next thing" in media or technology. As I explained when *Glow Kids* came out in August 2016, there is a growing and compelling mountain of clinical and neurological research showing that these devices are harming kids in ways that parents never anticipated.

What *I* hadn't anticipated when the book was first published was the overwhelming response that I would get from parents and young people who shared their horror stories of tech addiction with me. Many thanked me for finally identifying the real and present danger that had been destroying their families after having been ignored or, worse, ridiculed, by people—friends, therapists, spouses, teachers, psychiatrists—who failed to appreciate or understand the potential for adverse effects related to excessive screen time.

Of the hundreds of emails that I received, many described good kids who had become hooked on their devices and became aggressive and often violent when their parents attempted to cut back or limit their screen time.

One mother in Marin County described how her once-happy surfing and nature-loving 9-year-old who had become horribly addicted to video games "beat the sh-- out of me." He had attacked her with a "dazed look on his face—his eyes were not his." Afraid, she called the police; when they arrived, they were so shocked by his wild state, they asked what drugs the boy was on.

What they didn't understand was that the drug that had altered that 9-year-old boy wasn't pharmaceutical, but digital—and that his drug dealer had been his school, which gave him a tablet in first grade so he could play "edu-games," after which the boy became hooked.

Other parents described hospitalizations and visits to psychiatric emergency rooms because their once-sweet children had become so transformed by their screen or social media addiction that they had threatened to kill themselves—or hurt others—if or when their devices were taken away.

After publication, I wrote about some of these cases and the drug-like effects of screens on kids in two *New York Post* editorials: "Digital Heroin" (8/27/16) and "Kids Turn Violent as Parents Battle 'Digital Heroin' Addiction" (12/17/16). Those articles hit a nerve and went viral with more than four million views and shares. The term "digital heroin" entered the popular culture, and I appeared on several national television shows explaining the parallels between drug and screen addiction.

Yes, we can all laugh when Molly Ringwald talks about a *Breakfast Club* remake being entirely teens on their phones, but the negative impact of screens are real and they are significant. Not only have we undergone a seismic shift as a society in the last fifteen years—where we have changed the ways that we communicate, the ways that we think, the ways that we process information—but we have become entirely dependent on our devices as our interpersonal skills, memory, attention spans, cognitive abilities, and mood and mental health have all atrophied and deteriorated as a result of our beloved screen time.

How bad has the problem become?

Let me share with you an email I received from the U.S. Air Force. It was from the clinical director of the Air Force Family Program, a division of the Air Force Medical Operations Agency, asking me to speak at their annual gathering of mental health providers—a gathering of more than 350 psychologists, social workers, and nurses who treat Air Force families. And why would they want the *Glow Kids* and "Digital Heroin" author to address their mental health providers? Even I was shocked at what that email said:

"We have seen increased issues with gaming addictions in the (military) parents of young children and we have seen 5 cases where infants died as a result of physical abuse or neglect related to parents' constant gaming."

I was speechless. I knew from my friend and colleague Navy Commander Dr. Andrew Doan (whom I interview in *Glow Kids*) that young soldiers were gaming in record numbers. He told me that if I went to any barracks in the United States or around the world, I'd find many young soldiers escaping the horrors of PTSD or the boredom of military life through their video games. Because of frequent drug testing, video games had now become the new drug of choice for today's soldier.

But had it really become so bad that babies of military families were *dying* because of their parent's video gaming addiction? How come we hadn't heard about this in the news? I emailed back and asked for more information about this horrible statistic. The response was even more shocking— the problem was so significant that the Department of Defense (DoD) had created a new protocol to track child deaths related to what they termed "electronic distractions":

"I chair the Air Force Domestic Violence and Child Maltreatment Fatality Review Board. That is why I am aware of these gaming addiction-related fatalities. All of DoD is now, beginning this year, to track child deaths that have been identified for 'electronic distractions.'"

The email went on to further elaborate on the problem:

"If you google 'Stinky Airmen come from stinky houses' you might see an interview I did where we identified airmen with personal hygiene issues who are a red flag for gaming addictions as they don't take care of the house, themselves, the kids or even the pets when they are gaming. They don't even stop to go to the bathroom, they drink power drinks then they urinate in the bottles and they are lined up under the TV they are gaming on."

The fact that the problem was so severe in a place as disciplined and supported as the military was something I hadn't expected. Indeed, as the letter further explained:

"Our military families are some of the most healthy and resilient in the world. However, we have child maltreatment in the military, but it's only about half of the rate of child maltreatment among civilians in the United States. This should be no surprise to anyone because in the military there are fewer risk factors for child maltreatment (i.e., everyone has a job, no one is homeless, military people are generally not addicted to substances and are high-functioning individuals.)"

And yet, still, with all of that resilience, health, and support, some trained soldiers were becoming so addicted to video games that their babies were being neglected to the point of dying. So I ask: what chance does an *untrained* and *undisciplined* 17-year-old video gamer have? Or, worse, the 7-year-old whose parents were told that their games were educational and weren't warned about their addicting potential?

As you'll read about in this book, the addictive potential of video games is NOT an accident. I describe the multibillion-dollar gaming industry and their concerted efforts via behavioral psychologists and certain specific dopamine "hooks" built into the games to purposely make games addicting, in order to hook children at a young age—and hook them for life.

Since then, two prominent national TV news shows have done exposés on just that, as they interviewed video game and app designer "insiders." Both CBS's *60 Minutes* and ABC's *20/20* (a show in which I participated) pulled back the veil and candidly exposed the insidious and manipulative practices aimed at our youngest and most vulnerable.

During the *60 Minutes* piece ("Brain Hacking" 4/9/17), Anderson Cooper interviewed former Google product manager Tristan Harris, who told him, "Silicon Valley is intentionally engineering your phone, apps, and social media to get you hooked." He further explained how this addicting process works: "There's a whole playbook of techniques that used to get you using the product for as long as possible . . . every time I check my phone, I'm playing the slot machine to see, 'What did I get?' This is one way to hijack people's minds and create a habit."

In that same segment, Ramsey Brown, a computer programmer who is cofounder of the aptly named Dopamine Labs, a company that writes computer codes for apps, was even more blunt when asked by Anderson Cooper if these software developers were perhaps using an "addiction code":

"Yeah, that is the case. That since we've figured out, to some extent, how these pieces of the brain that handle addiction are working, people have figured out how to juice them further and how to bake that information into apps."

In the end, the full extent of how so few are manipulating so many was summed up by Google alum Tristan Harris: "Look, never before in history have a handful of people at a handful of technology companies shaped how a billion people think and feel every day with the choices they make about these screens."

And make no mistake: society is being reshaped. Beyond the clinical, social, and neurological impacts already discussed, we've seen a new socio-economic "failure to launch" phenomenon that was highlighted in an article in *The Economist* by Ryan Avent (April/May 2017) titled "Escape to Another World." There he cites the statistics of a shrinking young-adult workforce that seems to be substituting time that had traditionally been devoted to work to the escapist pleasures of video gaming. The sad reality is that as video games have become more realistic worlds of escape, young men with poor job prospects are checking out of the labor force in order to game.

Indeed, according to University of Chicago economist Erik Hurst, the "failure to launch" Millennial generation is not getting married, are increasingly living with their parents and are working less and less. According to Hurst, as the hours young men spent in work dropped in the 2000s, the hours spent in leisure activities rose nearly one-for-one, with video games accounting for 75 percent of that increased leisure time.

At the other end of the age spectrum, infants are also being profoundly adversely impacted by screens. In addition to ADHD and other clinical effects that I document in *Glow Kids,* there are developmental impacts as well. Shockingly, according to Britain's Association of Teachers and Lecturers (ATL), infants raised from birth on screen devices were "unable to use toy building blocks due to iPad addiction." Think about that. What used to be a developmental childhood rite of passage has now gone the way of the Edsel.

Addressing the 2014 ATL annual conference in Manchester, Colin Kinney, a teacher from Northern Ireland, said: "I have spoken to a number of nursery teachers who have concerns over the increasing numbers of young pupils who can swipe a screen but have little or no manipulative skills to play with building blocks or the like, or the pupils who cannot socialize with other pupils but whose parents talk proudly of their ability to use a tablet or smartphone."

My own wife, a former kindergarten teacher, has told me of children in her class who would "phantom swipe" at non-screen objects. One young student standing in front of a colorful fish on a field trip to the local aquarium kept swiping at the glass hoping to get a new fish to appear.

A seemingly depressing state of affairs. Where do we go from here? Can we un-ring the screen-effects bell? Unlikely. Technology, barring any dystopian Armageddon scenario, is probably here to stay. But not all parents are drinking the screens-are-wonderful Kool-Aid—some are fighting back.

Cindy Eckard, a mother of two, had launched a dynamic grassroots campaign to create legislation to limit screen time in schools in her home state of Maryland: "I was shocked to learn that the Maryland State Department of Education had no medically sound health guidelines in place before they put so many of our children in front of a computer every day. . . . The schools keep encouraging more screen time in the classroom without any regard for our children's well-being," Cindy told me. "Our children are owed a safe classroom environment, and right now they're not getting one."

She was able to get state legislators to draft the Maryland classroom digital device safety legislation, also known as HB866/SB1089—the country's first legislative effort to limit screens in schools. The bill had the support of Maryland State Medical Society and of the American Academy of Pediatrics Maryland Chapter.

Unfortunately, after a yeoman's effort on Cindy's part, the bill was voted down by the Maryland Senate Education, Health and Environmental Affairs Committee (EHEA). But the fight in Maryland continues—and Cindy has created the blueprint for other parents in other states to get involved politically to enact legislation to protect our kids.

Still other parents are fighting back in different ways. Longtime educator Debra Lambrecht created a new tech-free school model called the Caulbridge School, a distinctly "Finnish-style" school intended to serve as a template for future schools throughout the country.

"The argument for technology in the earlier grades is often rooted in the fear of children falling behind. It is true that most children will use technology in their jobs and everyday life. It is also true that most children will learn to drive a car," Debra told me. "Certainly we would not give a 7-year-old child the car keys to give them a jump-start to be a more skillful driver. In the same way, we want to ensure children can effectively use technology as a tool and will bring all of their best thinking, creativity, and innovation to bear."

What can the individual parent do? The one most important suggestion that I can give is to delay, as much as possible, your child's exposure to individual screen devices. Your children *will* be tech savvy; you needn't worry about that. But if you wait until they are at least 10 years old before you unleash the technology hounds, your little ones will be further along developmentally and better equipped to handle our amazing little screen marvels.

In the meantime, let your kids be kids—the way that nature and evolution had intended them to develop: let them play, explore, create, use their imagination, and just watch the miracles of their developing minds unfold. And very importantly: allow them the opportunity to be bored. There is no better master for innate creativity than a child compelled to entertain themselves. If at all possible, don't fall into the trap of feeling obligated to keep your little ones perpetually entertained. You will do more harm than good.

Finally, from the "fighting fire with fire" department, there have been some interesting developments in technology that can allow parents to regain control of their children's screen usage. I have been helping a new company called Zen Labs to create an app called Zen Screen that allows parents to control what their children access by using intelligent software and algorithms that can be set by parents to shut down certain apps (i.e., Snapchat or Facebook) after a predetermined number of usages. For example, after three views on Facebook, the app can then shut down Facebook. Or it can be set by time periods, disabling both tablets and phones at the parent's discretion.

Technology—yes. But technology that can be a practical tool in the fight against children's unfettered screen usage. In all of the talks that I have given around the country, that is the number one question that I'm always asked by parents—is there a practical tool that I can use to control my kid's screen time? Now there is.

We are all in strange new uncharted territory. This book will introduce you to the relevant research and information about our ubiquitous glowing screens. Your child will most likely have to be tech savvy and digitally versed—but they don't have to be Glow Kids.

GLOW
KIDS

INTRODUCTION

THE TROUBLE WITH TECH

CAPTAIN KIRK WAS *THE MAN*.

At least that's what I thought as an impressionable fifth-grader back in 1974. Watching *Star Trek* re-runs, I'd fantasize about being on the bridge with badass Captain Kirk and cool Mr. Spock, traveling to worlds *where no man had gone before;* heading at warp speed to exotic planets and confidently seducing green women—what more could a red-blooded young boy want?

Then there was all of that cool tech! That communicator that he'd so suavely flip open and command, "Beam me up, Scotty." Desperate to be one of his crew, I made hundreds of paper versions of that flip phone communicator while I was supposed to be paying attention to my teacher, Mrs. Legheart, as she droned on and on about the Pilgrims or fractions or some such . . . but certainly not *anything* as exciting as my *Star Trek*-inspired imagination.

I dreamed of a time when reality could catch up to my science fiction–fueled fantasy, not realizing the wisdom of the old adage "be careful what you wish for." Because, yes indeed, the tech of Kirk is here—but at a very, very high price.

Believe me, I didn't want that to be the case; I wanted—I yearned for—guilt-free tech. Unfortunately, it seems that we, as a society, have entered into a Faustian deal. Yes, we have these amazing handheld marvels of the digital age—tablets and smartphones—miraculous glowing devices that connect people throughout the globe and can literally access the sum of all human knowledge in the palm of our hand.

But what is the price of all this future tech? The psyche and soul of an entire generation. The sad truth is that for the oh-so-satisfying ease, comfort and titillation of these jewels of the modern age, we've unwittingly thrown an entire generation under the virtual bus.

C'mon—aren't you being a bit dramatic? you might ask. But look around you. Look at any restaurant that has families with kids; look at any place where kids and teens hang out—pizzerias, schoolyards, friend's houses—what do you see?

The head-down, glassy-eyed zombification of kids whose faces are illuminated by glowing screens. Like the soulless, expressionless people in *Invasion of the Body Snatchers* or the zombies in *The Walking Dead,* one by one our young people have fallen victim to this digital plague.

I had my first glimpse of this nascent global epidemic back in the summer of 2002 on the island of Crete. My newlywed wife and I had planned a trip to Greece—land of my parents and ancestors—as an escape from a hectic life in New York.

After the usual stops at Mykonos and Santorini, we decided to take the ferry down to the more rugged island of Crete and hike several hours down the ancient Samarian Gorge to the remote coastal village of Loutro. It is a magical place: Stunning, sun-drenched Greek beach with laughing bathers splashing around in the clearest blue water; a beautiful, tranquil place that time forgot . . . There are no cars, no convenience stores, no TV, no flashing lights—just traditional whitewashed houses and a handful of small waterfront inns and their beachfront tavernas.

Loutro is also known as a go-to family destination. The seclusion of the traffic-free village makes it an ideal playground for kids: kayaking, swimming, climbing of rocks, games of tag, leaps into the water—it is a kids' paradise.

During our first day there, after having spent the whole morning at the beach, we stopped by one of the cafés for a frappe. While there, I asked the waiter where the restrooms were and was pointed toward some steep stairs down to a dimly lit, low-ceilinged basement. Once downstairs, I could see an odd glow emanating from a corner in the darkness. Squinting to adjust to the darkened room, I was able to see the light source: it was Loutro's anemic version of an Internet café—two old Apple computers on a tiny table in a corner of the depressing cellar. As I looked closer, I could see the dark silhouettes of two pudgy American kids playing video games with their round faces illuminated by screens just inches away from their faces.

That's odd, I thought; one of the world's most beautiful seascapes, where the local Greek kids were playing from sunup to sundown was just a few feet away, yet these two were holed up in the darkness in the middle of a sunny afternoon.

As I chanced into that café a couple more times over the week that we were there, those two kids were always in that basement with their illuminated faces. Not being a parent myself yet, I didn't think that much about the pudgy kids with the glowing faces and wrote them off, rather judgmentally, I must admit, as probably just the unhealthy children of bad parents.

Yet I never forgot the hypnotized expressions of those boys playing in that horrible cellar while paradise was just over their heads. Slowly, as with the *drip, drip, drip* of a faucet, I began to realize that the hypnotized, glassy-eyed stares were spreading; like a virtual scourge, the Glow Kids were multiplying.

Is this just a harmless indulgence or fad like some sort of digital hula hoop? Some say that glowing screens may even be good for kids—an interactive educational tool.

But the research doesn't bear that out. In fact, there is not one credible research study that shows that a child exposed to more technology earlier in life has better educational outcomes than a tech-free kid; while there is some evidence that screen-exposed kids may have some increased pattern-recognition abilities, there just isn't any research that shows that they become better students or better learners.

Instead, what we do have is a growing mountain of evidence showing that there can be some very significant negative clinical and neurological effects on Glow Kids. Brain-imaging research is showing that glowing screens—like those of iPads—are as stimulating to the brain's pleasure center and as able to increase levels of dopamine (the primary feel-good neurotransmitter) as much as sex does. This brain-orgasm effect is what makes screens so addictive for adults, but even more so for children with still-developing brains that just aren't equipped to handle that level of stimulation.

What's more, an ever-increasing amount of clinical research correlates screen tech with psychiatric disorders like ADHD, addiction, anxiety, depression, increased aggression and even psychosis. Perhaps most shocking of all, recent brain-imaging studies conclusively show that excessive screen exposure can neurologically damage a young person's developing brain in the same way that cocaine addiction can.

That's right—a kid's brain on tech looks like a brain on drugs.

In fact, glowing screens are such a powerful drug that the University of Washington has been using a virtual reality video game to help burn victims with pain management during their treatments. Amazingly, while burn patients are immersed in the game, they experience a pain-reducing, morphine-like analgesic effect and thus don't require any actual narcotics. While this is a wonderful use of screen technology for pain-management medicine, we are also unwittingly giving this digital morphine to kids.

Ironically, while we've declared a so-called War on Drugs, we've allowed this *virtual* drug—which Dr. Peter Whybrow, director of neuroscience at UCLA, calls "electronic cocaine"; which Commander Dr. Andrew Doan, who has an M.D. and Ph.D. in neuroscience and heads addiction research for the U.S. Navy, calls digital "pharmakeia" (Greek for "drug"); and which Chinese researchers call "electronic heroin"—to slip into the homes and classrooms of our youngest and most vulnerable, seemingly oblivious to any negative effects.

Meanwhile, China has identified Internet Addiction Disorder (IAD) as its number-one health crisis, with more than 20 million Internet-addicted teens, and South Korea has opened 400 tech addiction rehab facilities and given every student, teacher and parent a handbook warning them of the potential dangers of screens and technology. Yet here in the United States, clueless and sometimes corrupt school bureaucrats are pushing to put glowing tablets—yes, electronic cocaine—into the hands of every kindergartener.

Why not? Tech in the classroom is big business, estimated to top $60 billion by 2018. Yet what I also discovered as I researched this book is that tech in the classroom is also the story of greed, scandal and FBI investigations.

Even if our schools are letting us down by not protecting kids from the dangers of age-inappropriate tech, surely parents are beginning to see the problems associated with screens? Unfortunately, many caring and well-meaning parents are either simply not tuned in to how damaging screens are, or those who do sense that there may be a problem remain in convenience-induced denial.

After all, it is difficult to hear that something that so many of us have come to love can somehow be bad for us and even worse for our kids. We've become so dependent on the digital babysitter or the so-called virtual learning tool that we don't really want to hear that our handy-dandy smartphones and our wonderful, all-knowing iPads can actually be damaging our kids' brains—say it ain't so!

But like it or not, it is so.

As one of the country's foremost addiction experts, I know addiction when I see it. And I'm seeing it in epidemic proportions in the obsessive video gaming, compulsive texting and hypnotized stares of the kids I treat. Indeed, in the past decade, I've done clinical work with over a thousand teenagers and have noticed the insidious and addictive effect of screens, which has led to a whole host of clinical disorders and a digitally induced adolescent malaise.

Yet as screens glaze children the world over, parents either ignore the problem or just throw up their hands and sigh, "It's just the way kids are today." But kids *haven't* always been this way; it's only been *six years* since the invention of the iPad—and in that blink of time, an entire generation of kids has been psychologically impacted and neurologically rewired.

I'm fully aware that I may get some pushback or even anger from tech lovers and video gamers. But neither this book nor I am anti-tech. Rather, this book is aimed at informing adults who care about the society they live in while also warning and informing parents about the clinical and neurological dangers that excessive screen exposure can have on their *kids*.

I love my tech. I also love driving my car; I just don't think that my eight-year-old twins should be driving it yet. So fret not, video warriors; my focus is tech effects on *children*. I am not here to advocate pulling the plug on those of you past the age of consent. Although you might want to think about getting outdoors a little every now and again. To quote the great William Shatner in his famous *Star Trek* convention parody on *Saturday Night Live* years ago: "Get a life!" And I don't mean a synthetic life or even a Second Life. I mean an honest-to-goodness, walking-outdoors, smelling-the-roses, having-a-girlfriend, feeling-the-grass-under-your-feet sort of life.

Please don't get me wrong; I really do understand the appeal. I'm not just an addiction expert, I'm also a recovering addict—the original masters of escaping reality. Truth be told, even though I have been in recovery from my addiction issues for many, many years, I find it increasingly challenging to maintain a healthy relationship with my seductive little smartphone.

Running a high-end rehab facility and treating many patients, I rationalized that I always need to be available in case of client emergencies. But the reality is that it's hard for me to unplug—even while on vacation. Like the cardiologist who smokes, I realize that I'm not immune to addictive tendencies creeping back into my life. And I'm also left wondering: if I'm having such a hard time managing my tech usage with my fully developed adult brain, with all of my training and addiction recovery work, what chance does an impulsive eight-year-old have?

Whatever we may think about tech usage for adults, a person doesn't need to be an addiction expert or a neuroscientist—or a Luddite—to see the undeniably negative effects of age-inappropriate tech, both in the latest research and in the everyday reality of plugged-in and tuned-out kids.

Yet as smart writers and witty bloggers debate the pros and cons of technology, the ever-increasing ubiquity of tech is doing real damage to kids *now*.

As the late, great Yogi would say, *it's getting late early*.

—*NK*
January 2016
Sag Harbor, NY

ONE

INVASION OF THE GLOW KIDS

LOST IN THE MATRIX

It was almost ten years ago when I had my "Houston, we have a problem" moment. Sure, I had first seen some disconcerting red flags in Greece years earlier, but up until 2007 I was still blissfully unaware of the severity of the problem; I hadn't yet fully grasped just how neurologically damaging and addicting hypnotic glowing screens could be for kids.

All of that changed one cool afternoon in October of that year. I thought that I knew a lot about addiction—after all, I taught the subject at a major university, was a professor of neuroscience on the doctoral level and specialized in the treatment of addiction in my clinical practice. So I had seen all of the various flavors of addiction—or so I thought.

I also thought that I had seen everything when it came to working with young people. As the mental health provider at a local high school, I had treated hundreds of teenagers; I'd seen sexually abused kids, drug-addicted students, antisocial teens, gang members, anarchists, pedophiles, schizophrenics, Columbine-style misfits, cutters, obsessive-compulsives and arsonists.* It was all in a day's work.

---

*Author's note: In the interest of medical confidentiality, the names of all of my patients, and any other identifying details about their cases, have been changed.

But I was entirely unprepared for "Dan," a young boy who was referred to me on that fateful day in 2007.

As he walked into my office, he looked dazed and disoriented . . . and terrified. He slowly sat down, nervously fidgeting in the chair across from my desk, constantly jerking his head as he kept fearfully looking around my office.

I asked him if he knew where he was; he didn't answer. He just kept nervously blinking and looking around, his head in perpetual motion.

"Dan, do you know where you are?" I asked once again.

Again, no answer.

After a long, uncomfortable silence, he abruptly looked toward my ceiling lights and squinted, trying to get his bearings. Still blinking hard, he looked down again, his dark brown eyes fixing on mine. His face reflected the terror and confusion of people who see things—sometimes horrible, sometimes mundane—that the rest of us can't. I recognized that frightened look; I had seen it many times in my work with schizophrenics.

Although this pale and greasy-haired 16-year-old high school junior wearing a weathered Metallica T-shirt didn't have any history of mental illness or substance abuse, he'd been sent to my office because he'd been acting very strangely.

I asked him again, more firmly: "Dan, do you know where you are?"

He blinked once more.

Then, finally, he looked straight at me and stammered in a tone of genuine confusion: "Are . . . are . . . we still in the game?"

No, we most certainly were not.

"Dan" was my first encounter—in what would eventually be many—of gaming-induced psychosis (also called Game Transfer Phenomena[1] [GTP] or the "Tetris Effect"[2]), a form of psychotic break that can occur when excessive gaming, often combined with sleep deprivation, blurs the line between what's real and what's fantasy. And, sure enough, Dan had been playing the fantasy game *World of Warcraft*—lovingly called "*WoW* crack" by many of its addicted devotees—for 10 to 12 hours a day and had become lost in the Matrix.

I would discover that *World of Warcraft* is a mythical role-playing game (RPG) that takes place in a fantasy realm called Azeroth and tells the story of the war between two factions, the Alliance and the Horde. Incredibly in-depth, with well-written lore and player-created and -administrated guilds, *WoW* offers a rich fantasy experience with opportunities for social interactions (via voice interface) with other gamers (these player-connected games are known as massively multiplayer online games, or MMOs).

Players become emotionally invested in these worlds, the progression of their characters, and the bonds with their fellow players. Indeed, with over ten million subscribers, *World of Warcraft* is the world's most popular massively multiplayer online role playing game (MMORPG) in the world.

As I sat there trying to assess Dan, I realized that kids getting lost in the fantasy of a video game was new territory for me. Reality blurring has long been the purview of psychedelic drugs; addiction psychologists are used to working with the substance-induced psychosis of LSD, mescaline and angel dust. Yet now it seemed that this new mind bending of the twenty-first century was the byproduct of a *digital* drug.

As Dan sat in my office, he was visibly scared and confused. He suffered from psychiatric symptoms of both derealization (not knowing what's real) and depersonalization (when people feel that they themselves aren't real); his brain had been fried by his complete immersion in his fantasy game.

In my work with psychiatric clients who had these kinds of dissociative experiences, I knew that *grounding techniques* could be helpful. Essentially, you help the client use his or her five senses to feel the immediacy—the physicality—of the present moment. Dan and I tried standing together and making a loud clapping sound; that seemed to help snap him out of his delusion for a moment. I asked him to grab and crumple a piece of paper, which he did.

"Where are we?"

"You're in my office talking to me. Are you still in the game?"

"No, I don't think so . . . but I feel weird . . . like I'm still not in my body."

Dan went on to describe his *WoW*-playing experiences. He was so addicted to *WoW* that he'd play straight through the night and wouldn't eat, sleep or go to the bathroom; when nature called, he'd simply pee in a mason jar next to his computer. I would eventually find out that peeing in jars isn't uncommon for *World of Warcraft* enthusiasts; the addictive gravitational pull of the game is so powerful that they've been known to wear diapers, like deep-space astronauts or long-haul truckers, so as to not miss a moment's playing time.[3]

Then he started to cry. "I'm scared. I don't know what's happening . . . am I going crazy?"

Because his symptoms would briefly get better, then abruptly worsen as flashback images of the game would overwhelm him again, he was sent to a psychiatric emergency room. The poor kid had to spend a month as an inpatient on the psych unit in order to get stabilized with pharmaceutical antipsychotic meds and psychotherapy so that he could eventually retether himself to reality.

While he was in the hospital, I spoke with his mother and asked her about his excessive all-night video game playing. His mother was a single mom with a limited education who worked at the local Walmart; while she was mildly concerned about his vampire-like hours, she was happy that at least he was "safe at home and not running the streets like other kids" when he was holed up in his room playing video games.

When he was released from the hospital, he asked for my help to stay off of the games. I encouraged him to throw all of his video games and gaming devices in the trash and to start reconnecting with things he used to like doing. He had, pre-video games, liked to play basketball in the local playground—I encouraged him to go outside and play again.

About a week later, I received an angry call from his mother.

"Do you know how much money those games and electronics cost that you encouraged him to throw away? Do you?!"

Taken aback, I responded: "Your son was just released from spending a month in a psychiatric hospital with problems that seem to be either directly related to, or at least impacted by, his playing of video games. He may have other underlying problems—we don't know yet—but those games were not helping."

I paused and then tried my best to help her understand that Dan wanted off of the games. "Listen, Mrs. Smith—he asked for help to stay off of those games. *He* asked for help."

I don't shock easily, but I was shocked by her reply: "Yeah, but now he wants to go outside and play! He wants to go to the playground and play basketball! God knows what could happen to him outside!"

Over time, it became clear to me: the video game phenomenon was about kids seeking *something* and parents, albeit misguidedly, thinking that they were keeping their kids *safe* indoors. Or, if they really wanted to feel better about the digital babysitter, believing that video games and screens might even be educational, or enhancing their children's ability to focus, or increasing their hand-eye coordination, or doing whatever else the game packaging might claim.

Unfortunately, since I worked with Dan in 2007, screen culture and video game playing has spread like wildfire. Today, 97 percent of all American children between the ages of 2 and 17 play video games.[4] That's 64 million kids. And those numbers are rising every year.

What's driving that growth—what's so appealing about playing a video game?

Sure, shooter games can create an adrenaline rush, and kids certainly like that; and match-three puzzle games like *Candy Crush* and building-block games with increasing levels like *Minecraft* certainly have their own highly addictive appeal. But what are we to make of the explosion of myth and fantasy games like *World of Warcraft* that appeal to tens of millions of kids? I've come to understand that, for some, the appeal here is much deeper and more fundamental than *just* adrenaline. Indeed, the need for mythical experiences may be hardwired into our human psyche.

The legendary Swiss psychologist Carl Jung and his devotee, the mythologist and writer Joseph Campbell, both wrote extensively about our need for myth and the soul-feeding role of archetypal experiences. On a very deep and human level, we *need* our myths—our creation stories, our hero's journeys, our parables and our morality tales.

Yet, by and large, we have lost that in our modern age. Almost 100 years ago, Jung wrote that the modern world had been "demystified" and was experiencing a "poverty" of meaning[5]; while the advances of science have certainly immeasurably improved our lives with everything from medical cures to useful household gadgets, the iconoclasm of science has also created a meaning void. Science has stripped us of our myths, telling us that there are no gods or demons, no heaven and hell, no Elysian mysteries, no Santa

Claus and no tooth fairy. Indeed, we are told by science that the world is a rather cold, mechanistic place without myth or meaning—the necessary life blood of the human psyche.

In that archetypal desert, myth-starved young people gravitate to fantasy worlds where they can play out the most fundamental of archetypes—the hero's journey. In *The Hero with a Thousand Faces* (1949),[6] Joseph Campbell describes this archetype, which can be found in the myths of every culture: A hero who has to overcome obstacles, pass initiation rites and cross various thresholds to achieve some transformational goal that's the object of his or her quest. In that sense, many of today's mythical fantasy games like *World of Warcraft* are nothing more than digital versions of the hero's journey writ small on a hypnotic glowing screen.

As I worked with hundreds of gamers, it became apparent to me that many of these kids were looking for some sort of deeper connection and a sense of purpose. Alienated and adrift in soulless and institutional high schools, the meaning-starved kid finds purpose in a digital fantasy realm of adventure where there are monsters to slay, competitors to vanquish and prizes to attain; there is a soul-satisfying sense of purpose—and, if the games are played with others, a *shared* sense of purpose.

As I treated and talked to my various young clients, another dynamic also revealed itself: escape. Imagine you're a teenager and just don't feel like you quite fit in. Or you don't like the way that you look or live with a dysfunctional family; or let's say that you feel alone and empty and are often depressed. You hate school and have no real friends. In the cruel dynamics of the adolescent hierarchy and pecking order, you are on the outside looking in—after all, there can be only so many kids sitting at the cool table in the school cafeteria.

Would you escape from that life if you could?

For some, the Matrix does have its appeal.

Sure, there are the old standbys of drugs and alcohol to help ease the discomfort of not fitting in or not feeling comfortable in your own skin. But today kids also have magical fantasy worlds to lose and reinvent themselves in; worlds where they can create strong and powerful majestic personas that get to shoot everyone into oblivion, all while pursuing some noble common goal.

Which would you choose: being on the outside looking in at the cool lunch table or being a magical warlock who can conquer entire worlds?

I had worked with one gaming-addicted 16-year-old boy named "Matthew" who couldn't stop playing *Final Fantasy*. *Final Fantasy*, like *World of Warcraft*, is also a fantasy RPG in which four youths called the Light Warriors each carry one of their world's four elemental orbs, which have been darkened by the four Elemental Fiends. Together, the Light Warriors go on a quest to defeat the evil forces, restore light to the orbs and save their world. It's a boilerplate hero's journey.

I could understand how Matthew became entirely consumed by this game: Matthew was a very sweet, sensitive and soft-spoken young man who lived in a filthy, dilapidated house with disabled parents. His father was a disabled veteran, his mother a homebound, mentally ill woman on disability. Their house was such an unsanitary pigsty that Child Protective Services was frequently at their home. In school, Matthew would be mocked with the nickname "Roach Boy" as, on several occasions, cockroaches literally fell out of his clothing and onto his desk.

No, it wasn't hard to figure out why Matthew preferred to spend most of his waking life as a Light Warrior in *Final Fantasy* rather than as Roach Boy.

But not all kids who become addicted to escape come from such dysfunction. Others come from beautiful homes with loving parents. In some of those cases, the kid isn't necessarily escaping from some terrible external reality; rather, he or she may be escaping intrapsychic demons or discomfort.

"Jonathan" was just such a young man. His mother was a beloved educator at a local school, his father a kind and supportive dad who owned his own business. Always introspective, Jon started having increasingly dark thoughts and began exploring the world of extreme conspiracy theories: 9/11 truthers, Illuminati, One World Order. He began gravitating to a group of goth kids, but eventually even they found his antisocial rantings to be too much. Isolated, he talked of moving into a cabin and getting "off the grid." Instead, he fell into the Matrix, as he too lost himself in *World of Warcraft*.

For the socially better-adjusted, the traps are different. If you *are* lucky enough to be part of the cool lunch table, escaping into a video game may not be as compelling. Sure, it may be fun on a sheer adrenaline level to play some shooter games, but you get to sit at the cool table, so who needs to escape

24/7? Yes, you may not be as into gaming if you're one of the cool kids—but social media, now *that's* another story.

Mean Girls—and Guys—are no longer limited to good old word-of-mouth gossip and verbal put-downs in maintaining the social pecking order; now they have the amplification of Facebook, Instagram, Snapchat, Twitter, Kik, and every other social media site at their disposal to add to their arsenal.

Here's the rub: video games for the alienated kid and social media for the cheerleader are both just as addicting as heroin is to a junkie.[7] With every burst of virtual gunfire, every text and tweet, there is a release—a little squirt—of dopamine, just as surely as cocaine tickles our dopamine neurotransmitters.[8] And, unfortunately, some kids, based on genetics and psychological temperament, may already be predisposed toward addictive personalities and thus might be more vulnerable to getting hooked on these various digital dopamine stimulants.

But I have learned one other very important lesson in my years of working with addiction. Even the "average" person or kid can get hooked—the kid without the lousy home life or internal demons can get trapped by addiction too. Regardless of *why* you do it, if you drink too much or play dopamine-activating video games all day, addiction can suck you in as well.

Surprisingly, digital drugs may be even more insidious and problematic than illicit drugs because we don't have our guard up about them; meanwhile, they're ubiquitous, continuously reinforced and more socially accepted than their reviled powdered counterparts, making them so much more accessible.

You certainly won't find powdered drugs in the classroom, but you'll definitely see tablets, Game Boys and smartphones with all of their addicting and potentially mind-altering effects. Even more disturbingly, the kids getting exposed to these digital drugs are getting younger and younger and younger.

THE TETRIS EFFECT

It's a typical suburban third-grade classroom: art projects on the cinder-block walls; eight-year-olds sitting at their desks in small clusters; an earnest young teacher standing at the front of the classroom.

The kids have just come back from recess, and there's an excited murmur in the class because reading time is about to begin—and that means iPads! The teacher walks over, unlocks the tech cabinet, and asks the kids to line up to get their tablets; there are smiles and giggles as the happy children get their devices. Once back in their seats, they log on to Raz Kids and go to *Animals, Animals,* the e-book where they left off the day before.

"Continue reading at your own pace—and let me know if you have any questions," their teacher soothingly instructs the students, who are all now fully immersed in their tablets. A pigtailed girl uses her finger to read about the humps of camels; a lanky boy sitting closest to the teacher is putting his face close to the screen to look at a photo of a hippopotamus.

Engaged and compliant students; a caring and supportive teacher—the ideal of tech-student-teacher synergy appears to be as promised.

But after a few minutes, a couple of the kids begin to fidget and tap their feet; two boys in one cluster toward the back of the class have switched off Raz Kids and have begun playing *Minecraft.* Fifteen minutes later, as the teacher asks the class to put down their iPads because reading time is over, the two boys are visibly agitated and defiant; the teacher has to move closer to them and repeat her request. While one boy acquiesces, the other remains defiant and shouts, "No, I don't want to!"

The teacher would tell me later: "Usually when I ask them to put away their tablets, a couple of the students always get agitated and defiant. What upsets me is how angry they can get when I ask them to stop; the one boy in particular almost always has an outburst."

Another third-grade teacher had this unsettling experience: "One day when we were doing reading club—out of a regular book—I asked Sam, a sweet and thoughtful boy, what he thought about the passage that we had just read. But he was just staring straight ahead with a vacant look on his face. I was really concerned. When I asked him, 'Sam, what are you thinking about right now?' he said, 'I can't get PlayStation 4 out of my head.'" Yet another shaggy-haired eight-year-old boy in a different class talked about not being able to get the cubes of *Minecraft* out of his mind and seeing them when he woke up in the morning.

Like my *World of Warcraft*-obsessed client Dan, these two boys were also experiencing a milder form of Game Transfer Phenomena, or the Tetris

Effect, a term that's been used to describe a phenomenon in which obsessive video gamers begin to see the shapes and patterns of their games intrusively in their waking thoughts and/or dreams.

The condition is named after the iconic 1980s video game of the same name that involved putting squared "tetrominos" together. After the game was introduced, people started reporting that they were experiencing hallucinations of the cubes or, in other instances, perceiving the real world as being made up of interconnecting shapes that could fit together. Still others reported seeing falling tetrominos on the periphery of their visual field or in their dreams.

But this electronic invasion of the mind has extended way beyond Tetris and squares. Professor Dr. Mark Griffiths and Dr. Angelica Ortiz de Gortari at Nottingham Trent University in Great Britain recently conducted three studies with more than 1,600 video gamers and discovered that they all had, at some point, experienced Game GTP.[9] Their symptoms included involuntary sensations, thoughts, actions and/or reflexes in relation to the video game—sometimes hours or even days after they had stopped playing.

Some reported that they were able to hear sound effects, music and characters' voices; sounds included those of explosions, bullets being fired, sword swipes, screams and even breathing from the game. One gamer reported hearing someone constantly whispering "death" for a few days after he had stopped playing; still others reported seeing images from their games pop up in front of their eyes.

Now, some might say that, well, if I read a book I might also fall asleep and dream of a character, or that maybe I would daydream about some aspect of a television show. That all may be true. But it seems that the intensive and hyperarousing digital imagery of our interactive screens creates more of an invasive and intrusive mental assault on our psyches than do books and television shows.

Participants in the study[10] described being terrified when adjusting to the real world—"I was freaked out when I went outside and trees were round and not square like the videogame I had been playing"—or of being consumed by thoughts of the game: "I cannot stop thinking about *Minecraft*. It's ruining my life." Yet others expressed concerns that they may confuse reality with the game: "It was scary because I would always worry that if I was tired or not paying attention I would by mistake switch over to *Grand Theft Auto IV* mode and drive over cars and people."

Clearly, these are more extreme experiences than just daydreams about a book that one has just read. According to Dr. Griffiths and Dr. de Gortari, their research indicates that some gamers cannot stop thinking about the games, while others display signs of confusing the video games with real life. These are exactly the conditions I had discovered among the gamers I had worked with. According to Dr. de Gortari, this video-game-vs.-real-world confusion can look like psychosis: "This research supports findings of previous studies into Game Transfer Phenomena, which show that video game playing can induce pseudo-hallucinatory-like experiences." While these auditory, visual and tactile hallucinations are usually temporary, in some instances they persist and are recurring.

In addition, as with any drug, the more you take, the worse the outcomes—and digital drugs are no different. Sure enough, the researchers found that excessive video gaming led to a higher likelihood of Game Transfer Phenomena, which, in turn, often led to sleep deprivation, which seemed to amplify the negative GTP effect. It's also important to keep in mind that, while the ages of the study participants ranged from 12 to 56, most were either teenagers or adults—not children. Knowing what we know about the brain and its development, we would anticipate that these negative GTP effects would be magnified in young children.

In addition to the study by Dr. Griffiths and Dr. de Gortari, there is other clinical research pointing toward screens and video games as contributors to psychiatric disorders that present as schizophrenia and/or psychosis. In 2011 researchers at Tel Aviv University published what they believed were the first documented cases of "Internet-related psychosis," indicating that tech was generating "true psychotic phenomena" and that "the spiraling use of the internet and its potential in psychopathology are new consequences of our times."[11]

Dr. Joel Gold, a psychiatrist at New York University (NYU), and his brother Ian, a psychiatry researcher and professor at McGill University, are investigating whether the reality-severing aspects of technology can lead to hallucinations, delusions and genuine psychosis.[12] At Stanford, psychiatrist and author Dr. Elias Aboujaoude is studying whether some digital avatars, popular in games such as *Second Life,* could clinically qualify as forms of alter ego that is often associated with what was formerly known as multiple personality disorder, now known as dissociative identity disorder in the *DSM* (the *Diagnostic and Statistical Manual for Mental Disorders*—otherwise known as the "Bible" of the mental health profession).[13] It's a profound question: do kids who create gaming avatars suffer from a version of multiple personality disorder? Are they becoming digital Sybils?

Not only are hyperarousing screens and video game imagery having a profoundly penetrating and searing effect on young people's psyches and mental health, but they're also affecting the neurobiology of their brains as well.

Aside from several brain-imaging studies that show the parallels between screen addiction and substance addiction, there is also a 2016 brain-imaging study published in the journal *Molecular Psychiatry* in which video games were found to affect the development of microstructural properties of the brain associated with negative psychological outcomes.[14]

The study looked at the brains of 114 video game–playing boys and 126 video game–playing girls. Using diffusion tensor imaging to measure "mean diffusivity" (MD), or microstructural properties of various parts of the brain, the researchers found that "video game playing directly or indirectly disrupts the development of preferable neural systems . . . related to the development of verbal intelligence" and that there was an association between increased video game playing and the delayed development of microstructures in extensive brain regions and of verbal intelligence.

In short, the researchers found that the more video games the kids played, the greater MD in key parts of the brain—and increased MD equates to lower tissue density and a decrease of cellular structures. Not good things.

Evolutionary neurobiological adaptation takes time; we still have essentially the same brains geared for hunting and gathering that our ancestors did. Our brains are simply not designed for the visual hyperstimulation with which recently developed digital technology bombards us. In my work teaching neuropsychology, it is well understood that brain development is a fragile process that can be easily disrupted by both understimulation and overstimulation—such as the overstimulation that the brain of a gamer experiences.

We've now seen research showing that hyperstimulating screen imagery can sear into kids' consciousness and haunt their thoughts and dreams—and now we're seeing that it's actually also "disrupting" their brain development.

And yet the march toward more and more screens in the hands of younger and younger children continues.

ADDICTING KIDS

Clearly, today's digital screens are not the innocuous, rabbit-eared TV screens of yesteryear. While people worried about television's effects, the hypnotic power of immersive and interactive digital screens on young minds is an altogether different animal. In addition to the just-cited studies, other research is indicating a more dopamine-activating—and thus potentially more addicting—effect than TV, as well as an increase in clinical disorders such as ADHD,[15] aggression,[16] mood disorders[17] and, as just discussed, psychosis.

One young mother told me of the time when she walked into her seven-year-old's bedroom in the middle of the night to check on him and was horrified by what she found: he had been playing *Minecraft* and had gone into a trance; he was sitting up in his bed staring wide-eyed, his bloodshot eyes looking into the distance as his glowing iPad lay next to him. Beside herself with panic, she had to shake the boy repeatedly to snap him out of it.

The mother of that boy was a caring and well-educated professional who had sacrificed and done all the right things to make sure that her son received the support and tools he needed to grow into a happy and healthy adult. Distraught, she could not understand how her once-healthy and happy little boy had become so addicted to the game that he wound up in a catatonic stupor.

Sadly, for many children, *Minecraft* and childhood have become synonymous. Indeed, with more than 100 million registered users, *Minecraft* is the best-selling computer game of all time.[18] Designed by the small Swedish software company Mojang—and recently sold to Microsoft for $2.5 billion—the game is hailed for its creative, Lego-like building capabilities.

Showing images of 3D cubes that represent materials like dirt, stone and various valuable ores, the game requires the player to gather these material blocks and use them to build a shelter to survive the night—when all the monsters come out. Once the player finishes a day (20 minutes in real time), he or she repeats the cycle, building more complex shelters and stocking up on vital resources in order to survive.

Yet *Minecraft* is in every way—clinically and neurologically—an addicting drug. *Minecraft* proponents will use the magic buzzword "educational" to deflect any concern but fail to produce any research or evidence that actually show that video games can lead to increased *learning*. Sure, there is some evidence that that video games can increase spatial awareness and pattern recognition—but at what cost?

History is full of examples of new "miracle" fixes that only worsened the problem that they endeavored to cure. Ninth-century Chinese alchemists invented gunpowder as a medicinal elixir that would help achieve immortality; but rather than lengthening life, gunpowder, as we all know, has ended more lives than any other substance ever created. Sigmund Freud believed cocaine was a "magical" drug that could cure depression and morphine addiction—not *cause* its own epidemic addiction; heroin was also initially hailed as a miracle drug when it was invented by the Germans in the 1870s as a "safe and non-addictive" alternative to morphine. We know how that wound up.

Video games in general, and especially video games in the classroom, are a problem. There is research—which we will examine—that shows us that this "educational" cure is indeed a digital drug in sheep's clothing, neurologically and psychologically damaging with only marginal potential benefits not worth the cost—although, of course, the manufacturers would tell us differently. Really, this is no different from 1950s America, when Big Tobacco told us that tobacco is great for you and Joe Camel told kids to puff away—cigarettes are cool and fun!

And just how is *Minecraft* an addicting digital drug?

The ever-increasing and never-ending "limitless possibilities" of the game create a very hypnotic grip on kids. That hypnotic pull along with the stimulating hyperarousing content creates a "dopaminergic" (dopamine-increasing) effect; that dopamine increase becomes the key ingredient in a primordial addiction-forming dynamic.

The most primitive part of our brains—the medulla and cerebellum—cradle our ancient dopamine-reward pathways. And when an action has a feel-good result—like finding food or discovering something new on the

Internet or in a video game—dopamine is released, which feels pleasurable and creates a more-we-get-more-we-want addictive cycle.

In addition, the game also creates the opportunity for novelty, something our brains are hardwired to explore. Dr. Peter Whybrow, UCLA's director of the Institute for Neuroscience and Human Behavior, has called computers and computer games "electronic cocaine" and describes this novelty-seeking addictive dynamic this way: "Our brains are wired for finding immediate reward. With technology, novelty is the reward. You essentially become addicted to novelty."[19]

What also makes *Minecraft* particularly addictive goes beyond the compulsive novelty of Lego-like block building and the dopamine increase; combining archetypal imagery with basic principles of behavioral psychology, Mojang created a game that relies on a system of rewards to keep kids playing. Since the rewards (the ores) are distributed randomly through the "earth," the player never knows which strike of the pickax will find that sought-after gold or diamonds. Just as in casino slot machines, this is known as a variable ratio reward schedule, the most habit-forming and addicting reward schedule—just ask any pensioner who has compulsively gambled away an entire paycheck, one quarter at a time, to the one-armed bandit.

And then there is the hormonal-arousal aspect.

According to Commander Dr. Doan of the U.S. Navy: "Anytime that there's arousal, there can be addiction because it feels good. Research shows that when the brain is stimulated, that arousal mechanism also stimulates the pituitary gland through the hypothalamus. So the hypothalamus-pituitary-adrenal axis (HPA) is also stimulated; that's the adrenaline rush that's essential with gaming. The kids' blood pressure goes up, their palms get sweaty, their pupils constrict—they're all revved up in a state of fight or flight mode. Then there's also the dopamine response in the dopamine-reward pathway which makes the kid want to chase that adrenaline rush again."

And, as any neuroscientist can tell you, adrenaline and dopamine make for a potent and addictive combination.

What we are discovering is that video gaming is perverting an ancient neural-hormonal network. Unlike our ancestors, who were in fight-or-flight adrenal arousal for only brief, acute periods of emergency—like being chased by a lion—today's tech keeps the adrenaline and the fight-or-flight response on perpetual high alert for hour after hour of game play. That constant adrenal stress is not a good thing; the immune system gets compromised, inflammation increases, and cortisol and blood pressure spike. And there are behavioral consequences as well.

According to Dr. Whybrow: "When the stress response is continuously in play, it causes us to become aggressive, hypervigilant, overactive." Dr. Whybrow draws parallels between symptoms of tech addiction and those of clinical mania: rapid speech and excitement over acquiring new things are followed by sleep loss, irritability and depression.

This addictive adrenal arousal is no accident. The video game business is a sophisticated, multibillion-dollar industry devoted entirely to creating addictive products aimed at defenseless kids and young people—like shooting fish in a barrel. According to Dr. Doan, the entire focus of the research and development departments of the gaming industry is to make games as stimulating and arousing to children as possible, because that's what amplifies the addictive effect and sells the most games.

"Gaming companies will hire the best neurobiologists and neuroscientists to hook up electrodes to the test-gamer. If they don't elicit the blood pressure that they shoot for—typically 180 over 120 or 140 within a few minutes of playing, and if they don't show sweating and an increase in their galvanic skin responses, they go back and tweak the game to get that maximum addicting and arousing response that they're looking for," Dr. Doan explains.

Can something so arousing to the brain and nervous system of a child somehow also be educational, as *Minecraft*'s proponents would have us believe?

As Lisa Guernsey, an education and technology journalist, discovered with her own daughters: "I have an acute love-hate relationship with this game [*Minecraft*]. One minute I'm mesmerized by its potential for encouraging children to get creative . . . the next I'm shrieking at my kids and issuing ridiculous threats" as her daughters play compulsively for hours and her eight-year-old proclaims: "I like *Minecraft* better than my homework."[20]

Other parents have become "*Minecraft* widows," lamenting that they have lost their children to the insidious game and have formed support groups with other parents. There's also Minecraft Anonymous, a 12-step program for those whose lives have been swallowed up by the "educational"-yet-habit-forming cubes of the game. As Guernsey warns: "You may rue the day you let this time-sucker into your household."

WHY JOHNNY CAN'T FOCUS

Addictive or not, the video game classroom is coming soon to a school near you. The narrative that the tech companies use is quite simple: kids just don't have the attention span these days for traditional education, so we need to jazz up the educational experience with a bit more stimulation—more bells and whistles and flashing lights to get little Johnny and Suzie to pay attention.

That is the beginning of a vicious and addictive ADHD cycle: the more I stimulate a child, the more I need to keep stimulating that child in order to hold his or her attention. As with a drug addict, tolerance and desensitization develop, and the hyperstimulated child needs ever-increasing levels of visual stimulation to continue to stay engaged.

Let's all do a little experiment. I ask adult readers of this book to watch the most high-speed and intense two-hour action film they can think of—something that really gets the old adrenaline going, maybe one of Liam Neeson's *Taken* movies, let's say. Or to simply take about two hours to surf the Net—rapidly skimming along as many hyperlinks as they can. At the end of those two hours, pick up any one of your favorite books and start reading. Now notice how far you get before your attention begins to wander.

If you're like most of us, you won't get too far. It takes time to calm down a hyperaroused nervous system; you can't just downshift from fifth to first gear.

Now keep in mind that, as an adult, you have a fully developed brain and nervous system; your frontal cortex—which controls your executive functioning, including impulsivity—is fully formed. Your adrenal and nervous systems—fully developed. And your attentional abilities have been hardwired since your childhood.

Yet you *still* have a hard time staying focused after just a couple of hours of intense, rapid scene changes in the movie or the rapid content shifting that occurs while you are surfing. Now imagine if hyperarousing screen stimulation was a condition under which you spent the bulk of your time—like the seven-plus hours a day that kids do. Do you think that there may be a link to the ADHD "epidemic" and the 800 percent increase that we've seen in the last 30 years?[21] Sure enough, research confirms this ADHD-screen connection—originally due to television effects and, more recently, as research has shown, to the amplified adverse attentional effects of interactive screens such as those of iPads.[22]

Now let's also imagine that after your two-hour hyperstimulating experiment, based on your poststimulation attentional drift, it was decided that, hey, maybe you really can't handle thoughtful and deep experiences like reading. Nah, you're a flashing-lights-and bells-and-whistles learner; let's not even bother to give you a book anymore. Sadly, you just don't have the attentional muscle to handle such things. So let's just keep you on a strict diet of Michael Bay smashup films, some *Grand Theft Auto* video games and some superquick hyperlink surfing about the Kardashians.

What do you think would happen to your attentional abilities? Hint: they would atrophy.

Unfortunately, that's exactly what's happening in our educational system. As schools are force-fed by ed tech companies the narrative that kids just do not have the attention span required for traditional learning anymore, they keep increasing the amount of flashing, stimulating lights they throw at students, thus further eroding the children's already compromised attentional abilities by feeding them a high-stimulation diet.

This video-gaming-the-classroom movement has made for some strange bedfellows: educators are now collaborating with game designers—you know, the people who brought us the ultraviolent *Grand Theft Auto* and *Call of Duty*—who are now charged with shaping our kids' classroom experience.

There is big money behind it, too. In addition to the previously mentioned *Minecraft* and Microsoft, the Bill & Melinda Gates Foundation, along with the MacArthur Foundation, has poured millions into GlassLab, a tech company researching video games in the classroom. Not to be outdone in the race to make video game–like classrooms, media mogul Rupert Murdoch pumped hundreds of millions into Amplify, the ed tech company run by Joel Klein, a former New York City schools chancellor, which employed 652 people in its "games" division in Brooklyn.[23]

There, advances like "gaze tracking" and the measurement of pupil dilation were being developed to gauge the cognitive responses of what little Johnny and Suzie are reacting to on the screen. Then a data profile of each child would be created, ostensibly to customize and optimize each child's learning/gaming experience, with the end result being that Big Data—and Rupert Murdoch—would literally know your child's every eye move.

Romper Room and *Mister Roger's Neighborhood* this is not.

Thankfully, Amplify has crashed and burned. Murdoch has sold his interest to Klein, whose company has had massive layoffs.[24] The ed tech profiteers grossly miscalculated in their strategic plan to video-game and tablet-ize the classroom. Unfortunately, there are many other edupreneurs lined up and salivating, ready to participate in what they perceive as an educational technology gold rush.

REAL EXPERIENCES VS. DIGITAL EXPERIENCES

Aside from the unsubstantiated claims that tech leads to better educational outcomes, some tech advocates are even shockingly claiming that immersive games can better present certain *nature* experiences for kids. According to Greg Toppo, author of *The Game Believes in You: How Digital Play Can Make Our Kids Smarter* (2015), 3-D games like *Walden, A Game* can capture the Walden Woods that Henry David Thoreau wrote about in his book—better than the book itself: "As a result, students can gain a better understanding of how Thoreau lived in the woods than they might have by reading the original book."[25]

The irony, of course, is that Thoreau's entire point was to stimulate an engagement with real nature—*not* a virtual copy of a pond in the woods. And here, in a nutshell, is the problem. The digital realm has usurped real-life experiences. Unfortunately, not only do we have a societal problem as we cross over into the Matrix where the simulation becomes preferred to the real world, but from a developmental and pedagogical perspective, we *really* have a problem as kids succumb to that preference, because nature experiences and real-life immersion are an essential part of a healthy developmental process for children.

Unfortunately, the push for virtual classrooms can blur that essential development process; playing a game called *Walden* is *not* the same as walking in the forest by an *actual* pond. As author Richard Louv points out in *Last Child in the Woods*, a kid who is perpetually plugged in and disconnected from nature and the real world can suffer developmentally from what he calls "nature deficit disorder"[26]; similarly, Harvard biologist Edward O. Wilson's "biophilia" theory also affirms that humans suffer when we aren't connected or exposed to nature.[27]

Indeed, a Cornell University study reported that the more nature a child encountered at home—including indoor plants and window views of natural settings—the less he or she was affected by negative stresses.[28] Another study at the New York State College of Human Ecology found that nature exposure led to "profound differences" in children's attentional capacities and that "green spaces may enable children to think more clearly and cope more effectively with life stress."[29]

Sadly, nature has become as rare as a magic unicorn for most kids, as we have had a fundamental shift in our society. For tens of thousands of years, human beings essentially lived either agrarian or hunter-gatherer lifestyles—both nature-based methods of survival. Even up until the early 1900s, 90 percent of the population of North America lived in rural areas. Now more than 90 percent of our society lives in urban areas flooded by the white noise and sensory overload of the information age.[30]

As a result, our technology has outrun our biology. While our society has undergone a seismic shift in the blink of an eye, our biology simply has not been able to evolve and adapt quickly enough. As Michael Gurian, author of *The Minds of Boys,* puts it: "Neurologically, human beings haven't caught up with today's over-stimulating environment, which is why many neuroscientists and psychologists theorize that we are seeing an explosion of developmental and psychiatric disorders."

This concept has parallels to the thrifty gene diabetes hypothesis proposed by Dr. James Neel, a genetics professor at the University of Michigan Medical School. According to the theory, the fat-storing "thrifty gene" developed in humans as an evolutionary adaptation over thousands of years, so that people could survive lean times (a good thing). Unfortunately, our biology has not been able to adapt quickly enough to our new calorie-abundant diets—an abundance that we initially viewed as a wonderful thing, until we discovered that our physiology and genes have not been able to catch up to our "new" way of eating. Thus we've seen an explosion of medical disorders like diabetes, obesity, high-cholesterol and heart disease as byproducts of what was once thought to be a very good and beneficial development—more food.

Similarly, powerful technology—while certainly often beneficial and potentially life-enhancing—is too stimulating and coming at us too fast for our brains—especially kids' brains—to adapt evolutionarily and handle the sensory bombardment. And just as with the thrifty gene diabetes hypothesis, we're now beginning to see the clinical byproducts of our modern digital age—increased ADHD, tech addiction, mood and behavioral disorders, psychosis—all as a result of our new and wondrous screen technologies.

Beyond those clinical disorders, the hyperstimulating and rapid-fire nature of modern screen media—even *nature*-oriented media—makes kids impatient with *real* nature, even when they do get the opportunity to be exposed to it.

According to author and education professor Dr. Lowell Monke: "In my discussions with teachers and parents about the importance of nature in children's lives, one of the most often expressed frustrations is that young people today typically show little patience when they are taken out to a pond or forest. Having been raised on Discovery Channel–type nature programs that compress hundreds of hours of footage into a half hour of exciting video, they expect to see the deer drinking, the fish jumping, the otters playing and the bears growling all at once and with no effort on their part."[31]

Expansive and slow-moving nature just can't hold a candle to the whiz-bang of a video or a video game. Simply put, the digital world creates a space-time compression effect, reducing the big and slow-moving macro real world into a neat and condensed fast-moving digital screen experience. Dr. Monke puts it this way: "Real space is too big, real time is too slow to match the excitement the child experiences watching a video or playing a video game." Who has the patience to read the whole book—nature—when you can get the CliffsNotes via a game?

The developmental and educational benefit can *only* be found, however, in the richness of the real and full experience—not in the more hypnotic digital shortcut. Further, we must ask ourselves what is the educational benefit of something that kids find so compelling—so addicting—that they prefer it to the real thing? According to Monke: "When the simulation becomes preferable to the real, there arises a real question of the simulation's true educational value."

Even the iconic granddaddy of historical nature-themed educational video games, *The Oregon Trail,* has been of dubious educational benefit. With the game's having sold more than 65 million copies since it was developed in the early 1970s and bundled into school computers from the mid-'80s to the mid-2000s, some have argued that it does students a disservice by presenting a pale, reductionistic copy-as-game version of a powerful historical experience.

Instead of activating students' rich imaginations by having them *read* about the hardships and epic struggles of one of the great American migrations—a journey that combined the stunning beauty of untamed nature with the brutal hardships of extreme suffering, freezing weather and life-threatening hunger—educators instead had students play a silly game focused on calculating resources and tallying points. Thus the real meaning of America's epic migration disappears into a two-dimensional who's-got-the-high-score video game.

This reduction of the rich, three-dimensional real world into a flat-albeit-glowing two-dimensional representation robs children of opportunities for multisensory learning. As child psychologist and author Dr. Peter Montminy puts it: "Children are hungrily exploring their world and literally absorbing their surroundings through direct sensory experiences. That is, their 'absorbent minds' are constructing, and being constructed by various multisensory interactions with nature, objects, and people that they can see, hear, touch, taste and hold." All things that are impossible to do in a video game simulation.

Even if a child can't experience something firsthand, then at least when he or she reads about it, the process ignites the child's imagination—another critically important developmental process. But if the child passively views something on a two-dimensional screen, rather than creating his or her own interior imagery of it, the imagery is programmed for them.

Nicholas Negroponte, the founding director of MIT's Media Lab, describes the imagination-enhancing aspects of reading this way: "Interactive multimedia leaves very little to the imagination. Like a Hollywood film, multimedia narrative includes such specific representation that less and less is left to the mind's eye. By contrast, the written word sparks images and evokes metaphors that get much of their meaning from their reader's imagination and experiences. When you read a novel, much of the color, sound and motion come from you."

Aside from having their imaginations dampened and the experience reduced to 2-D, did kids actually *learn* anything about the *Oregon Trail* from
playing the game? When I asked one of my clients, "Eric," a very intelligent yet gaming-addicted 17-year-old high school senior, if he had actually
learned anything while playing *Oregon Trail*—a game that he had played often over many years—he smiled and replied: "I didn't learn anything at all
about the Oregon Trail. The things that it was supposed to be teaching me
were lost in the game." Indeed, Eric's video gaming addiction has led this
inherently bright young man to almost flunk out of high school.

If you search "*Oregon Trail* video game" on YouTube, you'll find a
4-minute-and-46-second how-to-play clip by a young man whose screen
name is NickelsandCrimes; in it, he teaches the viewer the essentials of the
iconic game, which he claims to have grown up on. Before he gives his point-
ers, at 1:05 of the video, he says, tellingly: "But the great thing about this
game is that it's supposed to be this great big educational adventure where
you learned all about the Oregon Trail and how terrible it was for these
people to go through . . . but if you play the right way you won't learn a thing,
so don't worry!"[32]

Yes, don't worry. Our kids won't learn anything. In the new video game
classroom, learning is optional—while entertainment and stimulation are
everything. Buzzwords such as "educational" and "engaging" notwithstand-
ing, what's actually inside our wonderful "educational" screen Trojan Horses
are clinical and developmental disorders.

Worse yet, there is even research indicating that exposure to screen imagery is actually dulling our very senses. According to longitudinal research
conducted by the German Psychological Association (GPA) in association
with the University of Tubingen over a 20-year period, we are shockingly
losing sensory awareness at a rate of 1 percent a year.

This research began in the 1960s after teachers working at the university noticed that, after the proliferation of television viewing in the 1950s,
students seemed to suffer from a severe reduction in their sensory awareness;
they appeared less alert than previous generations to information from their
surrounding environment, which, in turn, was adversely affecting their ability to learn. The university then partnered with the GPA in order to quantify
this phenomenon.

The researchers conducted sensory tests on 400 undergraduates per year over that 20-year period—a total of 8,000 subjects. The results shocked even the researchers; each successive cohort was slightly less sensitized than the prior cohort: "Our sensitivity to stimuli is decreasing at a rate of about one percent a year," their report stated.[33]

According to pioneering, visionary educator Joseph Chilton Pearce, author of *Magical Child* (1992), who wrote extensively about the study in his 2002 book, *The Biology of the Transcendence*: "Fifteen years ago people could distinguish 300,000 sounds; today many children can't go beyond 100,000 . . . Twenty years ago the average subject could detect 350 different shades of a particular color. Today the number is 130."

The researchers concluded in their report that increasingly, "brutal thrill" was needed in order for our brains to register stimuli. Indeed, all we need to do is look around our world and the media landscape; the "brutal thrill" of more flashing lights, more piercing sounds is everywhere—in our commercials, our movies, our lives—all in order to grab our desensitized attention.

Keep in mind that the German study was concluded in the late 1980s— well before we really upped the hyperstimulating ante with immersive interactive screens. This leaves one wondering: if that trend of 1 percent desensitization per year has been continued—and very probably accelerated— by interactive screens, what level of sense acuity do today's bombarded Glow Kids have? In a few years, will they be able to see or hear anything that isn't shouted or strobed at them?

But, hey, don't worry. Hyperstimulating glowing screens are educational.

At least that's the bill of goods that we're being sold as we're creating an entire generation of kids raised in this hyperstimulating, addicting and reality-blurring landscape as huge tech conglomerates like Apple, Microsoft and Amplify perversely manipulate well-intentioned parents into believing that iPads, tablets, smartphones and hypnotic games like *Minecraft* are wonderful educational tools that will make kids smarter.

It's this combination of opportunistic tech companies, oblivious school districts and duped parents that has led to the head-down and glowing-faced epidemic that any moderately observant adult has witnessed over the last few years—the *Invasion of the Glow Kids*.

Yet, ironically, the most tech-cautious parents are the people who invented our iCulture. People are shocked to find out that tech god Steve Jobs was a low-tech parent; in 2010, when a reporter suggested that his children must love the just-released iPad, he replied: "They haven't used it. We limit how much technology our kids use at home." In a September, 10, 2014, *New York Times* article, his biographer Walter Isaacson revealed: "Every evening Steve made a point of having dinner at the big long table in their kitchen, discussing books and history and a variety of things. No one ever pulled out an iPad or computer."

Years earlier, in an interview for *Wired* magazine, Jobs expressed a very clear anti-tech-in-the-classroom opinion as well—after having once believed that technology was the educational panacea: "I've probably spearheaded giving away more computer equipment to schools than anybody on the planet. But I've come to the conclusion that the problem is not one that technology can hope to solve. What's wrong with education cannot be fixed with technology. No amount of technology will make a dent."[34]

Education psychologist and author of *Failure to Connect: How Computers Affect Our Children's Minds,* Dr. Jane Healy, spent years doing research into computer use in schools and, like Jobs, had expected to find that computers in the classroom would be wonderful for learning. Yet she found exactly the opposite and was dismayed by the lack of research indicating any benefit. She now feels strongly that "time on the computer might interfere with development of everything from the young child's motor skills to his or her ability to think logically and distinguish between reality and fantasy."

Jobs and Healy are not alone in their anti-tech-in-schools sentiments. Many tech execs and engineers in Silicon Valley put their kids in no-tech Waldorf Schools, according to an October 22, 2011, *New York Times* article. At the Waldorf School of the Peninsula in Los Altos, the majority of parents work at Google, Apple or Yahoo; yet these tech-savvy parents insist on no-tech classrooms precisely *because* they understand tech—and its dangers— better than most.

According to one parent, Alan Eagle, a Google exec with a computer science degree from Dartmouth: "I fundamentally reject the notion that you need technology aids in grammar school." These tech-savvy parents appreciate the importance of developing healthy minds and learning through creative hands-on tasks and understand that computers inhibit rather than strengthen the development of their children's young brains.

Another Waldorf parent, Pierre Laurent, a former Microsoft exec and father of two teenagers, says: "I love computers. They can do wonderful things. . . . But you can overuse technology, and become a slave to it. We allowed screen time for our son until he was two. Then I read a book called *The Growth of the Mind,* by Stanley Greenspan, which explains how we learn when we are small through our interaction with the world. . . . We decided that there's no harm in not exposing children to screens until they're big enough. It can only be beneficial."[35]

Laurent waited until his kids were 12 before letting them have access to smartphones and computers. He dismisses the idea of simply limiting kids' screen time when they're younger, indicating that the games are designed to be addicting and hypnotic. "You could offer an hour's screen time a day, but media products are designed to keep people's attention . . . it has a hooking effect. It looks like it's soothing your child and keeping them busy . . . but that effect is not very good for small children."

He talks openly about his time working in the 1990s at Intel, where he and his co-workers would engage with other tech companies in what they used to call a "war of the eyeballs"—a fierce competition to capture the attention of kids and thus create the most hypnotic and addicting products that they could sell.

Many parents have been led to believe that their kids will somehow lag behind in our technological world if their little ones aren't shot out of the womb with tablets in hand. Mr. Eagle counters that argument bluntly: "At Google and all these places, we make technology as brain-dead easy to use as possible. There's no reason why kids can't figure it out when they get older."

Let's remember: Bill Gates was a hands-on Boy Scout who never used a computer until he was 13; Steve Jobs was a mechanical tinkerer, using the hand-eye coordination required for hands-on building—the kind of effort that best develops neuronal synaptic connections—and he never used a computer until age 12. Other tech geniuses, like Google founders Sergei Brin and Larry Page, Amazon creator Jeff Bezos, and Wikipedia founder Jimmy Wales, all went to no-tech or low-tech Montessori schools, which also embrace a connection with nature experiences.[36]

On the Barbara Walters ABC-TV special *The Ten Most Fascinating People of 2004,* Larry Page and Sergey Brin credited their education as Montessori students as the major factor behind their success. Will Wright, designer of the groundbreaking computer game *The Sims,* has said, "Montessori taught me the joy of discovery. It showed you can become interested in pretty complex theories, like Pythagorean theory, say, by playing with blocks."[37]

What is becoming increasingly clear is that kids today don't need better gadgets to get ahead in our uber-competitive high-tech world—they need sharper minds. Yet we throw more and more technology at children when they are younger and younger, even as all the research is clearly showing us that screens are *dulling* rather than sharpening young developing brains.

That sentiment was expressed in a biting commentary by comedian and activist Paula Poundstone on the *CBS Morning News* on November 29, 2015, during her taped segment on screen addiction: "Research shows that the brain retains information better read from paper than a screen and that students who take notes by hand are more successful on tests than those who type their notes on a computer. Yet art, music, sports, play, healthy meals and green space—things we know help the developing brain—are on the chopping block of school districts' budgets annually. Even knowing this, at the suggestion that we get screen devices out of the classroom and away from our children, people *gasp:* 'But they'll need them for the world of the future!' Our children will need fully functioning *brains* for the world of the future—let's put *that* first."

It seems that the no-tech Waldorf parents and Paula Poundstone are justified in being concerned. Not only is tech exposure linked to clinical disorders and dulled sensory acuity, but groundbreaking research done by Dr. Marcia Mikulak in the 1980s further confirmed that kids living in more technologically advanced societies not only had duller senses, but apparently they were lousier students than their so-called "primitive" counterparts.[38]

In two parallel studies, Mikulak examined children from a number of cultures, including those in preliterate societies in Brazil, Guatemala and Africa as well as those in Europe and the United States. She found that sensory acuity and sensitivity to the environment were up to 30 percent higher in the children from the so-called primitive societies.[39]

Further research that she carried out in the late 1980s showed that children from preliterate low-tech societies in Guatemala and similar countries showed a prodigious capacity for learning. When these "deprived" children were given learning environments equal to those provided for North American and Western European children, they demonstrated an ability to learn estimated to be *three or four times greater* than that of their higher-tech peers, showing far superior attention, comprehension and retention.[40]

In other words, less tech equaled better minds and thus better learners.

To be clear: I—and by extension, this book—are not against technology, either in everyday usage or as a learning tool. The problem is the age of exposure; hyperarousing screens can be damaging to a young child's brain, which simply is not developmentally ready to handle that level of stimulation.

This developmental idea is echoed in an old Buddhist proverb: before you can be no one, you first have to be someone. That is, a person needs an ego before they can go beyond the ego. Technology is sort of like that. People need to first fully develop their brains—their cognitive, attentional, linguistic, emotional, spatial and reality-testing mental faculties—before their brains can go beyond those areas and handle hyperarousing and reality-immersing screens.

Yet the false narrative fed to most parents is clear: if you want your children to keep up in the race to the best schools, early tech is good and more tech is better—despite the dearth of research to back that up and in spite of the research that does show that interactive screens are not quite as harmless as we originally thought.

That's really the key here—if screens and age-inappropriate tech were *merely* ineffective as educationally enhancing learning tools, then we could just shrug our shoulders and shake our heads at the huge amount of money wasted—$13 billion a year—while more and more teachers and enrichment programs get cut.

But an ineffective intervention is one thing—a *damaging* intervention is quite another.

While tech companies and duped school administrators unfortunately operate under a different set of ethical standards from that of doctors, they would most certainly fail the fundamental aspect of the Hippocratic "do no harm" oath, as evidence is showing us that we *are* harming kids.

Like it or not, the reality is that in our glowing screen culture, we have essentially been giving our most innocent and most vulnerable an addicting and mind-altering electronic drug.

TWO

BRAVE NEW E-WORLD

I HAD RECEIVED A DISTRESSED EMAIL FROM "CATHY," A WELL-
known entertainer in Los Angeles. Cathy was desperate to get some help for
her screen-addicted 17-year-old son, "Mark." Cathy, a woman of means, had
been to 13 psychiatrists and psychologists in Los Angeles, and not one was
even remotely familiar with screen addiction. Rather than helping, Cathy
told me, "They actually did more harm than good by not understanding this
issue."

Mark, who had started by fiddling with a computer when he was five
because his well-intentioned mother thought it could be educational, fell into
a horrible screen addiction that was destroying his life. From the time he was
very young, his mother told me, his whole demeanor would shift when he got
in front of a screen; even the GPS in her car would hypnotize him.

Once he discovered video games at the age of ten, it was all over. He
would steal from his mother to buy video games and game consoles; he would
get violent and aggressive when he wasn't allowed to play; he lost all interest
in school and hobbies that he had loved: "He used to love to drum, now [the
drums] just sit there . . . he just wasn't the same kid anymore."

After the failed attempts to get help from the 13 uninformed therapists
("Let the boy play his games; if you take them away from him, he'll be hopeless"; "Video games are very important for boys socially"), Cathy read all
that she could about screen addiction and eventually pulled the plug on all

of Mark's electronics. His school was entirely uncooperative with her efforts to keep him screen-free, which then prompted her to enroll him in a residential therapeutic school that worked with her to keep Mark away from the electronics.

"Most of these schools are so tech whipped!" Cathy said in exasperation. "Even in some of the best therapeutic schools that I interviewed—that supposedly knew about tech addiction, they would say, yes, but for school he could use the computer . . . it's like they give the machines a free pass."

But in Mark's case, he had proven that he couldn't handle computers— even just for school use. He would lie to his mother that he had to use the computer (which she had to lock in her bedroom) to research various school assignments; after he had spent hours hypnotically surfing the Net on various topics, Cathy would find out that the alleged school assignments were nonexistent—like a true addict, Mark just *needed* to experience the *glow*.

Mark has been screen-free in his residential school for almost a year now and is doing quite well and even thinking about going to college—something that would have been unimaginable a year ago. And we are developing a plan, in conjunction with his school, to *slowly* reintegrate computers into his schoolwork, and I am working with Cathy to develop a tech plan for Mark when he moves back home in May.

"This was just like any other addiction—and, in some ways, worse because it's so new that we don't have a lot of precedent on how to deal with this problem," Cathy said. "We needed to treat this very seriously and carefully. Unfortunately, there just wasn't a lot of help or awareness of the problem out there."

ELECTRONIC SOMA

Although it may come as a shock to some—even to trained therapists—the idea that electronic screens could have an addicting drug-like effect is not a new concept.

In 1985, 25 years before Steve Jobs, in his trademark black turtleneck, introduced the world to the game-changing iPad, a soft-spoken, visionary intellectual NYU professor named Neil Postman wrote a prophetic little book called *Amusing Ourselves to Death*.[1] In it, he suggested that we were living in the equivalent of Aldous Huxley's *Brave New World,* only instead of Huxley's imaginary drug, soma, our addictive elixir was the "new" electronic medium—television.

It was a provocative idea: TV as a cocaine-like drug.

Postman believed that, like soma and cocaine, this visual medium was so highly addicting that it was creating an entire society of uninformed pleasure-seekers. Keep in mind that Postman's prophetic bit of wisdom was written well before the world had even glimpsed an Xbox, smartphone, iPad, tablet or laptop.

In fact, the insidious tech that Postman was referring to was the rather quaint—by today's standards—boob tube, with the hot-selling Sony Trinitron being the iPad of its day. The most popular content on this electronic scourge during 1985? The hardly nefarious-sounding *Cheers, The Cosby Show, Dynasty* and *Miami Vice.*

But that's the thing with visionaries like Postman—they can see further over the horizon than most of us. While the majority of people in 1985 probably didn't think that watching Ted Danson on *Cheers* was the harbinger of a dystopian future society zombified by soma-like tech, are we not a bit more concerned about tech effects and tech addiction in the year 2016, otherwise known as the year 6 A.i. (After iPad)? In fact, the research is showing us that if TV was soma-like cocaine, then the more powerful, hyperstimulating and interactive iPads can be considered the more addicting crack of the electronic media landscape.

Moreover, Postman didn't believe that electronic media was *just* an addictive drug; like philosopher and communication theorist Marshall McLuhan before him, he believed that television also marked a major shift in human development, fundamentally impacting not only the way that we communicate, but also the way that we think as well.

He argued that since television images had replaced the written word as the dominant communication medium, our ability to engage in in-depth rational discourse and the dialectical engagement of serious and complex issues—which had evolved over hundreds of years as a consequence of a reading culture—had now been compromised. We had effectively been dumbed-down as the depth of written language was replaced by the superficial visual images of television's information-as-entertainment.

An intelligent and thoughtful man not prone to emotional histrionics, Postman became deeply troubled by what he saw on the educational horizon as well. As a professor at NYU's prestigious Steinhardt School of Education and the chair of its Department of Culture and Communication, Postman knew a thing or two about education.

Aside from its addicting effect, he wrote that, from a pedagogical perspective, electronic media were simply not effective or appropriate for the classroom. He believed that the then-recently introduced personal computer (PC), like television, offered a passive and shallow top-down form of information transfer rather than the engaged and dynamic cognitive interaction that is required when reading complex written discourse. In addition, the "personal" aspect of the PC bothered him too, because it eliminated the dialectical engagement of the teacher-class dynamic which had always been a *group*—not an individual—process.

In 1995, ten years after the initial stir he caused with *Amusing Ourselves to Death,* Postman was interviewed on *The MacNeil/Lehrer NewsHour* (broadcast, ironically enough, on the dreaded electronic medium of TV—an irony that he noted). During the interview, he further elaborated on his opposition to the increasing use of PCs in the classroom, saying that he was opposed to them—and individualized learning in general—because they lacked the necessary group dynamic that was a critically important ingredient in both education and the socialization process.

Today, in a world of online education and virtual classrooms with 10,000 students—who are all "alone together" and isolated in front of their respective computer screens—one wonders what an educator like Dr. Postman would think if he had lived to see the exponential expansion of technology within education as a form of mass communication.

Postman had been stirring the cultural pot and creating controversy about his concerns regarding the media and technology his entire life. In 1982, three years *before* writing *Amusing Ourselves to Death,* he had penned an equally dystopian vision of the near-future entitled *The Disappearance of Childhood,* in which he suggested that the new electronic medium of television would cause childhood to go the way of the Edsel:

"I am going to argue that our new media environment, with television at its center, is leading to the rapid disappearance of childhood in North

America and that childhood will probably not survive until the end of this century . . . that such a state of affairs represents a social disaster of the first order."[2]

A prescient Postman suggested that the divisions that had developed between children and adults were eroding under the electronic barrage of television, which exposed kids to the previously taboo adult concepts of sex and violence.

Fast-forward three decades: the electronic "liberation" of previously adult themes that had started with television has only been amplified by the information free-for-all of the Internet. While the Web has democratized knowledge, it has also, unquestionably, exposed and sexualized kids and accelerated their development into adulthood. In our YouTube era, when any kid with a tablet can literally see anything ever recorded—from snuff films to porn—is there any doubt that the quaint notion of "childhood" is slipping away?

Recently, a therapy group of ninth-graders whom I had been working with—basically good kids with some emotional issues—were all talking about the beheading and dismemberment video that they had all just seen online.

"Don't your parents block that from your computers at home?" I naively asked. Jake, the group's leader, just smirked: "At home? We just watched that at school—we've disabled the security filter—it's easy."

Gone are the days when an adolescent boy who glimpsed a copy of *Playboy* had imagination fuel for the year; now, daily graphic images stream unfiltered into the eyes and minds of our kids, forever seared into their psyches. One of my 14-year-old clients, troubled by things that he couldn't un-see, tried to thoughtfully warn me: "Dr. K—don't ever look at that Web site—you'll never be able to get those images out of your head . . . I know that I can't."

Yet as technology and the information free-for-all rob kids of their innocence and blur the notion of childhood, it also paradoxically perpetuates and extends their adolescence. Historian Gary Cross describes this phenomenon as "delayed social adulthood," in which adolescence in the tech era is being redefined to extend well into people's twenties and even thirties.[3]

Postman foresaw this phenomenon decades ago, as he understood that hyperarousing glowing screens are addicting—and that if a kid gets hooked, he or she may be hooked for life in a state of perpetual pleasure-seeking adolescence.

Beyond television, who or what is the main culprit in this "failure to launch," where apathetic and emotionally stunted boys do not become men? Cross blames video games: "In 2011, almost a fifth of men between 25 and 34 still lived with their parents," a scenario in which many play video games and "the average player is 30 years old."

Dr. Leonard Sax (author of *Why Gender Matters*) writes extensively about this adolescent malaise in *Boys Adrift* (2009) as he, too, cites our video game culture as one of the main culprits in the "failure to launch" dynamic.

In addition to being addicting, according to Sax, video games do not engender the sense of resilience or the patience and drive that the real world requires. In real life, when people lose at sports, they have to lick their wounds and process those experiences as they learn to eventually get back on the horse to compete another day. All of that fosters resilience and emotional growth. When you lose in a video game, you hit the reset button. Game on.

Author and psychiatrist Dr. Mark Banschick adds: "From the psychiatric couch, I have come to see avoidance as being part of a generational style; at least in a sizable group. Boys in particular love their video games and have developed an expectation of instant gratification that makes schoolwork and other chores seem too much. The brain is a developing organ, and we've been feeding our boys (and to some degree girls as well) with brain junk food."[4]

Thirty-year-old adolescents . . . ten-year-olds who have "seen it all" on YouTube . . . how did this happen? How have we become a society of sexualized kids-as-adults but also, paradoxically, 30-year-old quasi-teenagers?

Perhaps a bit conspiratorially, Postman believed that there was a political subtext to addicting electronic media: just as soma in *Brave New World* was a mechanism of societal control, so too was our electronic addiction sedating the masses to make us more vulnerable to oppression. Having personally worked with hundreds of poor families of color, I can say that I've also been struck by the politically sedating effect that Xbox has had on some of these young disempowered boys.

NEW TECHNOLOGY: THE GOOD, THE BAD AND THE UGLY

Of course, Neil Postman wasn't the first person to cast a wary—perhaps even apocalyptic—eye toward a new form of communication technology;

history is replete with technophobic Chicken Littles who warned against the evils of everything from the typewriter to the telegraph to radio to moving pictures . . . all of those inventions had their detractors, who were convinced that the fill-in-the-blank latest technological advancement would bring about the end of civilization.

We can even go as far back as ancient Greece and Socrates for "this-new-medium-will-be-the-end-of-us-all" reactions. Unlike Postman, Socrates did not think much of books and the written word; as a proponent of oral storytelling, he thought the written word would kill our memory skills and make us all bloody idiots: "[It] destroys memory [and] weakens the mind, relieving it of . . . work that makes it strong. [It] is an inhuman thing."[5]

In addition to memory atrophy, Socrates was also concerned that books would allow information to be communicated without the author or teacher being personally present. Like Postman, he believed that true learning necessarily entailed a living, engaged give-and-take interaction between teacher and student that was dynamic (the dialectic); but, unlike Postman, Socrates believed that a book was a static form of information transfer. According to the wisest man in all of Athens, only fools thought that they were wise because they had learned something from teacherless books: "[Books], by telling them of many things without teaching them," will make students "seem to know much, while for the most part they know nothing."

But, luckily for us, unlike Socrates, his student Plato did write. Prolifically. That's why, ironically, I know about Socrates' aversion to books by reading about it—in a book . . . just as Neil Postman vented about the dreaded medium of television—on television (during that *MacNeil/Lehrer NewsHour* interview in 1995).

Perhaps it is true, as a long line of philosophers from Socrates to Marshall McLuhan and Neil Postman have told us, that technology inevitably changes us and that such changes always entail some level of loss.

But can new technology, as some have suggested, perhaps also change us for the better?

Maybe—although at a very high price.

In 2015 the journal *Addiction Biology* published a study, a collaboration between the University of Utah School of Medicine and Chung-Ang

University in South Korea, in which the brain scans of 200 adolescent boys described as video game addicts were examined.[6]

According to Doug Hyun Han, M.D., Ph.D., professor at Chung-Ang University School of Medicine and adjunct associate professor at the University of Utah School of Medicine, this was the largest and most comprehensive investigation to date of the way that the brains of compulsive video game players differ from the brains of non-gamers.

The researchers found indisputable evidence that the brains of video game–addicted boys are wired differently; chronic video game playing was associated with increased hyperconnectivity between several pairs of brain networks. What was more difficult to determine was whether those changes are good or bad.

"Most of the differences we see could be considered beneficial. However the good changes could be inseparable from problems that come with them," says senior author and researcher Dr. Jeffrey Anderson, M.D., Ph.D., associate professor of neuroradiology at the University of Utah School of Medicine.

Let's take a look at some of these brain changes.

The good: some of the changes can help game players respond to new information. This study found that in these gaming-addicted boys, certain brain networks that process vision or hearing are more likely to have enhanced coordination in the "salience network." The salience network helps to focus attention on important events, helping with a person's reaction time to enable taking action, if necessary—jumping out of the way of a moving car, for example. In a video game, this enhanced coordination could help a gamer to react more quickly to an oncoming attack from an opponent.

According to Dr. Anderson: "Hyperconnectivity between these brain networks could lead to a more robust ability to direct attention toward targets, and to recognize novel information in the environment. The changes could essentially help someone to think more efficiently."

The not-so-good: some of these brain changes are also associated with distractibility and poor impulse control. "Having these networks be too connected may increase distractibility," says Anderson; as we know, people who have quick reflexes and reaction times can be a bit jumpy and unfocused.

The bad: what the researchers found more troublesome is an increased coordination between two brain regions, the dorsolateral prefrontal cortex and temporoparietal junction; this is a brain change also seen in patients with psychiatric and developmental conditions such as schizophrenia, Down's syndrome, and autism.

Not a good thing.

Distractibility and poor impulse control are also hallmarks of addiction. The researchers point out that, benefits aside, those with Internet Gaming Disorder are so obsessed with and addicted to video games that they often give up eating and sleeping in order to play them.

So let's recap: kids can get addicted to games and not eat or sleep; they can also run the risk of developing ADHD and schizophrenia-like symptoms—but they can react and shoot targets like nobody's business!

The question simply comes down to one of cost/benefit: is having a re-wired brain that can see patterns and targets better and react more quickly worth the potential for developing impulse-control disorders—like addiction and ADHD—not to mention more serious psychiatric and developmental disorders, such as schizophrenia and autism?

Leaving autism aside for the moment, we saw in the last chapter in the research of Drs. Griffiths and de Gortari that gaming can indeed induce Game Transfer Phenomena and hallucinatory experiences. Is that really a risk that we want our kids taking so that they have better reaction times in a video game simulation?

The researchers concluded that what remains unclear is the chicken or the egg: whether the persistent video gaming caused the rewiring of the brain, or whether people who are wired differently are drawn to video games.

But as I'll point out in the next chapter, there is indeed a "pre and post" brain-imaging study from the University of Indiana School of Medicine that did brain scans of nongamers, then had them play video games for several weeks, and then did post-video gaming brain scans again. That study clearly showed neurobiological changes in the brain that were indeed a direct result of the video game playing—brain changes that, very interestingly, mirrored those of drug addiction.

Let's take a look at some other *possible* technology benefits.

In his pro-tech book *Smarter than You Think* (2013), Clive Thompson ex-tols quite a few technological virtues. Besides obvious tech-as-tool benefits such as the use of keypads for nonverbal autistic children and many other instances in which tech can be an invaluable tool for the disabled, Thompson discusses instances of tech-human hybrids that work more efficiently than humans can without tech.

As an example, he discusses chess "centaurs" as one form of superior tech-human hybrids. Named after the mythical creature that was half human and half horse, a chess centaur is a chess-playing dyad that consists of a human player collaborating with a computer to form a single player/ team. This man-and-machine dynamic is in stark contrast to the earlier man-vs.-machine model, in which, for example, chess world champion Gary Kasparov played against the supercomputer Big Blue in 1997 and suffered a humiliating loss—one so infamous that it led to the *Newsweek* cover story "The Brain's Last Stand."

Yet it was Kasparov himself who in 1998 came up with the if-you-can't-beat-'em-join-'em idea of collaborating with the computer, his former high-tech arch nemesis. Kasparov's innovative idea of creating a team composed of a human and a computer pitted against other half-human, half-computer teams came to be known as "advanced chess," with the first such tournament, held in 1998, featuring Kasparov as one half of a centaur team.

After that initial tournament, he analogized the experience with that of learning how to drive a race car: "Just as a good Formula One driver really knows his own car, so did we have to learn the way the computer worked."

Yet Kasparov's centaur team lost to a centaur with an inferior human player—one whom Kasparov had easily beaten four times earlier but who was apparently a better "driver" of his technology. In fact, lower-ranked players were often better collaborators with technology than the higher-ranked humans because, according to Thompson, they knew more intuitively when to rely on the computer's advice and when to rely on their own skill when making the next move.

But does knowing when to defer to a computer enhance a human being's skills? While the man-machine hybrid might do better, is the human half of that equation diminished by an overreliance on a computer?

In order to answer that question, let's also look at another human-computer hybrid: pilots and their computer navigation systems, which often fly the plane for the pilot. Question: do pilots who are more reliant on their flight computers—pilots who tend to fly-by-wire more—have better piloting skills than pilots who fly manually more often?

That question was answered in a fascinating 2009 piloting study conducted by Matthew Ebbatson at Britain's Cranfield University School of Engineering.[7] In the study, pilots had been asked to conduct a flight simulator landing of a Boeing jet with a crippled engine during rough weather. Ebbatson then measured indicators of the pilot's skill—things such as maintaining correct airspeed—during this difficult maneuver.

When he then looked at their actual flight records, he found a correlation between pilots' reliance on their autopilots and their skill-level; it seemed that the more pilots relied on technology, the more their human piloting skills had eroded. Clearly in this case of man-and-machine integration, technology was not enhancing the skills of the human.

If you don't believe that study's findings, just ask yourself this question: if the plane that you're on gets hit by lightning and has its electrical system debilitated, who would you rather have as your pilot—one who has flown manually before or a fly-by-wire high-tech hotshot?

Thompson also writes about other technology tools that allegedly enhance human ability; he mentions the "extended mind" theory of cognition, which essentially says that humans are so intellectually dominant because "we've always outsourced bits of cognition, using tools to scaffold our thinking into ever-more rarefied realms. Printed books amplified our memory. Inexpensive paper and reliable pens made it possible to externalize our thoughts quickly."

So do printed books amplify our memory? As I noted earlier, Socrates would certainly take issue with that statement, as he believed just the opposite: printed books weakened our memory.

Thompson also mentions today's digital tools, such as smartphones and hard drives, and talks about their "huge impact on our cognition" and the "prodigious external memory" that is the byproduct of today's tech.

While we can agree that technology offers incredible data storage and external memory capabilities, do we really believe that external memory tools like hard drives and smartphones actually *amplify* our human memory or in any way add to our human abilities or skills?

Here's a quick experiment that you can do if you have a smartphone: can you write down the ten most frequently called telephone numbers on your phone without looking into your phone's memory? If you're like most of us, you can't. We tend to forget our frequently called numbers because we don't need to remember them any more—our external memory device has it covered. Less than a decade ago, that wasn't the case; most people knew most of their frequently called numbers from memory.

So what, you might say. Big deal, I can't remember as many phone numbers as I used to, and I use my memory less because of my handy-dandy gadgets—what harm can that do?

Well, memory, like language, is a skill that requires practice and use, otherwise one's memory abilities—in true use-it-or-lose-it fashion—begin to atrophy. Conversely, as Socrates understood, memory was also a skill that one could increase by practice. And now, thanks to modern science, we have brain-imaging research that clearly shows that engaging in memory practice can actually strengthen our brains and increase our gray matter.

In a study published in 2011 in the journal *Current Biology,* Professor Eleanor Maguire and Dr. Katherine Woollett from the Neuroimaging Center at University College London studied the brains of a group of professionals who inspire awe with their prodigious memories: London cabdrivers.[8] Those individuals are required to memorize what is called "the Knowledge"—the complex layout of more than 25,000 labyrinthine streets and, additionally, several thousand landmarks including theaters and well-known pubs.

Developed before the prominence of GPS devices, it's a rigorous and brutal learning process that often took three or four years before the aspiring cabbie felt ready to take the licensing test—the Knowledge of London Examination System. Forget bar exams and medical boards—this test is so difficult that prospective applicants often make up to 12 attempts to pass, and even then, ultimately only *half* of the cabbie trainees are eventually successful.

So Maguire and Woollett thought that it would be illuminating to study the brains of these memory quasi-savants—"quasi" because these taxi drivers were not *born* with prodigious memories but, rather, *developed* them.

The researchers selected a group of 79 cabbie trainees and an additional control group of 31 non–taxi drivers. All 110 participants had their brains scanned at the outset of the study and were administered certain memory tests; initially, the researchers found no discernible differences, as all groups had performed equally well on the memory tasks.

Over the next several years, only 39 of 79 trainees passed the test, which then allowed Maguire and Woollett to break the participants down into three different groups: those who had trained and passed the test; those who had trained and did not pass the test; and those who had neither trained nor taken the test. Then, three to four years after the initial MRIs (magnetic resonance imaging) and memory testing—when the trainees had either passed or failed to acquire "the Knowledge"—the researchers again conducted MRIs and tested everyone on memory tasks.

This time around, Maguire and Woollett found significant changes in the brains of those who had passed the test: they had a greater volume of gray matter in their hippocampus than they had before they started training. The hippocampus, we should note, is essential in memory acquisition; in Alzheimer's patients, for example, the hippocampus is one of the first brain regions to suffer damage.

Interestingly, this increase in gray matter of the hippocampus wasn't present in the group who had studied but failed the test. The control group who had not studied also showed no brain increase. Perhaps, we can speculate, the group who studied yet failed—and subsequently did not show an increase of volume in gray matter—simply did not study enough to either pass the test or gain the desired brain change.

Regardless, the research clearly showed that the group who studied rigorously enough to pass the test did indeed change their neurophysiology in a beneficial way. This research also shows us that it's never too late to change your brain. According to Professor Maguire: "The human brain remains 'plastic,' even in adult life, allowing it to adapt when we learn new tasks."

Yet now we have GPS and don't have to remember streets or directions. We also have smartphones that remember, well, *everything* for us. And devices that can do all sorts of things for us—they can cook, clean, make dinner reservations, fly our planes, drive our cars . . . perhaps one day soon they will even be able to think for us.

But as technology advances, does humanity recede?

Does tech that externally remembers things for us—thus lessening our need to utilize our memory muscles—help our human memory or weaken it? Do chess computer-hybrid centaurs make their human halves better—or does the computer do most of the heavy lifting? Do tech devices—like calculators, which help us do math, or computers that help pilots fly on autopilot, convenient as all these things may be—do those technological wonders work as skill-strengthening tools or skill-dampening crutches?

Perhaps it's as Thoreau once said: "Men have become the tools of their tools."

As we continue to explore the effects of technology in our lives, we now also have, as we have just seen, the benefit of yet another technological tool—state-of-the-art brain imaging that wondrously and definitively shows us the negative impacts of technology on the brain.

The irony is rich: technology that shows us that technology is bad for our brains.

In *Smarter than You Think,* Thompson interestingly decides to not look at any of the brain imaging research: "If you were hoping to read about the neuroscience of our brains and how technology is 'rewiring' them, this volume will disappoint you." He goes on to rail against the latest brain imaging research as "premature" and of dubious benefit because our understanding of the brain itself is still a work in progress, as he concludes: "The field is so new that it is rash to draw conclusions, either apocalyptic or utopian, about how the internet is changing our brains."

While our understanding of the brain is admittedly incomplete, neuroscience, thanks in large part to brain imaging, is fairly far along. Several recent and compelling peer-reviewed brain imaging studies, which we'll examine in the next chapter—some that have come out after Thompson's book—do indeed show the damaging effects of tech on the brain, damage that, as mentioned, closely mirrors the effects of drug addiction.

So was Neil Postman prophetically correct in *Amusing Ourselves to Death*—is the new electronic media our soma? Thirty years later, in the age of iPads, smartphones, tablets, laptops, Google Glass, Twitter, Facebook, Oculus Rift and who-knows-what-else on the tech horizon, does it seem so ludicrous to view tech as a drug—the "electronic cocaine" that Dr. Whybrow considers it to be? Benefits aside, has digital tech become what Chinese researchers are calling electronic heroin?

Indeed, as we'll read in the next chapter, interactive glowing screens have become such a powerful drug that the U.S. military is literally using them as a form of digital morphine.

THREE

DIGITAL DRUGS AND THE BRAIN

DIGITAL MORPHINE

"I was on fire . . . I couldn't speak or see to unbuckle my seatbelt or open the door. I believe that my guardian angel just took me out of the truck."

First Lieutenant Sam Brown is lying in the burn unit of Brooke Army Medical Center (BAMC) in San Antonio, Texas, describing the horrible events that took place earlier that year, 2008, in Kandahar, Afghanistan, when his Humvee was hit by an IED and exploded. His body was engulfed in flames, and he suffered third-degree burns over 30 percent of his body; his injuries were so severe that he was kept in a medically induced coma for the first few weeks to help him survive.

While his eyes looked the same as in the pictures of the handsome cadet who had recently graduated from West Point, his face now bore the scars of badly burned flesh. As he would later tell NBC's Natalie Morales in a 2012 interview: "I literally thought that I was going to die and my instinctual reaction was to throw my arms up in the air and cry out to God. And I remember thinking 'how long will it take for me to burn to death?'"

But the IED explosion and the initial burn was only the beginning of what would be a very long and painful process. According to Dr. Christopher Maani, the anesthesiologist in BAMC's burn unit: "With burn injury, that rehabilitative process can go on for weeks to months, sometimes even years if the burn is significant enough as it was in Sam's case."

Sam had to endure more than two dozen painful surgeries, but the most excruciating pain came from the daily wound care and the physical therapy that followed. In fact, the procedures were so painful and unbearable that there were times when Sam's superior officers would have to order him to undergo treatment. As with many burn victims, narcotic painkillers are the only medication that can provide some relief from the daily ritual pain. While narcotic opiates have an analgesic effect that stimulates pain-dampening endorphin release, they are also highly addictive. As Sam grew increasingly concerned about his growing dependence on narcotics, Dr. Maani suggested a new experimental treatment to help Sam lessen his pain: a video game called *SnowWorld*.

SnowWorld is a cartoon-looking virtual reality game set in the arctic ice where a series of penguins march back and forth as Paul Simon's cheery song "You Can Call Me Al" plays in the background. During the game the player, who is wearing a wraparound plastic virtual headset, uses a joystick to throw snowballs at the cute penguins.

When I interviewed Sam, he said: "I went into this totally a skeptic, but was willing to give it a try." The game had been developed several years earlier at the University of Washington by Dr. David Patterson and Dr. Hunter Hoffman, two psychologists who had been working on non-opioid pain-management methods specifically for burn victims at Harbor View Burn Center in Seattle. Patterson and Hoffman discovered that while patients were immersed in virtual reality games, their sensation of pain greatly decreased.

Indeed, in 2011, the military conducted a small study using *SnowWorld* and got even more dramatic results: for soldiers in the most severe pain, *SnowWorld* worked even better than morphine.[1] The researchers were not exactly clear on what the exact mechanism of this video analgesic effect was as some ascribed it to "cognitive distraction."

But we know from a study by M. J. Koepp (1998)[2] that video games raised dopamine levels 100 percent—and those were old-school, 2-D 1998 video games, not immersive 3-D virtual reality games. Is it possible that, rather than just "cognitive distraction," Sam's neurotransmitters were being stimulated to release pain-killing dopamine and, perhaps, endorphins as well?

In my interview with the navy's Dr. Doan, he expressed the view that there is indeed an endorphin-increasing mechanism that is not entirely understood; as previously mentioned, he embraces the notion of screens acting as "digital pharmakeia."

When I asked Sam about this, he said: "I was for sure feeling less pain than I was with the morphine. I think it definitely could have been an increase in my dopamine or endorphins."

Even Dr. Hoffman is surprised when it comes to the success of video game pain-management therapy: "The fact that you're getting such huge reductions in pain using something that's not a drug is a paradigm shift," he said.

Brain imaging would eventually confirm that the burn patients treated with *SnowWorld* virtual reality were indeed experiencing less pain in the parts of their brains associated with processing pain. All of these stunning findings have led the military to further pursue the use of virtual reality and video games as a quasi-digital drug in order to help treat pain.

Most people are shocked to hear that a video game can actually be more potent than morphine. While this is a phenomenal advance in pain-management medicine and treatment of burn victims, it begs the question: just what effect is this digital drug—which is more powerful than morphine—having on the brains and nervous systems of seven-year-olds—or fourteen year-olds—who are ingesting very similar digital drugs via their glowing screens? And, further, if stimulating screens are indeed more powerful than morphine, can they be just as addicting?

TRAPPED DOWN THE RABBIT HOLE OF DIGITAL ADDICTION

As I stood in the heavy downpour and knocked on the door of the cedar shingle ranch house I felt a sense of apprehension. Although a bit dated and frayed around the edges, by all outward appearances it looked like a normal suburban house where a happy family with 2.2 kids might live, complete with a tan minivan in the driveway parked next to a free-standing basketball hoop and backboard. It all looked very Ozzie and Harriet.

Yet I knew that inside that innocuous suburban house lived "Peter," a sometimes violent 18-year-old video game-playing recluse; a digital Howard

Hughes who had become homebound for the past four years as he had become trapped by his own psychiatric demons that were fed by his gaming addiction. I was apprehensive because, although I'm comfortable around mental illness and addiction, I'm a bit more tense during the rare occasions that I have to do a home assessment because you can never be quite sure what you'll find once you get past the front door. And, perhaps most unsettling, if there is a problem, they have the home field advantage.

This is what I knew about Peter based on his case file and from phone conversations with his mother: He had always been anxious as a boy, but he became depressed after his father had died several years earlier. The tipping point came in the ninth grade when he was suspended for the entire school year for a prank that had gone terribly wrong. Alone at home with his anxiety and depression, he found escape in his Xbox; what had once been a weekend recreation had turned into a 16-hour-a-day addiction. He had now become so addicted that he couldn't stop playing and had become agoraphobic and unable to leave the house or go to school.

During the extremely rare occasions that he had to leave the house—for a doctor's appointment, for example—his mother and brother would have to sedate him and physically drag him out as he fought, kicked and screamed. When his mother tried to pull the plug on the game, he became violent and would punch holes in the walls or throw things at her. The poor woman had to get a restraining order while he still lived in her house. Overwhelmed and worn out, she eventually gave in and settled into a pattern of compliant enabling; she would just let him play all day and night and bring him his meals when he demanded them.

Psychiatrists confirmed his anxiety and agoraphobia diagnosis and the school district was forced to send tutors to his house for two hours a day to provide him some semblance of an education. The district had also tried contacting various agencies to help, but the problem was that, at 18, he was a legal adult and could refuse treatments and interventions. That's when the school asked if I'd be willing to go to his house to assess him to see if I could get a better sense of the severity of the problem and perhaps coax him into some kind of treatment.

After a minute or two in the rain, his mother finally opened the door and invited me in. I couldn't help feeling a sense of being stuck in a time warp as her low beehive hairdo matched the wood paneling and the 1970s furniture with framed photos of a happy family that no longer existed. Thrilled to have someone come to the house to try and help, she greeted me warmly and sat with me in the dining room as she spilled her heart out about her son's situation. I genuinely felt for her; she was a very decent woman who had tried her best to keep things together after her hard-working husband had died. When she was done, I asked if I could speak with Peter.

"He just woke up; he's in the living room eating his breakfast that I just brought him."

It was 1:00 p.m.

She walked me into the living room where Peter was sitting on a chair that Archie Bunker would have been proud of. I hadn't seen him in four years, since the last time he'd been in school. Since then, he had grown quite a bit—both vertically and horizontally; he had to be at least 40 or 50 pounds heavier. He was staring with a dazed look on his face at a large bulky old-style television that had the show *Cops* blaring on it. While his gaze was fixed toward the TV, his expression was blank—almost catatonic; I'm not even sure if he was watching the TV or just staring and zoning out in that direction. He had on a soiled white t-shirt and dirty red sweat pants; on the coffee table in front of him was a plate of eggs, bacon and toast that their huge Labrador was eating off his plate.

I slowly sat in an ottoman next to him as he just continued to stare straight ahead.

"Hi Peter. Do you remember me, Dr. Kardaras? We had met at school a few years back?"

He briefly looked at me out of the corner of his eye and almost imperceptibly nodded as he kept looking at the TV.

"I just wanted to come and see how you're doing and maybe ask you some questions. Are you OK with that?"

Again, the barely there nod.

I asked him a series of questions about his childhood, his schooling, his family, his anxiety. Mostly I got one or two-word low-mumbled responses. But then everything changed when I asked him about his gaming; that's when he sat up and actually looked at me.

"I . . . I like to play *Modern Warfare 2* . . . and *Modern Warfare 3*."

He still mumbled, but there was better articulation because he was now more engaged.

"What is it that you like about playing video games?"

He had a difficult time finding the words. He tried several times but couldn't say much.

I tried again. "Peter, try and finish this sentence: 'The thing I like the most about playing video games is . . .'"

He nodded and tried to answer, "The thing I like the most about gaming is . . . is . . . I love trickshot . . . I love the sensation I get when I get one."

He was half-smiling now as you could see he was fantasizing about this thing called "trickshot." He then sat up even higher and said, with more enthusiasm:

"I love the *sensation*. I've never had that doing anything else in my life."

"What's trickshot?" I asked.

He tried to mumble a description, but got frustrated because he wasn't able to verbally describe this panglorious thing called a trickshot. His face then lit up as he had a flash of inspiration: "Can . . . can I show you?" he asked.

"Sure. I'd love to see."

He slowly got up and ambled—you could tell that he wasn't used to walking—over to an adjacent doorway that led into a dimly lit room. My stomach tightened as I followed him into his own *Heart of Darkness:* a dimly lit dark-paneled room that was the gateway into the digital war games that his whole life revolved around.

In that room, there were three huge computer screens attached to two gaming devices set up at angles on a large table—it almost looked like pictures of a flight simulator that I had once seen. As he powered up, the screens came alive with flashing lights and the sound of machinegun fire. He began to explain that he was part of a Clan of about another 20 gamers.

He began to show me clips of prior trickshots; from what I gathered, a trickshot is a complex sniper maneuver where the player/sniper uses an array of spinning moves and employs a variety of combinations on the controller to create a unique "no scope" kill shot. This complex move often required weeks of coordinated play and effort in order to accomplish. Then, the Holy Grail of trickshots was to record them as a YouTube video with the hope that your clan can become popular enough to get on a YouTube gaming channel like SoaR.

As I watched him immerse himself in the virtual battlefield, he became an entirely different person than the quasi-catatonic young man that had been sitting in the living room just minutes earlier. Now he was an able commando fighter engaged on a mission that required agility, dexterity and co-ordination. He went from a catatonic kid without a passion or a purpose to a member of a Clan that all fought together to attain the oh-so-climactic trickshot. His mother would tell me that the first time he got a trickshot, her normally nonverbal son shouted and hollered so loudly that she thought he was being attacked.

That video gaming room was like a power source for Peter. Inside that room, he was alive and animated; but as soon as we left and walked back into the living room, he plopped back onto his Archie Bunker chair with all the energy and enthusiasm of a not-so-spry 98-year-old and was quickly back to catatonic Peter. The shift was so profound, it reminded me of *Awakenings*, the brilliant book by Oliver Sacks in which severely catatonic patients briefly come to life with the new "miracle" drug L-dopa—as portrayed by Robert DeNiro in the 1990 film by the same name—only to eventually go back to their catatonic state.

The only difference was that Peter didn't start out catatonic. Anxious and depressed, yes, but he had once been relatively normal and functional. Instead, his animating L-dopa—his video games—rather than being his miracle *cure*, seemed to have *caused* his non-gaming catatonia and malaise. Sure, the video game seems to animate him, but now he spends his entire waking life immersed in a digital fantasy war zone fighting with his clan and seeking to attain the orgasm-like trickshot—and when he's not playing, he's unable to leave his house and is a catatonic agoraphobic mess.

By any clinical definition he's an addict, except his addiction is to a screen—or, more specifically, to the dopamine-activating interactive world that the screen acts as a portal to. I got it. I understood. I gathered up my notes, thanked him and his mother and left; I didn't want to stay too long.

Being immersed in an interactive and exciting battleground where you're in full control has its addictive appeal—I just didn't want to pull a Colonel Kurtz and get pulled in too deeply myself.

Interestingly, Peter's case is also a perfect nature-versus-nurture experiment as he has an identical twin brother who didn't fall down as deeply into the rabbit hole of video game addiction and is subsequently much better adjusted psychologically.

I made several recommendations to both Peter and his mother about mental health programs where he might be able to slowly emerge from his game, leave the house, and slowly reconnect with the real world. At the time of this writing, Peter has refused all suggestions of help and still lives primarily on the battlefield of *Modern Warfare 3*.

And like any scared and trapped enabling family member of an addict, his mother keeps the electricity going and makes sure that the trays of food are still dutifully delivered to his gaming den whenever he yells out.

THE ADDICTION RIDDLE

How does someone like Peter get trapped down the rabbit hole of addiction? Yes, he had some emotional and psychological issues, but how did he become so obsessively and compulsively consumed by his gaming world that he became a Howard Hughes-like shut in?

But before we can fully understand *tech* addiction, we must first understand what addiction itself is.

If we were to watch daytime TV, we'd be convinced that the world is full of "love addicts" or people "addicted" to *Game of Thrones* or hot yoga. But I think that most of us understand true addiction as ingesting a substance or engaging in a behavior in a way that is pathological—that is, a person continues with the addictive behavior in a compulsive way despite adverse consequences. Think Amy Winehouse or John Belushi.

But adverse consequences can have a pretty wide range—dying isn't necessarily part of the definition of addiction—just ask Peter. Typically, in the addiction treatment field, we think of something as being an addiction if a person continues to ingest the problematic substance or engage in the problematic behavior despite consequences such as losing their jobs, jeopardizing their relationships, or negatively affecting their physical health or their schooling.

But beyond symptomatic criteria that help us to diagnose addiction, what is it *really?* I mean, at its *essence*—what is it?

For many, clinicians and researchers alike, the understanding of addiction is sort of like a riddle wrapped in a mystery inside an enigma. Many have a hard time categorizing it—is it a bad habit, a lack of willpower, a disease, a mental disorder, a moral failing, a genetic condition, a psychological condition? Etiological theories abound.

For most people, clinical definitions aside, it's sort of like the old line from Supreme Court justice Potter Stewart in 1964, when he tried to define the highly subjective notion of obscenity: "I know it when I see it." I think that's true for addiction; most of us know it when we see it.

But perhaps even more importantly, if we are really trying to understand addiction, we should ask the further question: why and how does someone become an addict? This is an important question, because if we're to understand how an iPad can be *electronic* cocaine, we need to understand how good old *powdered* cocaine can be so compulsively addicting.

I think most of us can understand why someone might try getting high—why someone might smoke a joint or do a line of coke; odds are that most people reading this have probably dabbled in a little mind expansion themselves. Hell, our last two presidents have even admitted skiing down a white line or two in their youth. Yet how come they didn't become full-blown addicts while others who dabbled did?

Is it our genetics? Or the result of trauma or a rough childhood? Perhaps people with addiction have a neurochemical imbalance? Or are addicts simply people with poor impulse control and minimal will power?

People who don't understand addiction often ask: just how can a person become so compulsive about ingesting a substance—be it alcohol, cocaine, heroin or a pill—or engaging in an addictive behavior like gambling, sex or Internet use, sometimes even to the point of total self-annihilation? To the nonaddicted, it just doesn't make sense.

Of course it doesn't—addiction *isn't* rational.

Certainly Peter's behavior wasn't rational by any definition of the word. Let me provide another example of addictive irrationality from my clinical work: When I was just beginning my career in mental health, I had the opportunity to work at a hospital rehab facility on the East End of Long Island where I was assigned to do the intake on a new patient who had just recently had a heart transplant.

Heart transplants, although somewhat more common these days, are still very risky, complex and involved medical procedures that require quite a bit of medical follow-up and medication management. After all, another person's heart is now beating inside the patient's chest—no small feat. So our new admit, "Michael," arrived with a bulging satchel of medications that he needed to take daily, from immunosuppressants to antibiotics.

I met Michael, who was 42, while the nurses were sorting through his prodigious number of medication bottles, and I found him to be very pleasant; he was smart and funny and laughed easily. In fact, if I hadn't known about his heart or addiction history, I never would have guessed that he had any issues at all.

As I did his intake, I got to know more about his story: charming Michael had once been a chef in the highly stressful restaurant scene of a major city who had coped with that stress for many years by drinking nightly; at some point, alcohol turned to cocaine and cocaine turned to crack. It was this sporadic crack addiction that not only derailed his career, but also did a number on his heart—thus the transplant. He emphasized that his cardiologist had told him to be careful walking up and down stairs so as to not strain his new heart, and that if he smoked crack again, he would die.

When I came to work the next morning, Michael was already up and about. He was at the nurse's station signing himself out AMA—against medical advice. He looked different from the calm, rational man I had spoken to just a day earlier; this Michael was agitated and wild-eyed.

"Michael, what are you doing?" I asked.

He avoided eye contact as he mumbled something under his breath. I tried again:

"Where are you going? What about what we talked about yesterday— getting clean and sober to save your life?"

His face was flushed, and he was sweating. He just looked at me and said: "I gotta go smoke crack . . ." He then tossed his big black duffel bag over his shoulder and ambled toward the elevators. I never saw him again.

His decision seemed so impulsive, so irrational. Yet the day before, I had been speaking to a sane, thoughtful human being. What had happened?

There are no simple answers.

In what I call the "perfect storm" model of addiction, we understand that various factors such as genetics, environment, psychology and neurobiology come together to create the explosive phenomenon of addiction.

But it's also important to keep in mind that no one person's perfect storm of addiction is exactly the same as anyone else's; the intensity and combination of factors contributing to the addiction are a unique amalgam within each person.

We also know that certain people are more prone than others to addictive behavior; for argument's sake, we might say that these people are more predisposed toward having addictive personalities. Further, we know that having addiction in one's family can predispose a person toward that condition and that the children of addicts are eight times more likely to develop an addiction problem.[3]

What is less clear is why. It's been debated whether that increased risk is a consequence of genetics, the modeling of addictive behaviors or simply dysfunctional family dynamics that can create the emotional and psychological conditions for addictive vulnerability. Or perhaps all of the above.

We know, too, that trauma and abuse correlate highly with addiction, by some estimates quadrupling the odds that a person will become an addict. Then there is Attachment Theory, according to which an addict is a person who may not have been consistently and appropriately nurtured in childhood and who then grows up prone to codependence, forming a pathological attachment to an external entity, be it a person, alcohol, cocaine or an iPad—all to help fill the void of nurturing.[4]

For all of these reasons, it's commonly accepted in the addiction psychology field that the problem is less about the particular substance or behavior than about the underlying perfect storm of genetic, psychological, environmental and neurobiological factors that make a person ripe for addiction—any kind of addiction.

Harvard's Dr. Howard Shaffer, one of the world's foremost addiction experts and a friend and colleague of mine, has developed a "syndrome model" of addiction. He analogizes addiction to a virus that compromises the immune system and compares the multiple expressions of addiction (i.e., alcoholism, gambling, opiate addiction, video games) to opportunistic infections that an addictively predisposed person needs to come into contact with in order to "catch." For example, the addictively predisposed person with the weakened addiction immune system who comes into contact with alcohol is more likely to become an alcoholic; if that same addictively predisposed person, however, is exposed to pain pills, then pill addiction it is. And so on.[5]

Having said that addiction is more about a person's vulnerability to addictive substances and/or behaviors, we do know that certain substances or behaviors have a stronger magnetic pull for the vulnerable person; crystal meth tends to be more addicting than alcohol, for example.

Why is that?

As Dr. Steve Hyman, the former director of the National Institute of Mental Health, asks:

"Why does the brain prefer opium to broccoli?"[6] Why do our brains gravitate toward certain substances—or behaviors—more than others? And how might highly stimulating technology act in the same way as a highly addicting drug?

Understanding the addiction riddle—how a person can pursue something so compulsively and often so self-destructively, be it crack or technology—will require an exploration of some interesting concepts along the way: the dopamine tickle. Myelin. And Rat Park.

THE DOPAMINE TICKLE

In order to fully understand addiction, we need to understand the brain's reward system and the impact of dopaminergic substances or behaviors on that reward pathway.

How dopaminergic (dopamine activating) a substance or behavior is correlates very highly with the addictive potential of that substance or behavior. Dopamine is the feel-good neurotransmitter that's the most critical element in the addiction process. When a person performs an action that satisfies a need or fulfills a desire, dopamine is released into the nucleus accumbens, a cluster of nerve cells beneath the cerebral hemispheres that are associated with pleasure and reward, also known as the brain's pleasure center.

In simple terms, engaging in a dopaminergic behavior increases dopamine levels so that the dopamine-reward pathway is activated, thus telling the individual to repeat what he or she just did in order to get that feel-good dopamine reward (or what I like to call the dopamine tickle) again.

As an evolutionary adaptation, the dopamine tickle is a survival mechanism; it rewards and, thus, incentivizes essential biological functions such as eating and procreation. Eating and sex feel good because they increase dopamine; we then remember that and seek out those activities again in order to recapture the feel-good dopamine high.

Natural dopaminergic activities—eating, sex—usually come only after effort and delay and, as mentioned, serve a survival function. But addictive drugs and addictive behaviors, like gambling and video gaming, provide a shortcut to this reward process, which floods the nucleus accumbens with dopamine without serving a biological function.

Unfortunately, evolution hasn't provided an easy way to withstand that dopamine onslaught, so that when people become addicted, they experience a dopamine reduction or shutdown in order to give some relief to their overwhelmed receptor cells. With this reduced capacity to produce dopamine naturally, the addicted person then needs to ingest the addictive substance or engage in the addictive behavior just to maintain his or her dopamine levels.

Then, as a double whammy, chronic exposure to addictive substances or behaviors then negatively affects the frontal cortex—the brain's decision-making center, which is associated with impulse-control, otherwise known as a person's "braking mechanism"—which in turn compromises a person's ability to refrain from the addictive substance or behavior, making it harder to "just say no."

Research has also shown that people who are predisposed toward addiction have lower baseline levels of dopamine and other feel-good neurotransmitters such as endorphins and norepinephrine; thus they're more likely to get hooked on any substance or behavior that increases dopamine—anything that gives them that dopamine tickle—simply because their brains crave it more than those of people who have normal baseline neurotransmitter levels.[7]

We also know that certain substances or behaviors tickle dopamine more than others. For example, brain imaging research shows us that eating—especially eating craving foods like chocolate—can raise dopamine levels by 50 percent; while sex can raise dopamine by 100 percent; snorting cocaine increases dopamine by 350 percent; and ingesting crystal meth creates a whopping 1,200 percent increase in dopamine.[8] That's why we'd say that crystal meth has the highest dopaminergic effect—and thus the highest addictive potential—amongst the substances just mentioned.

So how dopaminergic are virtual experiences? According to one groundbreaking study by Koepp in 1998, video games increase dopamine as much as sex does, about 100 percent. And keep in mind that those are positively quaint 1998 video games, not the 72-inch LCD, ultrarealistic, hyperstimulating and highly arousing games of today.

Think about it this way: we'd be horrified if our young children were exposed to something as inappropriate and stimulating as sex, yet we're letting them get virtual brain orgasms every time they play video games. Knowing that, is it really any wonder that kids are so hooked on their electronics?

As the navy's Dr. Andrew Doan puts it: "The problem is that video game playing (VGP) is estimated to increase brain dopamine levels equivalent to sex; thus, VGP is risky in young minds that cannot say 'no' as VGP literally hijacks their thoughts."

There's one other very important factor that we need to keep in mind in trying to fully understand the addictive potential of video games: the reward schedule, also known as the schedule of reinforcement, a term used by psychologists to describe the pattern or frequency of dopamine-tickling rewards.

As mentioned earlier, natural dopaminergic activities require time and effort: if I get a dopamine tickle when I eat a piece of chocolate cake, we can say that that event has a buildup (I get the cake and cut it), an actual engagement period (I eat the cake) and a coming-down period (I digest the cake). The same can be said for sex—arousal, fooling around and then climax; for the young and vigorous, maybe a rinse-and-repeat. But I'm not repeatedly rewarding myself (getting the dopamine tickle) continuously over a period of hours.

Drugs and virtual stimulation, however, can be quickly repeated, over and over again. I can keep playing *Minecraft* or shooting the target in a shooter game as my dopamine squirts in rat-tat-tat fashion, and it's that rapid reward schedule of a continuous brain orgasm that creates such a powerful addiction dynamic.

While an adult may have the willpower to refrain from engaging with tech as powerful and addicting as sex, from a developmental standpoint, since the brain's frontal cortex—the brain's "braking mechanism," which control impulsivity—isn't fully developed until well into a person's twenties, a child simply doesn't have the neurobiological apparatus to handle that level of stimulation.

Thus once little Johnny and Suzie experience that feel-good, electronic orgasm-like dopamine tickle, they want to push the repeat button again . . . and again . . . and again . . . and again . . .

How compulsive are video games? Here's a telling factoid: according to the manufacturer, gamers have played the *Call of Duty* series—one of the more popular first-person-shooter games—for 25 *billion* total hours. (In a first-person-shooter game, the player sees through the eyes of the shooter and controls the gun.) That adds up to 2.85 million years—longer than the course of human existence![9] And that's just *one* game franchise.

A rather prophetic episode of *Star Trek: The Next Generation* called "The Game," which aired 25 years ago, back in 1991, vividly depicts this addictive brain orgasm effect; the crew of the *Enterprise* is given a virtual headset game that produces an intensely euphoric sensation. They become so addicted to the devices that they walk around in a perpetually trancelike state—not unlike that of Google Glass wearers—and are almost taken over by another species while in their euphoric stupor.

But addiction is about more than just dopamine; we also need to understand myelination, another critically important neurological factor in the addiction process, which can, in turn, better help us to understand tech addiction.

MYELIN—THE BRAIN'S HIGH-SPEED BANDWIDTH

In 2001 the pioneering UCLA neurologist Dr. George Bartzokis, in his groundbreaking "myelin model" of brain disease, was able to prove the existence of another very important brain dynamic associated with addiction: the role of myelination, otherwise also known as the brain's "white matter."[10]

When talking about the brain, most people tend to think of "gray matter," the network of roughly 100 billion neurons* that form the brain and give it its

---

*Recent research by Brazilian neuroscientist Dr. Suzana Herculana Houzel indicates that the oft-repeated 100 billion number is overstated; in a unique and innovative process wherein she analyzed healthy postmortem brains in a "brain soup," she discovered that the actual number of human neurons is actually closer to 84 billion.

pinkish-gray color. But in addition to gray matter, we also have white matter, also known as myelin, a pale lipid composed of cholesterol that, like cable insulation, envelopes the trillions of stemlike parts of neurons called axons that connect neuron-to-neuron to form a single, functioning neural network.

Without myelination, our brains would be as frustratingly slow as a dial-up connection. According to Bartzokis, "Think of the Internet. Myelination makes axons more efficient; it increases bandwidth. Axons are able to do more so that our brains are able to do more."[11]

Okay, a faster-working brain; but why else is myelin so important?

Myelination occurs as part of a healthy developmental process. As we grow and learn, our myelination increases in areas of the brain that need it. According to Dr. Robert F. McGivern, a San Diego State University research psychologist, "If you take a very young brain, say a three- or a four-year-old, the brain organizes itself around experience. You can train that child to learn to read very early and the brain will be well-myelinated in those parts of the brain needed for reading." Reading thus becomes hardwired via myelination.

But how does this happen?

A newborn infant is born with billions of brain cells; each brain cell—or neuron—has branching appendages called dendrites, which reach out to make connections with other neurons. When electrical signals pass from neuron to neuron, synapses are stimulated; as those synapses are stimulated over and over again, those neural connection patterns become hardwired via myelination, which forms in those heavily used areas.

Neurologists call this the "sled on a snowy hill" phenomenon: the first exposure to something or the first time we learn to do something is like the sled first making tracks on fresh snow. On subsequent tries, your sled will tend to follow those grooves; as we repeat those sled rides over and over again, we learn as our brains myelinate in the areas devoted to those activities.

Recent brain imaging research has confirmed the existence of this hardwiring myelination process and has allowed us to see that there are physical differences between a child's brain that has been appropriately stimulated and one that hasn't been appropriately stimulated; connections that aren't appropriately stimulated by repeated exposure and/or experience atrophy, creating a use-it-or-lose-it situation.

That's what happens with language. When an infant is exposed to the complexities of language, the neural pathways devoted to language myelinate—the sled forms tracks in the snow—and become hardwired, making language acquisition permanent and relatively effortless and organic. But if there's no language stimulation during those critical early years, there are no "snow tracks," and so the language-development window closes and language connections atrophy as the brain loses its ability to hardwire and myelinate for language.

Interestingly, that same brain imaging is now also showing us that it's not just understimulated neural pathways (as in feral children) that can lead to neurological differences and developmental problems—but that the over-stimulation of the glowing, flashing screens of iPads and video games can damage myelin in neural pathways as well.

That's because myelin is extremely vulnerable to disruption; oligoden-drocytes, the brain cells that produce cholesterol for proper myelination, are easily damaged by things such as head trauma, environmental stressors, toxins, stress hormones, certain drugs—and overstimulation. What problems can develop as a result of this myelin-destroying overstimulation? Our ability to pay attention and focus, our ability to feel empathy and our ability to discern reality can all be adversely affected by overstimulation during key developmental windows.

That's why Bartzokis's myelin model research in the early part of the new millennium was so important, as he was able to show the critically important role of myelination in healthy human brain development.

Just as importantly, he was also able to prove the correlation between impaired myelination and various brain disorders. Bartzokis believed that those myelination abnormalities drive various neuropsychiatric disorders across our entire life cycle—everything from ADHD and autism in infants and children to schizophrenia and drug addiction in teens and young adults to Alzheimer's in seniors.

And Bartzokis was able to prove it. His brain research was the first of its kind that empirically showed that drug addiction can damage myelin. In his 2002 study published in the *Journal of Biological Psychiatry*, he compared the brains of 37 male cocaine-dependent subjects with those of a control group of 52 non–drug dependent subjects, all between the ages of 19 and 47, and clearly showed the adverse impact of cocaine on brain myelination.[12] "If you look at the data," Bartzokis says, "you will see that the average 40- or 45-year-old cocaine addict has the same amount of white matter as the average 19-year-old."

In his earlier research, Bartzokis had discovered that healthy brains continue to grow and myelinate until we're roughly 50 years old; now, his addiction research clearly showed that drug use stunted myelin growth and development. Bartzokis concluded, "The [healthy] age-related expansion in white matter volume occurring in normal control subjects was absent in the cocaine dependent subjects." These decreased-myelination results were repeated in other studies using other drugs, including alcohol, opiates and marijuana.

And now, a little over ten years after Bartzokis's original work, we have research from several recent brain-imaging studies that show us that tech exposure can also alter brain structure and myelination in exactly the same way that drugs can.

Yes, that's right: that iPad that your child's school thought would be so wonderful as a first-grade learning tool is making your child's brain resemble that of a drug addict.

The recent research: In 2012 a research team led by Dr. Hao Lei of the Chinese Academy of Sciences discovered that the brains of people who had been diagnosed with Internet Addiction Disorder had myelin (white matter) integrity abnormalities in brain regions involving executive attention, decision making and emotional generation. Their study compared the brains of 17 IAD subjects and used as a control 16 healthy subjects. In their findings, published in the *Public Library of Science*, Dr. Lei states: "The results . . . suggest that IAD may share psychological and neural mechanisms with other types of substance addiction and impulse control disorders."[13]

In other words, screen addiction looks like drug addiction in the brain.

In 2013 a brain-imaging study entitled "Decreased Functional Brain Connectivity in Adolescents with Internet Addiction" in *PLOS One*, conducted on 12 adolescents diagnosed with IAD and 11 healthy control subjects, concluded that "Internet addiction is associated with a widespread and significant decrease of functional connectivity."[14] As I've mentioned, functional connectivity relates to the brain's white matter/myelination.

This study shows that gaming is associated with a decrease in all-important myelination.

A September 2014 brain-imaging study in *PLOS One* entitled "Disrupted Brain Functional Network in Internet Addiction Disorder: A Resting-State fMRI Study," by Wee et al., also found similar myelination and connectivity problems with gamers.[15] The researchers indicated that "there is significant disruption in the functional connections of IAD patients, particularly between regions located in the frontal, occipital, and parietal lobes. Our findings . . . suggest that IAD causes disruptions of functional connectivity and, importantly, that such disruptions might link to behavioral impairments."

There was also an amazing American study done at the Indiana University School of Medicine in 2011. In this study, by taking brain scans at both the beginning of the study and then again after subjects had spent one week playing violent video games, the researchers showed cause-and-effect brain changes after just *one week* of video game playing.[16]

Yes, measurable brain changes after just one week.

For the study, 28 healthy young adult males, ages 18 to 29, all with low past exposure to violent video games, were randomly assigned to two groups of 14. Members of the first group were instructed to play a shooting video game for 10 hours at home for one week and refrain from playing the following week. The second group did not play a video game at all during the two-week period. Each of the 28 men underwent functional magnetic resonance imaging (fMRI) analysis at the beginning of the study, with follow-up exams at one and two weeks.

The results showed that after one week of violent game play, the video game group members showed less activation in the left inferior frontal lobe and less activation in the anterior cingulate cortex than in their baseline results and the results of the control group.

"For the first time, we have found that a sample of randomly assigned young adults showed less activation in certain frontal brain regions following a week of playing violent video games at home," claimed Dr. Yang Wang, the lead researcher of the study. "The affected brain regions are important for controlling emotion and aggressive behavior."

The frontal brain regions that Dr. Wang mentioned are the same brain regions that are affected by drug addiction; and now, for the first time, researchers had shown a direct relationship between playing violent video games over an extended period of time and a subsequent change in those brain regions associated with executive functioning.

Interestingly, after the video game group refrained from game play for an additional week, the executive regions of their brains returned to a state closer to that of the control group. It would seem that the brain's plasticity—its ability to bounce back and compensate—was clearly at work. But what if a person continued playing violent video games? "These findings indicate that violent video game play has a long-term effect on brain functioning," Dr. Wang says. "These effects may translate into behavioral changes over longer periods of game play."[17]

All of this recent research linking screen exposure to neurobiological changes has excited academics in the field of brain science. Indeed, Professor Gunter Schumann, chair of biological psychiatry at King's College in London, told the BBC, "For the first time . . . studies show changes in the neuronal connections between brain areas as well as changes in brain function in people who are frequently using the Internet or video games." Neurologist and Oxford professor Baroness Susan Greenfield believes that video game addiction can even cause a form of what she describes as "dementia" in children.[18]

When looking at this brain-imaging research, some ask the inevitable chicken-or-the-egg question: is screen exposure causing the brain changes, or are those with preexisting and underlying brain abnormalities gravitating toward addictive gaming and screen time? Since most of the brain imaging studies (with the notable exception of Dr. Wang's) are looking at the brains of gamers without having a baseline reading of that brain before the problematic gaming, it is a valid question.

Certainly we know that in substance addiction there can be a vicious cycle: sometimes people with underlying brain abnormalities or chemical imbalances are more likely to self-medicate and become substance addicted, and then the addiction further impairs or damages the neuroanatomy or neurochemistry of the brain, which then only further exacerbates the addiction.

Author and adolescent psychiatrist Dr. Victoria Dunckley describes that chicken-or-the-egg dynamic this way: "In gaming and Internet addiction research in general, the chicken and egg question is a legitimate one, but research suggests there are bidirectional influences that create a vicious cycle. In other words, vulnerable brains are more vulnerable to screen addiction, and then the addiction contributes to psychiatric pathology, which worsens the addiction."

Let's also keep in mind that Dr. Wang's study did indeed do pre- and post-brain imaging and did show a causal relationship between excessive screen exposure and abnormalities in the frontal regions of the brain. So while it can be true that those with preexisting brain disorders can be gravitating toward gaming, it does also seem to be the case that excessive gaming changes brain structure—even in so-called normal brains.

Now that we've explored the neurobiology of addiction via dopamine and myelination, let's take a look at the role that environment plays in the perfect storm of addiction.

RAT PARK: ADDICTION AND THE CAGE

Nature vs. nurture. Most of us have heard that phrase since grade school as a framing of the two competing theories of human nature: biological determinism vs. learned behavior or behavior shaped by our environment. The consensus these days is to reject the proposition as an either/or statement in favor of the more inclusive and comprehensive "and," as in: it's nature *and* nurture creating a perfect storm that determines who we are and how we behave.

Just how important our environment is in shaping who we are and how we behave was proven in an exquisitely simple yet illuminating experiment conducted in the late 1970s by Canadian professor Dr. Bruce Alexander. Dr. Alexander had been skeptical of earlier addiction studies done on rats in the 1960s; in those earlier experiments, the poor little furry rodents were put in Skinner boxes (named after the behavior guru B. F. Skinner). These boxes were small, cramped solitary-confinement cages where often-starved rats could get tiny pellets of food, provided that they pushed a little lever on the side of the box over and over and over again.

In the addiction experiments of the 1960s, a rat would be tethered to the box's ceiling, with tubing that included a surgically implanted needle going into its jugular vein. Yes, it was as horribly unpleasant as it sounds. When the rat pushed the lever, the sweet relief of morphine would instantly surge into its little bloodstream (in other experiments, cocaine water was used).

Not surprisingly, these poor trapped rats hit those morphine levers like a retiree at the quarter slots in Atlantic City, and the little creatures became hopelessly addicted. That drugs-lead-to-addiction research then became part of the War on Drugs media campaign, which hyped the evils of illicit drugs; for most people, the evidence was in: drugs = hopeless drug addiction.

But Dr. Alexander was troubled by these conclusions. If the power of addiction lay in the drug, why didn't all people who ingested them become addicted? He understood that rats, in their natural state, are highly social creatures not designed by nature to be isolated in Skinner boxes; was it possible that the prior experiments were merely indicating that an isolated and trapped rat might be more likely than a "free" rat to choose an anesthetic escape from an intolerable existence?

Rats share this strong social aspect with human beings, and as Dr. Alexander understood, solitary confinement often drives humans insane. It's well known that if inmates in isolation have access to mind-numbing drugs, they invariably take them. Thus, Dr. Alexander reasoned, couldn't it be the isolating Skinner box and *not* the morphine that was driving these similarly incarcerated rats to drug addiction?

With that in mind, Dr. Alexander and his colleagues set about designing a study with two separate groups of rats: one group was kept in the isolation of Skinner boxes while the other got to frolic in what came to be known as "Rat Park," a large open area filled with things that rats love: platforms for climbing, tin cans to hide in and running wheels for exercise. Oh, and it was coed. Apparently rats, like humans, enjoy sex as well.

The results were shocking: the rats in cages became addicts. But the rats in the freedom of Rat Park, not so much; in fact, they barely touched the drug water that was made available to them. Alexander concluded that addiction was less about the magnetic, addictive pull of the drug and more about the condition of a rat's life; without healthy socialization and connection, a rat seemed to be much more vulnerable to addiction.[19]

But what about people?

As Dr. Alexander speculated, "People do not have to be put into cages to become addicted—but is there a sense in which people who become addicted actually feel 'caged?'"

Years later, he wanted to see if he could test these findings on humans. Ethical considerations precluded him from caging people and offering them drugs; most universities tend to frown on such practices. But he was able to study the historical records of just such a "natural" experiment: the colonization of Native people and their subjugation on reservations.

Alexander realized that the Native peoples of Canada and the United States had been effectively put in their own Skinner boxes, which robbed them of their traditional cultural ties and normal socialization. He also discovered that before this colonization period, there were scant records of addiction: "There was so little addiction that it is very difficult to prove from written and oral histories that it existed at all. But once the [N]ative people were colonized, alcoholism became close to universal; there were entire reserves where virtually every teenager and adult was either an alcohol or drug addict or 'on the wagon.'"

Western researchers used to blame the higher incidence of alcoholism among Native peoples on "genetic vulnerability"; English settlers would cite a variation of the racially charged "Indians just can't handle their liquor" and would impose strict alcohol prohibition on reservations. Yet, very tellingly, on reservations where alcohol was available but Native culture was preserved, Native people were able to incorporate alcohol into their traditions without too much difficulty; in those cases, there were instances of alcohol consumption and some abuse, but no widespread alcoholism.

Today, most addiction experts have rejected the genetic-vulnerability explanation. Indeed, Rat Park—and the colonization of Native peoples—has shown us that social beings put in physical, mental or cultural isolation—"cages," if you will—are more susceptible to addiction, including behavioral addictions like excessive Internet use.

According to Alexander: "The view of addiction from Rat Park is that today's flood of addiction is occurring because our hyperindividualistic, hypercompetitive, frantic, crisis-ridden society makes most people feel socially and culturally isolated. . . . They find temporary relief in addiction to drugs or any of a thousand other habits and pursuits because addiction allows them to escape from their feelings, to deaden their senses, and to experience an addictive lifestyle as a substitute for a full life."

According to this perspective, today's epidemic of glowing screens is less about the screens and more about the isolating "hyperindividualistic, hyper-competitive, frantic, crisis-ridden society" that our kids inhabit.

When I interviewed Lt. Sam Brown about his experiences using virtual reality therapy, he made an insightful observation about another important addiction dynamic when he described how many of his soldier friends were getting addicted to video games: "Look, people are looking for purpose in their lives. Some of these games give you that. Whether you're on a shared mission in *Halo* or whatever, if you don't have a sense of purpose, these games can fill that void." He added: "Probably the only reason that I didn't get hooked those first couple of years is because I couldn't use my hands well enough to handle the control board."

How many kids today feel adrift and purposeless? Add to that the "hy-percompetitive" and "hyperindividualistic" dynamic that Dr. Alexander mentioned, mix in a little stress, social disconnect and the seductively addict-ing escapism of glowing screens, and voilà!

Tech addiction.

Sure enough, according to the latest research, tech addiction is affecting young people more than adults: *The American Journal of Drug and Alcohol Abuse* found that 8.2 percent of Americans suffer from Internet addiction, but ac-cording to *Internet Addiction: A Handbook and Guide to Evaluation and Treatment*, the disorder affects more than 18 percent of college-age Internet users.

The idea that we can become addicted to virtual tech is not a new one to some clinicians. Back in 1999, Dr. Peter Greenfield published a small, well-written book called *Virtual Addiction*, years before any of the most recent brain-imaging research and well before the intensity and pervasiveness of this generation of iTech. Instead of brain imaging, Greenfield used good old clinical criteria to assess that many people were developing increasingly problematic—even addictive—relationships with their technology.

That's an important point that shouldn't be understated. Brain imaging can be wonderfully illuminating, but the way that psychiatrists, psychologists and psychotherapists diagnose a mental disorder is by diagnosing clinical symptoms, not by using brain imaging. To point: I've diagnosed or worked with hundreds of alcoholics and addicts (who were drug or alcohol "dependent," according to the older *DSM-IV*), and not one was diagnosed via an MRI.

I think it's fair to say that if a person is using a substance or engaging in a behavior in such a compulsive way that it negatively affects—or even destroys—his or her life, then we can say that addiction is at hand.

In the next chapter, in order to get firsthand insight into the addictive and hypnotic power of hyperarousing screens, we will meet an amazing addiction researcher, neuroscientist—and recovering video game addict.

FOUR

INTERVIEW WITH DR. DOAN*

NEUROSCIENTIST AND RECOVERING VIDEO GAMER

I WAS FIRST INTRODUCED TO DR. ANDREW DOAN WHILE WRITING this book and became quite fascinated by him, as I believe that he has a unique perspective to add to our understanding of tech addiction. That's because Dr. Doan is not just a Johns Hopkins–educated M.D. who also happens to have a Ph.D. in neuroscience and has extensively researched and studied tech addiction; he's also a recovering video game addict. To the best of my knowledge, he's the *only* neuroscientist/recovering video game addict.

But his bona fides are even more impressive: as previously mentioned, he's a commander in the U.S. Navy and the head of addiction research for the navy and the Department of Defense.

I was amazed that this kind, compassionate, physically fit and respected physician had once been a very unhealthy, overweight and rage-filled video game addict. Interestingly, beyond coming to understand that his video game addiction was ruining his own life, he became aware of some of the darker aspects of tech addiction when he started realizing that many military vets who were involved in violent episodes—homicides and suicides—were also violent video gamers, and that more often than not, they were *sleep-deprived* gamers.

---

*Opinions and points of view expressed are those of Dr. Doan and do not necessarily reflect the official position or policies of the U.S. Navy or the Department of Defense.

I think his story of video game addiction can help us better understand how even an intelligent medical student can get seduced by screen addiction. The following interview has been culled and edited from our talks together as well as from an interview that he gave to Vee Williams on September 17, 2014; it is both very personal and quite illuminating.

Q. TELL ME A LITTLE ABOUT YOUR GAMING ADDICTION. AND WHAT EVENTUALLY WAS YOUR BOTTOM?

When I was in medical school, about 16 years ago, I was really heavily addicted to video games. For over ten years and all through medical school, I played 50 to 100 hours a week. . . . I was utilizing the games as a form of digital drug to reduce anxiety, to deal with stress, and to allow me to feel the adrenalin rush of online head-to-head competition.

I had played all the time and had just assumed it was a hobby. But the first time I thought that there was a problem . . . I wouldn't sleep very much. So my schedule would be, I go to school—I had a full-ride scholarship at Hopkins—I used to joke around, look at all these losers—they have to pay money to go to med school and I got a full ride. So in a way, I was cocky and arrogant.

So I'd go to school, come home around five, get dinner ready for the kids (we had two young children) and then maybe attend to my wife for a little bit; spend some time with her. She was a nurse at the time working a hard schedule. She'd go to bed early, like 8:30. And I was like "sweet!" I'd sneak out of bed—I'd already played a couple of hours before dinner, then I'd play from 8:30 till 4:30 in the morning. It was customary for me to hear the birds sing in the morning . . . sleep a couple of hours and repeat the cycle again. So I'd be gaming eight hours a day and at school eight hours a day. I had two full-time jobs, basically.

So I was a functional addict, but the problem was that I was always sleep-deprived, so I was raging. I became real rageful and abusive to my wife. And so she left. She left with the kids and filed a restraining order. So I thought that the problem was just my rage, that it was my temper. So I promised her I'd work on it—you know, come back and let's go to church together, I promised to change, get marriage counseling—all of that stuff.

But of course, in denial of the video game addiction because there's no diagnosis, right? I'm a medical student at the time and I never heard of this addiction. So it's not an addiction—it's a hobby. I tried to moderate, but then the addiction starts building up again. So then I would only play four hours a day, but then four became six then eight then ten then 12. And before you know it, I was full-blown playing all the time like I used to.

Finally what kicked in, it was 2003 and I had been playing addictively for almost 11 years, when I finally developed carpal tunnel from clicking the mouse in the real-time strategy games. Because I played Starcraft—*real-time strategy was my drug of choice. I loved playing* StarCraft, Warcraft, Warcraft 2, Warcraft 3 . . . *and I'd be clicking the mouse 80 hours a week.*

I had pain from my clicking finger all the way up to my forearm. And my cortisol levels were shot—through my hypothalamus-adrenal-pituitary (HPA) axis, so I was getting fat because I had all of this cortisol floating around. I didn't exercise, so I was retaining more body fat. And then finally my HPA axis was all disregulated so I was more prone to infection—I had pimples all over my face, I had stretch marks beginning. And then, finally, I got an infection in my armpit!

So in addition to the carpel tunnel, I had this armpit infection that was streaking down my arm. And on top of that, because my blood pressure was going up because of the gaming adrenaline rush—my blood pressure was high, my cholesterol was high. And because my blood pressure was high and I was sitting all the time, I had hemorrhoids the size of walnuts—I mean, literally! I was a young man—I was pissed off. Why do I have hemorrhoids like some pregnant women do? We're talking bloody, painful hemorrhoids.

So I had this triad—you know, I had carpel tunnel, this armpit infection and these hemorrhoids. I was in surgery at the VA and I go, man, I'm killing my career; I can barely operate or work as a physician without taking these maximum pain killers.

So finally, I was like, man, maybe I can't play video games. But still calling it a "hobby"—that's causing me hemorrhoids, carpel tunnel and an armpit infection! So finally in 2004 I stopped playing completely.

But I did have a relapse in 2007. One of my residents dropped a CD-ROM of World of Warcraft [WoW] *on my desk. Now I knew I was more prone to real-time strategies, but I'm also a fanatic for RPGs [role playing games]. So I'm like, man, maybe I can play and moderate now because I'm a staff doctor now, I make plenty of money and there's less stress in my life so I don't have to use it to escape.*

Uh-uh. I was wrong. I played a year of that . . . and all of my old habits came back. My son, who was in his early teenage years—and I looked over at him one day and he was bawling his head off because I was yelling at him for not being able to keep up with me. Yelling at him! Here's my son who all he wants to do is spend time with me, but because of my rageful, addict nature when I was playing these games, that bad side came back again.

So what I started noticing [was that] my marriage started going back to the way it was before; my relationship with my kids was hurting; I was being rageful, I kicked the dog . . . I was not sleeping a lot so I'm more grouchy because [with] this kind of addiction, you have to trade something, and most gamers who are addicted trade sleep. That's the number-one thing they trade. So they stay up until two or three in the morning. I did too.

So I started falling asleep at the wheel. There are days when I drove—I had like a 60-minute commute one way—there were days when I dozed off in the car and woke up five minutes later, not knowing where I am. I should be dead, you know?

That's when I finally saw that I had this addiction and I started using the word addiction. And then you know what it was? I saw my son—I saw my son getting addicted at around 12 or 13 where he was sneaking out in the middle of the night playing Call of Duty. *And then you know when you see a quality of someone else that you know is a quality that you have? It really irritates you, right? I saw that and it really irritated me. And I'm like, I'm really getting irritated at my own son for doing the same thing I do!*

So we finally took him away from gaming and he just blossomed! *He went from this kid who was insecure who—I used to not pour into him, so he used to run into the bathroom at school and cry. When we took the gaming away, he found his love in track and field . . . he's getting recruited by 15 Division I schools now, his confidence is up, everything is going better for him. So I saw how gaming damaged him as well.*

So I'm convinced that if people are addicted to this thing, it's going to ruin your lives. It almost ruined mine—and it almost ruined my son and almost destroyed his confidence and his opportunities.

As mentioned, Dr. Doan has come up with the term "digital pharmakeia" to describe digital screen drugs and their effects on the brain. He believes that such screen drugs are dopamine-elevating stimulants that hyperarouse our HPA axis. He also believes that some are more potent than others. TV can be considered the mildest on the stimulation continuum, then perhaps a game like *Tetris,* culminating with high-arousal games like *Call of Duty* or *World of Warcraft.*

From both his own experience and his work in the military, he also came to understand the important role that sleep deprivation plays in gaming addiction. "With alcohol, people usually pass out and sleep with severe intoxication. In contrast, video games require being awake in order for the addict to engage in the behavior. As a result of sleep deprivation, there will be HPA dysregulation."

HPA dysregulation is associated with depression, anxiety, psychotic breakdowns and mental disorders. Dr. Doan described one sleep-deprived video gaming marine whom he worked with who was homicidal and wanted to cut people's heads off. According to Dr. Doan, the solution was removing video games and removing sleep medications that were not working because of excessive gaming and stimulation from gaming. "With sleep and rest, the homicidal ideation dissipated."[1]

Would that marine have gotten violent if he hadn't unplugged and taken a nap? We can't know for sure; human behavior is hard to predict. But Doan believes that many of the suicides and homicides committed by PTSD (Post Traumatic Stress Disorder, a mental disorder that used to be commonly referred to as "shell shock") vets are also influenced by violent video games and sleep deprivation. "Many of these soldiers—they're young kids who are already gamers when they come into the military. Then when they're on base, they can't drink or do drugs because they get tested for that, so they play video games for hours on end as an escape. Add in some combat trauma and sleep deprivation and you have a recipe for disaster."

The attack by the infamous Washington Navy Yard shooter Aaron Alexis, who shot and killed 12 people in 2013,[2] was the incident that first got Dr. Doan to look more closely at veteran violence and video games. Alexis seemed to have some psychotic symptoms (hearing voices, he believed he was being influenced by electromagnetic waves)—but he was also a sleep-deprived gamer. He would play the ultraviolent *Call of Duty* for up to 16 hours a day, and in the weeks before the shooting, he went to the VA emergency room seeking medication for his insomnia. Did the sleep deprivation and gaming cause the psychotic symptoms that pushed him over the edge? We will never know. But we do know that Dr. Doan's other homicidal marine patient became "normal" after he stopped gaming and got some sleep.

Neurologically, Dr. Doan uses a five finger/hand analogy to demonstrate the effect that gaming has on the brain. "Observe your left hand. The thumb will represent the cortical areas associated with all the benefits of video gaming and use of technology: quick analytical skills, improved hand-eye coordination, and perhaps improved reflexes. The index finger will represent the cortical areas associated with communication skills. The middle finger will represent behaviors associated with social bonding with family and friends. The ring finger will represent the capacity to recognize emotions of both self and others (empathy). Lastly, the little finger will represent the cortical areas associated with self-control."

In essence, with excessive gaming, just one part of the brain is being developed—or overdeveloped: the thumb, representing the region associated with quick reflexes and pattern recognition. But this creates a potential imbalance as that gamer grows up: "As the brain matures, the possible end product is a young adult who is all thumbs in their thinking: possessing quick analytical skills and quick reflexes, but not as developed in communication skills, having few bonds with people, exhibiting little empathy, and showing minimal self-control."

Finally, Dr. Doan also brings up a subject that most people may not consider when they think of gaming: that it may be a national security threat as terrorists are turning to social media, Internet discussion forums, and online gaming to seduce new recruits. According to Doan, gamers are easy pickings: "Internet addicts are isolated, lonely, and low-hanging fruit for recruitment."

Dr. Doan's compelling personal narrative, describing his descent deeper and deeper into gaming addiction—and how his health and family life suffered as a result of it—reads like the story of any other drug addict. Even the manner in which he rationalized his way into a relapse after a period of abstinence, thinking that he might be able to moderate his usage, is familiar territory in drug addiction.

Despite stories like Dr. Doan's and the growing body of research that shows the drug-like effect of digital media on the brain, there are still screen-addiction "deniers," both laypeople and some mental health experts, who haven't quite tuned in to the potential depth and severity of the growing problem. Yes, video games can most definitely be a hobby for some, but they are quite clearly an addiction for others.

We should also keep in mind that screen addiction and other problematic clinical disorders are not just limited to video game effects. In our hyperconnected world, we have a couple of other suspects as well: social media and texting.

But how can that be, you might ask. As social animals, what can possibly go wrong with a little technology-assisted connection?

FIVE

THE BIG DISCONNECT

TEXTING AND SOCIAL MEDIA

"I'M GOING TO KILL YOU WHILE YOU'RE BOTH ASLEEP!" THE wild-eyed 13-year-old girl said as she flailed and kicked her father before biting his arm. This was the second time in less than a week that "Heidi" had flown into a violent rage because her parents had taken away her Chromebook and her access to social media. It would also be the second time that she would have to be taken to the psychiatric emergency room.

When her parents, "John" and "Melanie," first called me to help with their daughter, they described a sweet, happy, loving girl whom her teachers had always described as their favorite student. With a tendency to gravitating toward overachievers, she loved playing soccer and hiking and would take mountain-bike rides with her dad—the man she bit.

John and Melanie, supportive suburban New Jersey parents with college degrees and their own tech business, were blindsided by Heidi's social media addiction. "It all started when she came home in seventh grade with a Chromebook that the school had given her." Ostensibly given for school purposes, the Chromebook came loaded with Google Classroom—which also, unfortunately, included Google Chat and various Google Chat communities.

Once the "educational" Trojan Horse entered their home, John and Melanie found that Heidi was more and more preoccupied with the social media chatrooms within that Chromebook and that she would spend hours every night on those various chatrooms. Since the chatrooms were part of the Chromebook platform, John and Melanie were not able to disable them. Then Heidi started becoming preoccupied with raunchy YouTube videos and also started playing *Squarelaxy,* an addictive progression game similar to *Minecraft,* which allowed her to be online with other *Squarelaxy* players.

Eventually, Heidi's parents discovered that she was chatting with strange boys all over the country; when confronted, she admitted that she had been talking to a boy in Texas who had bragged to her that he had just killed his mother with a hanger the night before. In her next breath, she asked if she could go visit the boy in Texas. Increasingly concerned that their sweet little 12-year-old was being exposed to very corrosive influences, John and Melanie asked the school for help. The school suggested that they use a filter called OpenDNS to block their daughter from the problematic sites. Heidi's tech-savvy parents found OpenDNS "absolutely worthless," and Heidi's problem's continued to escalate.

After a year with her Chromebook and social media addiction, Heidi had transformed from a sweet, innocent girl who loved spending time with her parents into a sexualized, foul-mouthed and violent terror who has kept her parents hostage. And, sadly, a girl who now has a psychiatric profile after her two hospitalizations. I'm currently working with John and Melanie, who are beside themselves with fear, to explore treatment options for Heidi.

The question some might ask: How did the "miracle" of social media connection go so terribly wrong with this young girl?

———————————

Best-selling author Johann Hari is standing on the famous red dot, well-known to viewers of TED Talks, as he looks out at the packed auditorium at the Royal Institution of Great Britain, in London.

He is presenting his powerful and well-received TED talk on addiction (almost four million views) where he discusses a new addiction paradigm that stresses the importance of human connection and heavily references the work of Professor Bruce Alexander and his Rat Park research. He concludes his talk by saying that he's come to understand that "the opposite of addiction isn't sobriety—the opposite of addiction is *connection*."[1] The crowd then breaks out into thunderous applause as he gets a standing ovation.

Social connection. It's not only the most essential part of being human but also a key ingredient in our happiness and health as well. Yet a few minutes earlier in his talk, Hari had looked out into the crowd and said: "It might sound weird to say . . . I've been talking about how disconnection is the major driver of addiction, and it's weird to say [addiction has] grown, because we're the most connected society that's ever been, surely."

He's right. We are indeed the most connected society that's ever lived— each *second* we send over 7,500 tweets, 1,394 Instagram photos, over two million emails and view over 119,000 YouTube videos.[2] And we keep texting and texting as if our lives depended on it: Americans send 69,000 texts a second, with over six billion texts sent in the United States every day; globally, that number is 23 billion daily texts and 8.3 trillion annually.[3]

And, as we would all suspect, the younger the texter, the more texting. According to a 2011 Pew Research Poll, cell phone owners between the ages of 18 and 24 exchange an average of 109.5 messages on a normal day—more than 3,200 texts per month—while in the adult population, users send or receive an average of 41.5 messages on a typical day, with the median user sending or receiving only ten texts daily.[4]

As for social media, according to a 2015 report by *Digital, Social and Mobile,* more than two billion people have active social media accounts—who knew the young and awkward Mark Zuckerberg would change the world in 2004 from his Harvard dorm room? Beyond social media, a little over three billion people on the planet are active Internet users.

That's a lot of connecting. For a species that's hardwired for social connection, that should be a wonderful thing; we should all be walking around with smiles on our faces.

Then why the hell are we so depressed and lonely? That shouldn't be the case—the more connected that we are, the happier and more fulfilled we should be. Yet we're not. As Hari points out during his TED Talk, "We're one of the loneliest societies that has ever been."

Recent studies back up the theory that as social media and technology have made us more connected, we've become increasingly depressed.

In a 2014 study published in the journal *Social Indicators Research,* Dr. Jean M. Twenge, a San Diego State University psychology professor and the author of *Generation Me* (2006) and co-author of *The Narcissism Epidemic* (2010), analyzed data from nearly seven million teenagers and adults from across the country and found that more people reported symptoms of depression than in the 1980s.[5]

According to that study, compared to their 1980s counterparts, teens are 74 percent more likely to have trouble sleeping and twice as likely to see a professional for mental health issues.

Another study indicates that people are ten times more likely to suffer from depression today than in 1945, with women and teenage girls twice as susceptible as men.[6] Even more depressingly (pun intended), the World Health Organization (WHO) predicts that by 2020 depression will be second to heart disease as the leading cause of disability globally,[7] as suicide rates have increased by 60 percent over the past 50 years.[8]

Again, that doesn't appear to make sense; if we're social animals with a hardwired need to connect, then why are we getting more depressed as we get more connected? Someone's got some 'splaining to do.

Let's start by looking at our need for human connection. We know that we can get both physically and psychologically ill without human contact. In fact, we can go crazy.

That's what happened to Sarah Shourd.[9] The 32-year-old American was hiking with two others in the mountains of Iraqi Kurdistan in July of 2009 when, having inadvertently strayed over the Iranian border, she and her friends were arrested by Iranian troops. Accused of spying, she was sentenced to solitary confinement in Evin prison in Tehran, where she endured a little over a year with minimal or no human contact before she was freed.

According to Sarah, she began to lose her mind after about two months in solitary confinement. She started hearing phantom footsteps and seeing flashing lights, and she spent most of her day crouched on all fours, listening through a gap in the door.

"In the periphery of my vision, I began to see flashing lights, only to jerk my head around to find that nothing was there," she wrote in the *New York Times* in 2011. "At one point, I heard someone screaming, and it wasn't until

I felt the hands of one of the friendlier guards on my face, trying to revive me, that I realized the screams were my own."

Being alone doesn't agree with us. Biologists believe that human beings evolved as social animals because being with others had an evolutionary benefit: a group had a better shot at survival than a nomadic loner. This led to a hardwiring of social/tribal connection that, in turn, also helped to define the social and emotional life of the group member.

Being social creatures, we find purpose and meaning and bolster our emotional states largely through the social and cultural context created by contact with others. Without the group to act as a sort of mirror to help us contextualize our feelings and our self-concept, before very long we are gazing, as it were, into a fun-house mirror—and the distorted perceptions and irrational thinking that occur can look very much like psychosis.

This insanity-creating effect of isolation was also confirmed in several human experiments. The most notorious of these, involving not only isolation but sensory deprivation as well, took place at McGill University Medical Center in Montreal in the 1950s.[10] Initially motivated by a desire to better understand alleged "brainwashing" by the Russian and Korean military, psychologist Dr. Donald Hebb and his researchers enlisted mostly college students as paid volunteers—$20 per day—to spend several weeks by themselves in soundproof cubicles, deprived of human contact.

The researchers' aim was to eliminate social contact and perceptual stimulation to see how their subjects would behave when left totally alone. In order to also minimize what the volunteers could feel, see, hear and touch, the researchers fitted them with translucent visors, cotton gloves and cardboard cuffs extending beyond the fingertips. The volunteers also had to lie on U-shaped foam pillows to restrict noise, and air conditioners were set up to create a continuous hum to mask any additional noise.

After only a few hours, Dr. Hebb's volunteers started to crave stimulation; many began talking, singing or reciting poetry to themselves to break the monotony. Later, many of them became highly emotional and anxious and were unable to perform simple math and word-association tests.

But anxiety, restlessness and adverse cognitive effects weren't the worst of it. The most shocking thing that happened to human beings in isolation with minimal stimulation, the researchers discovered, was psychosis. Test subjects started hallucinating, seeing points of light, lines or shapes. Eventually the hallucinations became more bizarre, as subjects reported seeing squirrels marching with sacks over their shoulders or processions of eyeglasses filing down a street. The test subjects seemed to have no control over what they saw: one man saw only dogs; another, babies.

Beyond visual hallucinations, some subjects had auditory hallucinations as well, hearing a music box or a choir, for instance. Still others had tactile hallucinations: one man had the sense that he had been hit in the arm by pellets fired from guns; another reached out to touch a doorknob and felt an electric shock instead.

The results were so disturbing that the researchers had to cut the experiment short; the subjects became too disoriented and distressed to keep going. Hebb had originally hoped to observe his subjects for six weeks, but in the end, only a few lasted beyond two days, and no one lasted for an entire week. Afterward, Hebb wrote in the journal *American Psychologist* that the results were "very unsettling to us . . . to find, in your own laboratory, that merely taking away the usual sights, sounds, and bodily contacts from a healthy university student for a few days can shake him, right down to the base."

In 2008 clinical psychologist Ian Robbins re-created Hebb's experiment in collaboration with the BBC for a reality television show called *Total Isolation*.[11] In the show, six volunteers were put in soundproof rooms in a former nuclear bunker for 48 hours. The results were similar. The volunteers suffered anxiety, extreme emotions, paranoia and significant deterioration in their mental functioning. And, like Hebb's participants, they also went a bit insane and hallucinated.

One of the volunteers, the comedian Adam Bloom, started getting paranoid after just 18 hours, fearful that he'd be trapped in the bunker. After 24 hours he began to pace endlessly. According to Dr. Robbins: "This behaviour is often seen in animals, as well as people, when they are kept in confinement. It's a way of providing input into your life physically."

Forty hours in, Bloom started to go insane. He described vividly seeing 5,000 empty oyster shells: "I could see the pearly sheen on the oyster shells as clear as day," he explained, adding, "then I felt as though the room was taking off from underneath me."

Two other volunteers also described their hallucinations. Mickey, a postal worker, was frightened when he saw mosquitoes and fighter planes buzzing around his head; Claire, a psychology student, didn't mind the little cars, snakes and zebras but was scared when she suddenly felt that somebody else was in the room.

We also know that like human beings, our cousins the primates don't do well in isolation either. One of the most graphic examples comes from psychologist Harry Harlow's experiments on rhesus macaque monkeys at the University of Wisconsin–Madison during the 1960s, in which he deprived them of social contact after birth for months and, in some cases, even years. They became "enormously disturbed" after only 30 days. After a year of isolation, they were "obliterated" socially, incapable of interaction of any kind.[12]

So we've seen that being alone can drive a person—and a monkey—crazy. But it's not just being alone that's problematic. Not getting the right kind of human contact and nurturing support at key developmental periods in childhood can lead to profound emotional and psychological problems.

We know this from the seminal work of psychiatrist John Bowlby in the 1930s at the Child Guidance Clinic in London, where he treated many emotionally disturbed children. Bowlby observed that children experienced intense distress when separated from their mothers; even being fed by other caregivers didn't diminish the children's anxiety.[13]

From all of these studies, we clearly see that we need social connection as much as we need oxygen. But interestingly, human beings also appear to have a couple of other basic psychological needs: the need for reward and a thirst for *novelty*.

Let's start with our need for novelty, also known as *neophilia*. Evolutionary biologists have come to understand that our exploration for something *new* had certain life-sustaining implications. As Winifred Gallagher points out in her book *New: Understanding Our Need for Novelty and Change* (2011), our human brains are biologically primed for novelty, which, in turn, has helped us to survive cataclysmic environmental change: "Our genius for responding to the new and different distinguishes us from all other creatures, saved us from extinction 80,000 years ago, and has fueled our progress from the long epoch of the hunter-gatherers, through the agricultural and industrial eras into the information age."[14]

Gallagher points out that from the time a baby can crawl, it seeks the new and different, a trait that has fueled our ability to create life-sustaining and life-enhancing innovations from the bow and arrow to the refrigerator to the computer. Unfortunately, as Gallagher points out, this hardwired thirst for novelty can be overwhelming in the information age, when every hyperlink, tweet, text, email and Instagram photo can be an opportunity to experience something new and novel; as with an alcoholic in a liquor store or a chocolate lover at Willy Wonka's, the multitude of opportunities for novelty can be exhaustingly hyperstimulating.

And what about the human need to experience reward? We know that humans like dopamine-activating rewards—a lot. As was pointed out in chapter three, evolution incentivized us via the "dopamine tickle" to pursue certain life-sustaining activities like eating and sex because dopamine made us *feel* good. But we've discovered that digital stimulation feels pretty good, too, and similarly lights up our dopamine-reward pathways.

So then where does modern digital technology, which plays off of these intersecting human needs of connection, reward and novelty, leave us? Short answer: Addicted. Or, at the very least, vulnerable to the potential for screen addiction.

According to Dr. Whybrow, "Our brains are wired for finding immediate reward. With technology, novelty is the reward. You essentially become addicted to novelty" as those new dopamine-tickling texts and social media updates feed into our ancient pleasure pathway.[15]

That's the problem—many adults and kids have developed compulsive and addicting texting and social media habits precisely because they quench our thirst for novelty while tickling our dopamine-reward pathways.

And, like all addicts, they can go into withdrawal without it.

THE TEXT EFFECT

In a 2010 study at the University of Maryland, 200 students were asked to give up all media, including texting, for 24 hours. Many showed signs of withdrawal, craving and anxiety. "Texting and IM-ing my friends gives me a constant feeling of comfort," said one student. "When I did not have those two luxuries, I felt quite alone and secluded in my life." Another student put it in even more direct terms: "I clearly am addicted and the dependency is sickening."[16]

According to a more recent 2015 Pew Research Center study of millennial communication habits, published in the American Psychological Association's journal *Psychology of Popular Media,* "Text messaging has increased dramatically over the past 10 years," and many teenage texters share addict-like symptoms and behaviors. In fact, the researchers indicated that such teens have a lot in common with compulsive gamblers, including loss of sleep because of the activity, problems cutting back on it and a tendency to lie to cover up the amount of time they are doing it.[17]

Perhaps even more shockingly, the study of more than 400 eighth- and eleventh-graders found that only 35 percent of teens socialize face-to-face anymore, compared with a whopping 63 percent of teens who now communicate mostly via text message and average 167 texts per day.

The study also clarified the difference between compulsive texting and simply sending a large number of texts, as frequency of texting does *not* by itself equate to compulsion, just like drug quantity does not always equate to addiction. The key is the *effect* that the substance or behavior is having on a person and his or her life.

As Dr. Kelly Lister-Landman, lead author of the texting study, explained: "Compulsive texting involves trying and failing to cut back on texting, becoming defensive when challenged about the behavior, and feeling frustrated when one can't do it." Based on those criteria, although boys texted with the same frequency as girls, the study determined that a significantly higher percentage of girls had texting-related problems: 12 percent of the girls met the criteria for "compulsive texters," while only 3 percent of the boys did—a ratio of four to one.

This indicates that while boys and girls text with the same frequency, the girls have more of an emotional/psychological attachment to the texting behavior and, thus, more difficulty controlling it. To put it in alcoholic terms, two people can drink the same amount of alcohol, but the one who is unable to cut back on drinking or lies about it would be considered the person who has the more serious drinking issue—just as, apparently, girls are developing a more problematic relationship with texting.

Compulsive texting has even led to a condition known as "text neck" and there's even a medical institute that specializes in treating it. Chiropractor Dr. Dean Fishman coined the term and created the Text Neck Institute in Plantation, Florida, after seeing a huge influx of young patients complaining of neck, back, arm and shoulder pain related to their phone usage.[18]

According to Dr. Fishman: "Whenever kids came to the office with pain, I noticed they were always on their phones." Not only that, he realized that they were assuming a troublesome phone posture: "They would be positioned at 'forward head posture,' but that term wasn't resonating with parents. After I started calling it 'text neck,' we got an emotional response and decided to trademark the name to help change the way people hold their mobile devices."

Compulsive texting can also lead to other problems as well. While the 2015 Pew study found a link between compulsive texting and poor academic behavior, an earlier study found a link between what they termed "hyper texting" (120 daily texts) and behavioral and psychological problems.

According to that 2010 research study done by Case Western Reserve University School of Medicine, 20 percent of teens engaged in hypertexting.[19] These hypertexters were shown to be at higher risk for unhealthy behaviors and mental health problems: they were twice as likely to have tried alcohol, 41 percent more likely to have used illegal drugs, nearly three and a half times more likely to have had sex and 90 percent more likely to have had four or more sex partners.

What are we to make of all of these statistics that show that more texting leads to more behavioral problems? I would look at this data a couple of different ways. First of all, a person's being a "compulsive" or addicted texter indicates to me that that person has an impulse-control problem. People who have a harder time controlling their impulses also naturally tend to be more impulsive in other areas of their lives: trying drugs, drinking excessively, having sex.

It's sort of like inferring that a person who is overweight—barring any thyroid issues—might also have other self-control issues or tend toward compulsive behavior. Indeed, we know from Dr. Shaffer's syndrome model of addiction that an addictive personality can manifest itself in a variety of ways.

So by that analysis, the compulsive texting isn't "causing" the other problem behaviors, it's merely reflective of an impulsive personality type.

However, we can also view it through another lens as well. According to Social Learning Theory, we model our behavior after that of our peers. What if I have hundreds of peers who text and use social media? I then increase the likelihood of getting exposed to certain problematic behaviors.

For example, if I hang out with ten kids and one of them smokes pot and has multiple sex partners, the influence on my own behavior might be minimal. Now, through social media, I'm hanging out with several hundred kids—and what if 40 or 50 of them have multiple sex partners? Or are taking Vicodin or Xanax? The impact of that larger—and potentially more troublesome—group on my own behavior is now greater.

SOCIAL MEDIA AND THE ILLUSION OF REAL CONNECTION

But perhaps even more worrisome than the addictive nature of our new digital way of connecting is the idea that electronic connection does *not* seem to satisfy our deep-seated need for true human contact. What in fact seems to have been spawned has been the *illusion* of social connection, via a medium that has our dopamine receptors on perpetual high alert as we anticipate, like Pavlovian dogs, the next "ping" that promises to offer us the novelty and pleasure of a text, IM, tweet, Facebook update or Instagram photo.

Perhaps it's as Johann Hari concluded in his TED Talk: "I've increasingly begun to think that the connections we have—the connections we think we have—are like a kind of *parody* of human connection." He went on to explain: "If you have a crisis in your life, you'll notice something—it won't be your Twitter followers who come to sit with you. It won't be your Facebook friends who help you turn it around. It'll be your flesh and blood friends who you have deep and nuanced and textured face to face relationships with."

Hari's insights are backed up by Oxford anthropologist and evolutionary psychologist Dr. Robin Dunbar.[20] Almost two decades ago, he proposed a now-famous theory that a person can maintain about 150 acquaintances but only five or so *close* relationships—our brains simply can't handle any more. The figure 150, also known as Dunbar's Number, was a measurement of the "cognitive limit to the number of individuals with whom any one person can maintain stable relationships."

He developed this theory while studying primates' grooming habits and social groups. When Dunbar started working with primates in the 1980s, the Machiavellian intelligence hypothesis (now known as the social brain hypothesis) was in vogue. According to that theory, a large primate developed a large brain—with a particularly large neocortex—by living in a complex social group. The larger the social group, the larger the neocortex, particularly the frontal lobe. So theoretically, if neocortex size is a function of social group size, then based on the size of the neocortex one should be able to predict the group size for that particular primate *or* human.

Dr. Dunbar did the math using a ratio of neocortical volume to total brain volume and mean group size to come up with his magic number of 150; his research indicated that anything beyond that would be too much for our social brains to handle and process.

The Dunbar Number, though, actually represents a range of several different numbers. The number 150 represents the high end of casual friends or acquaintances. From there, that number changes according to a precise formula that Dunbar called the "rule of three": the next step down is the 50 or so people we call friends—you see them often, but not so much that you consider them to be truly close friends. The step after that is the circle of fifteen: the friends you can turn to and confide in about *most* things. Finally, the most intimate Dunbar Number is five: these are your *closest* friends—the small circle of trust—whom you call in the most serious situations, like those 3:00 a.m. crises.

Amazingly, Dunbar discovered that these numbers have remained constant throughout human history: the size of a typical hunter-gatherer community was about 150, just as the average size of a small village has been throughout the ages.

Interestingly, social media hasn't really affected this dynamic. When Bruno Gonçalves and his colleagues at Indiana University looked at whether Twitter had changed the number of relationships that users could maintain, they found that the number of individuals whom people could manage to follow was still between 100 and 200 stable connections.[21]

Yet the important number is that small circle of close friends with whom we keep in face-to-face contact. Dunbar attributed this to the nature of what he termed the "shared experience" effect: when you laugh or cry with someone; when you go to a social event or have dinner together; when you *experience life* together, there is a deepening of the social bond that can't be replicated by social media.

In social media, you can "share" and "like" something with your Facebook friends, or you can watch the same hysterical YouTube clip of a dancing chimp, but it's not the same as if you had done something together—which is the phenomenon that Dunbar referred to as the *synchronicity* of shared experience. Let us look beyond social media: if I tell you to watch a funny movie that I saw last week, it's just not the same in terms of deepening our social bond as if we had watched it together.

There may also be a *physiological* aspect of friendship that Facebook friends can never replace. Over the past several years, Dunbar and his colleagues have been looking at the importance of physical contact: "We underestimate how important touch is in the social world," he said. He already knew that in primate grooming, the endorphin system was activated; now we know that the same is true for humans. In a series of studies, Dunbar and his colleagues showed that light touch triggers an endorphin response that's important for creating a personal bond. According to Dunbar, our skin has a set of neurons, common to all mammals, that respond to light stroking, but not to any other kind of touch.

"We think that's what they exist for, to trigger endorphin responses as a consequence of grooming," Dunbar said. Just as dopamine incentivizes eating and procreating, it seems that endorphins released with physical touch incentivize human touch and bonding. Facebook friends just can't replicate that; they can't pat us on the back, rub our knees or give us hugs.

Dunbar is also concerned about the negative developmental impact that our new digital world will have on children. From past research on social interaction, we know that early childhood experiences are crucial in developing those parts of the brain that are dedicated to social interaction, empathy and other interpersonal skills. If we deprive a child of interaction and touch early on because they mostly socially interact via screens, those areas won't fully develop.

What would that digitally raised Glow Kid look like as an older person? "This is the big imponderable. We haven't yet seen an entire generation that's grown up with things like Facebook go through adulthood yet," Dunbar said. "It's quite conceivable that we might end up less social in the future, which would be a disaster because we need to be more social—our world has become so large."

Yes, ironically, we will be more socially stunted in the social media age. As Hari pointed out, we have created a parody of real connection; our 500 Facebook friends have given us the illusion of being socially connected, oftentimes at the expense of real flesh-and-blood friendships.

What then happens to a person—particularly a kid—who doesn't have those real-life connections and is already feeling a bit alienated and sad? In those instances, the *illusion* of connection actually does more harm than good. The great social-media-as-genuine-and-meaningful-social-connection myth has been debunked by several studies that correlate social media with mood disorders and a higher incidence of mental health problems.

Facebook, with its 1.23 billion active users, has not led to happiness; instead, it has led to a phenomenon known as "Facebook depression," whereby the more "friends" one has on Facebook, the higher the likelihood of depression. There is also, as mentioned, the double whammy that the more time spent on social media and the more texting a person does, the higher the likelihood of not *just* depression but tech addiction as well, which only further amplifies the isolation and disconnect from healthier activities and true, meaningful face-to-face social contact.

The previously mentioned Case Western Reserve University School of Medicine hypertexting study also looked at "hypernetworking"—more than three hours per school day spent on social networking sites. The 11.5 percent of students who met the criteria for hypernetworkers were linked to higher rates of depression, substance abuse, poor sleep, stress, poor academics and suicide. These are *not* good outcomes. Perhaps not so shockingly, hypernetworkers were also found to have more permissive parents.

It gets worse: hypernetworking teens were found to be 69 percent more likely to have tried sex, 60 percent more likely to report four or more sexual partners, 84 percent more likely to have used illegal drugs and 94 percent more likely to have been in a physical fight.

According to the lead researcher, Dr. Scott Frank: "The startling results of this study suggest that when left unchecked texting and other widely popular methods of staying connected can have dangerous health effects on teenagers." He added: "This should be a wake-up call for parents to not only help their children stay safe by not texting and driving, but by discouraging excessive use of the cell phone or social websites in general."

With that warning in mind, let's take a closer look at the dynamics of Facebook depression. A 2015 University of Houston study published in the *Journal of Social and Clinical Psychology* confirmed that Facebook usage can lead to depressive symptoms.[22] The mechanism for this increase in depressed mood? A psychological phenomenon known as "social comparison."

I call it the "class reunion effect": it's a natural tendency that we all have to compare ourselves with our peers or former classmates; and if they seem to be living wonderful, fulfilling lives and we happen to be in a bit of a rut, it makes us feel worse. On Facebook, it's the constant stream of "look-at-me!" vacation highlight reels and cute baby pics that can make a person already feeling down feel even more envious and blue.

According to the study's author, Mai-Ly Steers: "It doesn't mean that Facebook causes depression, but that depressed feelings and lots of time on Facebook and comparing oneself to others tend to go hand in hand."

For a 2014 study called "Facebook's Emotional Consequences: Why Facebook Causes a Decrease in Mood and Why People Still Use It," published in 2014 in the journal *Computers in Human Behavior,* the researchers Tobias Greitmeyer and Christina Sagioglou, from the University of Innsbruck, in Austria, conducted three different studies with three different sets of participants.[23]

Their first study showed that the longer people are actually on Facebook, the more negative their mood is afterward. The second study provided "causal evidence for this effect by showing that Facebook activity leads to a deterioration of mood compared to two different control groups." As the experimental group was instructed to spend time on Facebook, the control group was instructed to browse the Internet without going to any social media site.

Why do the researchers think that Facebook made people feel worse? They pointed to a reason other than just the previously mentioned "social comparison" effect: "It appears that, compared to browsing the internet, Facebook is judged as less meaningful, less useful, and more of a waste of time, which then leads to a decrease in mood." When the participants were asked afterward how they felt and how "meaningful" they felt their time spent online had been, the researchers found that "meaningfulness" directly correlated to mood.

According to Sagioglou: "The meaningfulness actually accounts for the mood effects. It's not surprising that if you do something you don't consider very meaningful, you're not in a good mood afterward."

But if Facebook makes people feel like crap, then why do they keep using it?

That was the $64,000 question that the third study attempted to answer. Contrary to their prior experiences, participants still indicated that they had the *expectation* that they would feel better after getting on Facebook—even though the opposite was true. The researchers call that "affective forecasting error." It's similar to thinking, "Eating that chocolate cake is going to make me feel *great!*"—and then having the depressing post-cake reality hit.

In the addiction field, we know this phenomenon quite well. I would explain it this way: things that initially and *briefly* make us feel good—chocolate cake, Facebook, heroin—can tempt us because they are all dopaminergic and may have, once upon a time, felt good. So we focus more on that remembered short-term feel-good dopamine surge that we may have experienced in the past—this is known as "euphoric recall"—and tend not to consciously remember the less pleasant and more recent realities of our engagement with the formerly feel-good activity. From a neurological standpoint, we know that dopaminergic temptations can sometimes override the you-should-know-better rationality of our frontal cortex.

Indeed, recent research shows that Facebook can lead to social networking addiction; one recent study had participants who met all diagnostic criteria for substance addiction. In that 2014 study, conducted by the State University of New York at Albany, out of 253 undergraduate participants who completed a modified version of an assessment that measures for problem drinking, almost 10 percent were found to have "disordered online social networking use"—a fancy way of saying that they had an addiction-like problem related to using Facebook. This included showing signs of withdrawal, craving and increased tolerance—all benchmarks of substance addiction.[24]

Some more Facebook research:

An article titled "Too Many 'Friends,' Too Few 'Likes'? Evolutionary Psychology and 'Facebook Depression,'" published in the *Review of General Psychology* in 2015 by Charlotte Rosalind Blease of University College Dublin, provided an overview of the research into Facebook depression.[25]

Blease concluded that Facebook users may be more "susceptible" to "causal triggers" for depression (a) the greater the number of "friends" the user has online, (b) the greater the time that the user spends reading updates from this wide pool of friends, (c) the more regularly the user does so and (d) the more the content of the updates tends to a bragging nature.

In addition to the previously mentioned social comparison effect, Blease points out the extremely negative comments that Facebook users may leave as contributing to low self-esteem and depression. Going as far back as 2004, psychologist John Suler coined the term "online disinhibition effect" and described the tendency for people to be more forward, taunting, mean or aggressive when interacting online as opposed to in person, an effect that was amplified if the poster was anonymous.[26]

We know that people are more polite in person and tend to be more cruel or abusive the greater the distance separating them from others. Also, eye contact deepens the personal bond, which also makes it more difficult to look someone in the eye and say something hurtful. That's why some people choose to end relationships via text: it's easier because it's less personal. Just as it's easier to be cruel behind someone's back—or anonymously, on a blog post—than it is to say the same thing to a person's face.

MEAN GIRLS, SOCIAL MEDIA AND SUICIDE

As has been noted, there appears to be a gender divide in kids' digital habits: in the Brave New e-World of addicting screens, if video games are digital cocaine for boys, then social media and texting are the electronic equivalents for girls, as the majority of hypertexters and hypernetworkers are female.

Unfortunately, social media *amplifies* already existing young-female dynamics. Insecurities are magnified; Mean Girl cyberbullying attacks are tweeted and retweeted in a virtual echo chamber as social media decreases the quality of socialization and increases isolation. So-called Facebook depression and epidemic levels of female teenage suicides linked to social media cyberbullying are all byproducts of this social media phenomenon.

I've done probably about two dozen suicide risk assessments over the last couple of years; invariably, the depressed and suicidal young person is a plugged-in social media devotee. In fact, many young people who get referred to me for suicidal ideations are feeling that way because of some type of social media trouble—cyberbullying, sexting gone wrong, being defriended by key friends.

"I don't want to live anymore."

'Why?" I asked the young girl with blue hair sitting across from my desk.

"A boy who I liked—who I had dated . . . he posted a picture of me that I had sent him—a naked picture—on Instagram . . . now there's a page up with my pictures on it and everyone is making fun of me and I just can't handle it anymore."

Commonly known as "slut pages," these are the new scarlet letters for the teenage crowd. A young girl succumbs to pressure to send nude photos, only to have them show up on publicly viewed sites where the girl gets shamed by both the boys and the girls in her school. Social media has seemingly set the women's movement back several generations.

After determining that my blue-haired client was not what we would call "acutely suicidal," I contacted her parents and she eventually withdrew from school and enrolled in a private school.

Other times the suicidal ideations can be more acute and require psychiatric hospitalizations. Recently, I had just such a case.

"Emily" had recently transferred schools and was trying hard to fit into her new school. She was pretty, social and, outwardly, seemed fairly well adjusted. Unfortunately, as part of her effort to fit in and assimilate, she was sucked into the social media vortex and the accompanying drama at her new school as she started running with the Mean Girls. She also succumbed to the pressure of her handsome-yet-slimy new boyfriend to Instagram several explicit pictures of herself to him. Sadly, while that relationship proved to be short lived, the shelf-life of those explicit photos was not. Soon, everyone had gotten Emily's nude photos.

But unlike my blue-haired client, it wasn't the mass dissemination of her private photos that sent her over the edge; instead, it was the threat by her mother of cutting her off of all social media. Her mother had texted her as she sat in my office that she was on her way to get her and that she would lose the use of her phone and computer indefinitely.

As Emily sat in my office, she began to shake, sob and hyperventilate; I tried to calm her down and encouraged her to breathe as I tried to reassure her that everything would be alright. But her hyperventilating only got worse and she had a full-blown panic attack as her entire body shook.

In between gasps and sobs she cried: "Now I'll be all alone . . . all alone!" as she rocked back and forth while her body shook. The way she kept repeating "All . . . alone . . . all . . . alone!" was heartbreaking. You could palpably feel the existential anguish and fear of being so utterly isolated that the loss of her telephone represented for her. By the time her mother arrived, she had indicated that she was going to go home and hang herself. With that, she earned herself a ride to the psychiatric hospital where she was held for several weeks and treated with heavy psychiatric medications.

Sadly, her time at the adolescent wing of the psych hospital was not a pleasant one. *Girl, Interrupted* was a walk in the park compared to her horrific experience; she was jumped and violently assaulted by three other Mean Girls of the very psychiatric variety and loaded with enough psych meds to drop an elephant. Her mother was beside herself with horror at what had happened to her little girl. In what had seemed like the blink of an eye, a once pretty and social girl was now a beaten-up and overmedicated psychiatric patient—all because of the soul-crushing fear that she might lose her phone and be "all alone."

Clearly, her phone represented a lifeline and connection to her social world; while obviously addicted to her phone, it also provided her with a soothing sense of anxiety relief.

It reminded me of the double-edged sword of anti-anxiety medications like Xanax and Klonopin: they are incredibly effective in lessening anxiety but are also highly addicting. Unless the underlying causes of the anxiety are treated—trauma, negative self-concept, etc.—the anxiety worsens and the dependence on the pharmaceutical crutch grows.

Similarly, with social media, it may temporarily relieve the loneliness and isolation that a person may feel, but it does not address the underlying need for real in-depth connection. Without those real friendships, the dependence on the phone and the various social media sites grows. Take away that crutch—that false lifeline to social connection—and you get the sort of meltdown that Emily had.

Unfortunately, cases like Emily's are becoming increasingly more common in high schools and even in middle schools. And, sadly, there have been several instances of teenagers who have indeed committed suicide related to social media issues and triggers.

But to be very clear, anytime that a person takes their own life there necessarily has to be an emotional or psychiatric vulnerability that can make a person more susceptible to negative outcomes if triggered by social media shaming or bullying. Having said that, we do also understand that social media can act as an accelerant on a psychiatric fire.

The following is a sampling of such cases.

MEGAN MEIER (1992–2006)

Megan was an overweight girl who struggled with ADD and depression. She found brief happiness in 2006 when a 16-year-old boy named Josh Evans asked Megan to be friends on MySpace. The two stayed in frequent contact online, although they never met in person or spoke on the phone. According to Megan's mom: "Megan had a lifelong struggle with weight and self-esteem, and now she finally had a boy who she thought really thought she was pretty."

But by October, Josh started sending cruel messages and saying that he didn't want to be Megan's friend anymore. As the messages got more and more hurtful, Megan received this final message from Josh: "The world would be a better place without you." Things got even worse as the cyberbullying escalated when classmates and "friends" on MySpace began writing even more hurtful messages.

Megan hanged herself in her bedroom closet. Her mother found her twenty minutes after she had gotten off her computer. She died the following day, three weeks before what would have been her fourteenth birthday. Shockingly, later that fall a neighbor would tell Megan's parents that Josh didn't even really exist—the MySpace account had been created by another neighbor, Lori Drew, her 18-year-old employee Ashley Grills, and Drew's teenage daughter, who used to be friends with Megan.

One year later, the case began receiving national attention. While the county prosecutor declined to file any criminal charges in the case, federal prosecutors charged Lori Drew with one count of conspiracy and three violations of the Computer Fraud and Abuse Act for accessing protected computers without authorization. A federal grand jury indicted Drew on all four counts in 2008, but U.S. District Judge George Wu acquitted Drew in August 2009 and vacated the conviction.

In addition to forming the Megan Meier Foundation, her mother also worked closely to help Missouri legislature pass Senate Bill 818, unofficially known as "Megan's Law" in August 2008. In April 2009, U.S. Representative Linda Sánchez of California introduced the "Megan Meier Cyberbullying Prevention Act"—but unfortunately it was never enacted.

JESSICA LOGAN (1990–2008)

Jessica Logan was an 18-year-old Sycamore High School senior who sent a nude photo of herself to her boyfriend. Unfortunately, after the couple broke up, the photo was sent to hundreds of teenagers in at least seven Cincinnati-area high schools. The cyber bullying continued through Facebook, MySpace and text messages. Unable to handle the virtual taunting any longer, Jessica hanged herself after attending the funeral of another boy who had committed suicide.

HOPE WITSELL (1996–2009)

In a similar case, 13-year-old Hope Witsell's boyfriend also shared a picture of her breasts that she had sent to him to students at six different schools in Florida. Soon, a "Hope Hater Page" was started on MySpace that led to additional cyber bullying. Unable to stand the ridicule, Hope hanged herself.

Jessica's parents, Albert and Cynthia Logan, filed a lawsuit against Sycamore High School and the Montgomery police for not doing enough to keep their daughter from being bullied and harassed following the nude photos incident. They also filed a lawsuit in April 2011 against Hillsborough County school officials for failing to take appropriate action after learning that Hope had suicidal thoughts.

In February 2012, Ohio Governor John Kasich signed House Bill 116, also known as the Jessica Logan Act, into law. The legislation addresses cyber bullying and expands anti-harassment policies.

RYAN HALLIGAN (1989–2003)

Ryan was a special education student who had been the regular target of a school bully. But in February 2003, Ryan fought the bully and the harassment ended, and Ryan even seemingly forged a friendship with his now former bully.

Unfortunately, after Ryan shared an embarrassing personal story with his new "friend," the boy started a rumor that Ryan was gay. The teasing continued into the summer of 2003, although Ryan thought that he had struck a friendship with a pretty, popular girl through AOL Instant Messenger (AIM). Instead, he later learned that the girl and her friends had set him up to think that the girl liked him so that they could make fun of him and have him share more embarrassing material—which she copied and pasted into AIM exchanges with her friends.

On October 7, 2003, Ryan hanged himself in the family bathroom. After his son's death, his father found a folder filled with IM exchanges from that summer that made him realize "that technology was being utilized as weapons far more effective and reaching [than] the simple ones we had as kids."

Although there were no criminal charges filed because there was no law on the books that applied, seven months after Ryan's death, Vermont's Bully Prevention Law (ACT 117) was signed into law by Governor Jim Douglas and Ryan's father John Halligan also authored Vermont's Suicide Prevention Law (ACT 114), which passed unchanged in April 2006.

AMANDA TODD (1996–2012)

On September 12, 2012, Amanda Todd made a YouTube video entitled "My story: Struggling, bullying, suicide, self-harm," in which the British Columbia teenager uses flash cards to tell about her horrific experiences of being blackmailed and bullied. Amanda met a stranger on video chat when she was in the seventh grade who convinced her to bare her breasts on camera. The stranger then attempted to use the photo to blackmail Amanda, and the picture began circulating on the internet, including a Facebook profile that used the topless photograph as the profile image.

"The Internet stalker she flashed kept stalking her," Amanda's mother, Carol Todd, explained. "Every time she moved schools he would go undercover and become a Facebook friend."

Her poignant YouTube clip received 17 million views.

A little over a month after she posted the video, Amanda hanged herself in her home on October 10, 2012. Canada's *CTV News* reported that lawmakers would consider a motion for a national bullying prevention strategy.

SOCIAL MEDIA, VULNERABLE GIRLS AND SEXUAL PREDATORS

Back in the pre-social media days, to be sure, there were sexual predators, miscreants and lurking men waiting to take advantage of a girl who may have felt a bit lost or restless or who maybe had a fight with her parents. But these were tangible boogey men that the wary parent could look out for: the leering man at the playground; the overly friendly store clerk or the creep lounging around the mall.

But now they're in your daughter's bedroom; they've made it right past the front door, past your protective parent-armor and landed literally in her lap—with her lap top. No longer limited to luring victims in the street, sexual predators and sex traffickers can now message thousands of young girls through Instagram, Facebook, Kik, Tagged and Twitter, with a growing trend toward WhatsApp and Snapchat where messages evaporate over time, thus erasing the predator's electronic trail.

"If just one of them answers . . . traffickers can make thousands of dollars off that girl very quickly," said Andrea Powell, founder and director of FAIR Girls, a U.S.-based NGO which helps trafficked girls worldwide.[27]

The Huffington Post recently did a story about a young 17-year-old girl named Hope. "It all started because I posted on a social media site that I hated my mother," she recalls. "A woman messaged me back telling me that I could go stay with her, and we'd go partying. She showed up within the next 45 minutes. I was gone."[28]

She was then taken to a motel room, where a male accomplice beat her, drugged her and then trafficked her for sex—with up to 20 men a day. After three weeks and eight states, she was finally rescued. "I could never be Hope again after that; I was never going to be the same girl," she says.

Sadly, there are millions of stories like Hope's. Globally, nearly 21 million people are victims of human trafficking, a $150 billion industry, according to the United Nation's International Labour Organization. An estimated 4.5 million of them are forced into sex work.

According to Andrea Powell at FAIR Girls, about 90 percent of the people they helped in Washington D.C. and Maryland had been sold online. Young girls are often lured by sex traffickers who contact them on social-media sites and invite them to parties, to meet at the mall or to just become friends.

I interviewed Anastasia Karloutsos, the Executive Director of Hope House, a residential home where victims of sex trafficking can find safety and a place to heal. A tall and imposing woman with a master's degree in social work, Karloutsos is passionate about helping these young women.

"There is an epidemic in our country. We are literally allowing the selling of our children through websites such as Backpage. There are thousands of underage children whose bodies are being sold and lives are being devastated. Many rescued children describe being raped 20 times a day by different men."

She proceeds to describe the seduction process: "Some are runaways who get picked up by a pimp with the promise of food, shelter and family. Others are seduced over the internet with the idea of a nice boyfriend. He is a faceless man that the girls meet on line. He is nice to her [or him], pays attention to her, listens to her problems about her parents, her friends at school, her teachers. He is a willing ear, someone who understands, someone who says he can make it better."

But that is just the lure. "Then he asks for a picture. Then, another. Typically, the pictures he asks for at first will not be explicit, but little by little the requests will get more sexual in nature. He is grooming his victim. By the time they meet in person, he already has her. By the time they meet he can already tell her about all the things he knows about her *and* then what he can show her family—the pictures—the shame of that, will make it hard for her to go back. Once you are started down the rabbit hole, it's very hard to feel that you are able to turn around and go back."

I ask her if she ever worries about traffickers and pimps coming to find the girls who have escaped. The answer is heartbreaking. "No, we aren't afraid. We aren't afraid because these men will not come for the women. Unfortunately, there are so many other potential victims that they will not 'fight for them.'" With an almost endless pool of victims to troll for online, the girls are considered to be easily replaceable spare parts by the predators.

Anastasia expressed exasperation that websites like Backpage, notorious for sexual trafficking, are allowed to continue to operate. But they have been shielded by first amendment protections and the ads often use code words for various ages and typically advertise for legal "escort" services.

But all is not lost. In 2015, the New York attorney general's office announced a partnership with Facebook to help combat child sex trafficking, which includes technical assistance to help law-enforcement officials find perpetrators and rescue victims. And North Dakota congresswoman Kristi Noem has written a bill that's in front of congress called the Stop Advertising Victims of Exploitation Act (SAVE) that would give law enforcement the resources and ability to prosecute companies that help sex traffickers advertise.

According to Congresswoman Noem: "76% of all sex trafficking that occurs in this country occurs over the internet. And we have over 5,000 different websites that sell children and women for sex every day."

Noem points to the profit motive: "Backpage makes millions of dollars a month selling people for sex and they do it under the guise of some kind of escort services."

Her proposed legislation is opposed by many free speech groups. But it is hard to defend sites that advertise thinly veiled ads for sex-trafficked kids—something which Backpage's attorneys have conceded occurs on their site.

Years ago, there was a famous PSA commercial geared toward parents that would run in New York: "It's 10 o'clock—do you know where your children are?" Today, answering *yes* to that that simple question could still be a problem; if there is a computer in that bedroom, your child is not alone and could potentially not be safe. Instead, the new PSA for this millennium needs to say "It's 10 o'clock—do you know who your kids are online with?"

I think that most reasonable people can understand that texting as a way to communicate and social media as a way to stay connected both have a place in our society. But if you want healthy and happy kids, it's vitally important that they have supportive, caring relationships with flesh-and-blood people in their lives.

If they absolutely must have Facebook accounts or phones with texting capability—although some parents now opt for nontexting "dumb" phones—at least wait until the children are further along developmentally and less likely to fall victim to tech addiction, Facebook depression or hypertexting. And even then, the research shows that closely monitoring your child's digital habits and virtual friends is critical in the new social media and texting landscape.

But what should a parent do when it comes to school? Obviously they can't monitor phone or computer usage once their little ones are within the confines of school. So what should they do?

To phone or not to phone—that is the question.

THE QUESTION OF PHONES IN SCHOOL

Certainly a child does not *need* a phone in school or in the classroom—the myth that parents need kids to have phones at school in order to be able to reach them is ludicrous. For decades, parents would call schools to contact their children. Now, under the pretense of "staying connected with mom and dad," kids who have phones in school can text friends, play music, watch YouTube videos, tweet, post photos on Instagram and play video games to their hearts' content.

The unfortunate teachers who work in schools with "out of sight" policies, which allow phones in school buildings but, ostensibly, not in classrooms, are engaged in a constant, disruptive "put-your-phone-away" struggle that takes away from class time.

Over the past few years, school policies have been shifting on this issue. In 2006, in the largest school district in America—New York City, with its 1.1 million students—Mayor Michael Bloomberg banned phones in all schools. That policy drew cries of racism, as the schools with metal detectors, traditionally in poorer neighborhoods with more students of color, were the only ones able to ensure that no phones entered the buildings. As a result, most kids in poorer neighborhoods would have to check their phones each morning at food trucks or bodegas that established a profitable dollar-a-day phone drop-off system; kids at more affluent schools, without metal detectors, became proficient at sneaking their phones into their schools and hiding them throughout the day.

Then, in March of 2015, Mayor Bill de Blasio, together with the schools chancellor, Carmen Fariña, reversed Bloomberg's ruling, indicating that doing so would reduce inequality. Let the texting begin!

But recent research from Great Britain clearly demonstrates the negative effects on academics when phones are allowed in school and indicates further that already marginalized poor students and special education students are the *most* adversely affected. Louis-Philippe Beland and Richard Murphy, whose study was published by the Centre for Economic Performance at the London School of Economics, looked at how phone policies at 91 schools in England have changed since 2001, comparing that data with results achieved in national exams taken by 16-year-olds. The comprehensive study covered 130,000 pupils.[29]

The researchers found that following a ban on phone use, the schools' test scores improved by 6.4 percent. Interestingly, the impact on underachieving students (mostly poor and special ed) was even more significant: their average test scores rose by 14 percent.

"The results suggest that low-achieving students are more likely to be distracted by the presence of mobile phones, while high achievers can focus in the classroom regardless of the mobile phone policy," the researchers said. All told, they estimated that the academic gains of banning phones were the "equivalent of adding five days to the school year."

In the study, "Ill Communication: The Impact of Mobile Phones on Student Performance," the British authors even take a swipe across the pond at New York City mayor de Blasio's ill-advised plan lifting the school cell phone ban: "de Blasio's lifting of the ban on mobile phones with a stated intention of reducing inequalities may in fact lead to the opposite. Allowing phones into schools will harm the lowest-achieving and low-income students the most." They added: "Schools could significantly reduce the education achievement gap by prohibiting mobile phone use in schools, and so by allowing phones in schools, New York may unintentionally increase the inequalities of outcomes."

Unfortunately, New York City's lifting of its phone ban is indicative of a national trend. Liz Kolb, an assistant professor at the University of Michigan School of Education and author of *Toys to Tools: Connecting Student Cell Phones to Education,* says that close to 70 percent of schools that had cell phone bans five years ago are reversing their policies.

"First it was a very slow domino fall, and now we're seeing more of a tidal wave," Kolb explains. "Part of it is because it's hard to fight the tidal wave and there's so many students with cell phones."

Yet some schools are not raising the white flag. Schools in Great Britain are trending in the opposite direction. In a survey conducted in 2001, no school in England had banned phones. By 2007, 50 percent of schools had done so, and by 2012 some 98 percent of schools either did not allow phones on school grounds or required them to be handed in at the beginning of the day.[30]

In addition to citing decreased academic performance, some critics of phones-in-the-classroom policies also express concern about increased cyberbullying and sexting during school hours; others point to opportunities to cheat with smartphones.

Ultimately, however, the main concern revolves around the battle to get students' attention. According to Greg Graham, who teaches writing at the

University of Central Arkansas and is a teacher-consultant with the National Writing Project: "Teachers are vying for their students' attention. Of course, this is a venerable struggle, but in the past students' only options were looking out the window, passing notes, or throwing spit wads at each other. Most teachers will tell you the struggle is much tougher today; it's one of those things they talk about at meetings and lunch breaks."[31]

Personally, having worked within public school buildings for many years as a mental health provider, I've sat in on countless classrooms to do student observations. In doing so, I've had the opportunity to see the various phone abuses firsthand: kids texting nonstop in class, listening to music on their headphones or playing video games on their devices. I've witnessed exasperated teachers trying to fight the good fight and constantly redirect kids to put their phones away, and, worse, I've seen frustrated or just cynical teachers who have grown apathetic and just allow their students to stay plugged in and disengaged.

"I tried and tried. But eventually I just had to give up" was what one well-respected high-school science teacher told me. "It would take so much classroom time away from the other students who did want to learn to constantly keep saying 'put your phones away' that I just decided that I had to focus on the kids who wanted to learn."

I asked her in an average class how many students were having problems with their phones. "It can vary. Sometimes 5 kids; other times it's 10 or 12 kids. In a class of 25, I just have to focus on the ones who really want to learn."

I had a meeting with the high school principal of that suburban school where that science teacher works. I have known him to be a very thoughtful, well-educated and caring administrator. Yet, when I presented him with the complaints of the vast majority of his teachers—as well as the London School of Economics study that showed that test scores increase if phones are removed from the classroom—his response surprised me.

"Nick, we just can't change the culture; the parents won't allow it."

"Change the culture? It's a 'culture' that's only been around less than 10 years, it's not some time-honored tradition to have phones in the class."

I then appealed to increased test scores: "What about justifying it by showing them the research—test scores will increase—6 percent across the board and up to 14 percent for special needs kids and kids from tougher socio-economic backgrounds—the kids least equipped to handle the addictive temptation of their phones?"

He stood his ground: "We just won't be able to do it." And then he effectively blamed the teachers: "I really believe that a great teacher who can engage their class effectively can overpower any addictive pull of a phone."

"You're wrong. This stuff is like digital crack for some kids; I don't care if you have Katy Perry in front of the class teaching algebra on a unicycle—the gravitational pull of the phone is just too powerful for some of these kids."

Meanwhile, the whole time that we were talking, his assistant principal was also in the office—checking texts on his phone the entire time.

In this case and in many others, the problem goes above the principals and into the district offices and the superintendents. Some get it and have put the brakes on screens in elementary schools and banned phones from the high schools. In this particular school district, the superintendent is a former technology teacher; her mandate has been clear: the district was going to go all in on tech, research to the contrary be damned. That's meant smart boards, Chromebooks, a computer-based curriculum, and a superintendent's meeting where she encouraged teachers to "text the kids their homework" and embrace the technology that the students were using.

While some parents hear about how wonderful it is for teachers to be able to text a homework assignment to their students or how kids can use their phones to research topics, the reality is that the overall negatives of the distraction effect far, far outweigh the alleged benefits of phones in school.

But that doesn't stop the tech companies from shilling their products. I recently attended a presentation of an app that teachers and students could both use. It was a terribly sterile affair, where an overly enthusiastic presenter waxed poetic to morose teachers about the app's benefits. The presenter then demonstrated how the teachers could use the app to ask their students a question from a question bank and then walk around the room to scan the students' responses with their smart phones.

As this was demonstrated, the assembled teachers acted the part of the students; there were, of course, glitches and burps in the technology that led to snickers and giggles—this from adults with master's degrees; one can only imagine the disruptive fun this would provide for distracted 16-year-olds. As

I sat in the back watching, I thought: all of this scanning and smartphone usage just so a teacher can ask a damned (pre-programmed) question?

Have we really drifted so far from the Socratic ideal of the dialectic that we need to invite this distracting and addictive digital drug into the classroom to scan an answer? Do we *really* need a smartphone to teach 20 kids sitting in a circle? According to Greg Graham, an *actual* educator and not a sales rep for a tech company: "There never has been—nor will there ever be—a more dynamic learning context than face-to-face in close proximity. Everything possible should be done to protect that timeless environment from interruption and distraction." Amen.

Regardless of school district policies, parents should be the ultimate arbiters of whether or not their children have phones and whether or not they are allowed to take those phones to school. If parents do allow their children to take phones to school, then, at the very least, they should put restrictions on the phones.

And, as we'll see in the next chapter, in some cases where children show signs of clinical disorders, what may be needed is more than just a phone ban.

SIX

CLINICAL DISORDERS AND THE GLOW KIDS EFFECT

SEVERAL YEARS AGO, I HAD BEEN WORKING WITH A YOUNG MAN named "Robert" who had Asperger's syndrome—a developmental disorder considered to be on the higher-functioning end of the autism spectrum. Robert was originally from down South but had moved up North to live with his lovely grandmother after his mother died suddenly, when he was 13.

When I met him, he was a very soft-spoken 16-year-old with very poor interpersonal skills—he made no eye contact, for example, and had no sense of how to engage in a back-and-forth conversation. He would also engage in some bizarre behavior that didn't help him fit in at school: he carried around a stuffed monkey and, on occasion, would crawl under his desk and refuse to move. And there was one more thing: Robert was an out-of-control video game addict, totally consumed by the *Final Fantasy* RPG series.

He had a Game Boy that he constantly played with at school and a computer at home that he would game on from the moment he got home to the time he fell asleep—which he often did at the computer table. His poor elderly grandmother, who had her hands full trying to rein in his behavior, would cry, "I can't stay up all night chasing him off the computer!" In school he was borderline mute, and in group counseling he would barely participate—until the subject of video games came up; then he would sit up straight in his chair and talk in a rapid monotone about the various minutiae of the game.

When Robert failed all of his classes due to lack of interest, his grandmother finally shut down the electronics—cold turkey. She felt his explosive wrath for a couple of days, but eventually he calmed down. In school, the poor kid would try to borrow other students' devices, but because of his poor social skills, it was a challenge since he didn't have any friends and couldn't express himself clearly, often mumbling and looking off in another direction. Robert had about three or four meltdowns in school, standing on top of his desk and screaming or banging his head against the wall. In hindsight, I realized that he was going through screen withdrawal.

In trying to figure out a way to connect with Robert, I noticed that he was an excellent writer. Sure, his fictional stories dealt with aliens and fantasy worlds, but the kid could write. So I asked him to write a science fiction story for me, complete with narrative arc and characters. Sure enough, he came in with a detailed manuscript in microscopic handwritten print, along with illustrations.

He began to tell me, in animated fashion, about his story. As he talked, I noticed something: he was looking at me in the eyes. He had been unplugged for about a week and a half at that point, and he was making eye contact! In group, I asked him to tell the other kids about his rather fascinating intergalactic tale. While still a bit awkward in the group setting, he was now talking more fluidly and pausing to hear feedback—all great signs of improvement.

At one point I noticed that Robert was looking at a copy of *The Lord of the Rings* that I had on my bookcase. I grabbed it off the shelf and handed it to him. He looked at me a bit perplexed.

"Read this. I think you'll really like it. It's a fantasy—almost like your *Final Fantasy* video game—but you have to *read* it."

I saw a little crooked smile creep along his face as he thanked me—another first.

Robert wound up doing fairly well. Over the few months that he was screen-free, his social skills progressed dramatically as he continued to read Tolkien and write his fantasy stories. At some point his grandmother gave him back the games because he had been improving so much in school. He did have a couple of setbacks, but he had moved the needle considerably on his social skills and was able to graduate.

His stuffed monkey now sits ornamentally on my bookcase. I smile whenever I look at it—as I also do when I invariably have to answer the "Hey, Dr. K . . . what's a stuffed monkey doing in your bookcase?" question.

ELECTRONIC SCREEN SYNDROME

Dr. Victoria Dunckley has boldly gone where no child psychiatrist has gone before.

Having worked with hundreds of kids with a variety of psychiatric, developmental and behavioral disorders, she realized something very profound: perhaps these disparate disorders had the same underlying cause. Maybe kids with ADHD, oppositional defiant disorder, sleep disorders, mood disorders like depression and bipolar disorder, or behavioral issues like aggression—even kids with autism—maybe they were all part of an underlying syndrome that presented itself in a variety of different clinical expressions.

As she looked at the data, she saw that visits for kids diagnosed with pediatric bipolar disorder had increased *40-fold* from 1994 to 2003; that between 1980 and 2007 the diagnosis of ADHD had increased by nearly 800 percent, while prescriptions for psychotropic medications given to kids had sharply increased over the past two decades.[1]

What was happening? Was this just a case of more awareness and, thus, more diagnosis, or were there really more psychiatrically distressed kids? And, if so, what might be causing these spikes in clinical cases? Dr. Dunckley wondered if there could be some common environmental stressor causing these epidemic increases. Perhaps, she reasoned, even if all of these disorders weren't being entirely *caused* by the environmental stressor, could they be getting amplified by a mitigating environmental factor?

As she looked over the child landscape trying to figure out what could have been the common denominator that kids had been getting exposed to, one thing glowingly stood out: screens.

The more that she looked at the problem, the more she began to understand what she began to call electronic screen syndrome (ESS). Dr. Dunckley came to believe that the unnaturally stimulating nature of an electronic screen, regardless of its content, wreaks havoc on the still-developing nervous system and mental health of a child on a variety of levels—cognitive, behavioral and emotional.

She began to conceptualize ESS as a disorder of dysregulation; that is, an inability in children to modulate their moods, attention or level of arousal in an appropriate or healthy manner.

Dunckley hypothesized that interacting with screens overstimulates the child and shifts the nervous system into fight-or-flight mode, which then leads to dysregulation and disorganization of the various biological and hormonal systems. These disrupted systems can then create—or exacerbate—disorders such as ADHD, depression, oppositional defiant disorder and anxiety.

But electronic screen syndrome isn't just limited to kids with pronounced psychiatric or behavioral disorders. Dr. Dunckley observed that *all* kids were getting impacted on some level—even those with so-called "moderate" screen exposure were showing signs of "subtle damage," such as chronic irritability, inability to focus, a general malaise, apathy or, oftentimes, a state of being "wired and tired." (That is, they're agitated but exhausted.)

Many of these kids fell below the threshold of a clinical diagnosis but still had troubling symptoms: "Many of the children I see suffer from sensory overload, lack of restorative sleep, and a hyperaroused nervous system, regardless of diagnosis . . . these children are impulsive, moody, and can't pay attention."

There's an old axiom in the medical community (placebo effects aside): if the cure works, you probably have the disease. That is, if a particular treatment works on an ailment, we might reasonably infer that the patient had the ailment that the treatment was designed for; if an antiviral drug reduces symptoms, we can infer that a virus was at play. If an antibiotic does the trick, then we would suspect a bacterial infection.

In similar fashion, Dr. Dunckley set about to confirm her electronic screen syndrome hypothesis. If screens were indeed the underlying culprits in these various disorders, then, certainly, the removal of this theorized environmental "toxin" should alleviate some of the symptoms in the hundreds of children she was treating.

Toward that end during the past decade she has prescribed four- to-six-week "tech fasts"—the removal of all electronic screens—to more than 500 children, teens and young adults. Here's what she has found: for those who strictly adhered to the fast, the results have been dramatic—if electronic screen syndrome was observed along with a true underlying psychiatric disorder, the tech fast was effective 80 percent of the time and typically reduced symptoms by at least half; in cases where there did not appear to be an underlying psychiatric condition, she often found "complete resolution of symptoms."[2]

To illustrate how amazingly successful the removal of screens can be in transforming troubled kids, Dr. Dunckley wrote in detail about one particular student whom she treated:

"Mikey" had been a real problem. In the year before he was treated, the fifth-grader had become increasingly resistant to doing homework and had become more and more oppositional and defiant. If he was told "no" about anything—*especially* regarding his electronics—he would fly into a rage and would typically destroy school property. These explosive rages were wreaking havoc in his classroom, as he often would throw chairs and knock desks over.[3]

The ten-year-old had been diagnosed with mild autism and ADHD; there were also whispers of bipolar disorder. Not sure what to do, the school district insisted that Mikey undergo a psychiatric evaluation. Luckily, he was referred to Dr. Dunckley.

She discovered that Mikey had been playing video games since age seven and would play his nonviolent games for several hours a day, usually starting as soon as he got home from school. When he was out with his family, he would play with his sister's or father's iPhone; at school, he had daily computer time and often watched cartoons.

But things had gotten worse in the past year: he'd become more resistant to doing homework and was now playing his video games to the exclusion of all other interests. In addition, his oppositional behavior had started to escalate, and his violent rages increased and had become more violent. Although bipolar disorder was discussed as a possible diagnosis, there was no history of it in his family.

Before prescribing any medications, Dr. Dunckley suggested a four-week electronic screen fast, to both assess the role that screens may have been playing in his behavior as well as to help him reset and downshift his obviously overaroused nervous system. His family supported the decision to remove *all* screens—including television—for four weeks. They also bought him Legos and puzzles and set up tennis and park outings in order to restructure his life with screen-free activities.

After one month, he'd only had one episode of aggression at home and none at school. In addition, Dr. Dunckley reevaluated his medication needs and concluded that no meds were necessary at that time. One year later, this boy who had had almost daily rages amazingly had not had any incidents of aggression.

He has also been able to slowly integrate some electronics back into his life; he doesn't play video games, but he does watch some TV on the weekends (though no cartoons). He has some computer time at school, but his parents have requested that it not be daily.

In light of the severity of his aggression and the concerns for his own safety as well as that of others, in 99 cases out of 100, a boy behaving this way would have invariably been put on strong psychotropic medication and perhaps even sedating antipsychotic meds. And as any mental health provider can tell you, once the medication merry-go-round begins, good luck getting off.

Luckily Mikey had been referred to Dr. Dunckley and averted a collision with a prescription pad; all that was required was a removal of the hyperstimulating screens that were raising his arousal thermostat to the point where he couldn't shut it off.

The navy's Dr. Doan also talks about the hyper-arousing nature of screens and video games, which activate the HPA axis and where adrenaline and blood pressure are consistently raised as kids go into chronic fight-or-flight mode and are unable to reset their adrenal thermostats.

In the past 14 years that I have worked with teenagers with emotional, cognitive, behavioral or developmental issues, I have had the opportunity to participate as a committee member in over one thousand Committee on Special Education (CSE) meetings for those various teenagers. And, like Dr. Dunckley, over the past seven or eight years, I also began to see a pattern—a connection—between many of those teens that had been classified with a disability and their addiction to screens—either video games, phones or social media.

I began to start tracking those numbers, and fully ninety percent of the students that had been classified with either an attentional, behavioral, emotional or developmental problem also had a problematic relationships with screens. At a recent CSE meeting, an intelligent, high-functioning boy with ADHD and a mild autism diagnosis was not doing well in school and falling asleep in all of his classes. These somnolescent tendencies were so severe, that the boy would often snore loudly and would be difficult to awaken by his flummoxed teachers.

The parent mentioned making an appointment for a sleep study for apnea and was also making an appointment to see a neurologist. I asked the obvious question to the boy: "Are you doing anything that's keeping you up late at night?" The mother began nodding her head as the boy's eyes lit up as he mentioned a particular video game that he played for hours and hours: "I just LOVE it! I love it!! I can't help it, but I love that game so much that I play until 3 or 4 in the morning. I can't help myself!"

Shockingly, the mother looked at me and asked: "Do you think the game has got something to do with this? Do you think that's part of the problem?" I said that it very well could and suggested that she try an experiment: "Unplug the boy for 4 weeks and let's see what happens." As the boy loudly protested and shot me a dirty look, his mother agreed: "As of tonight—no more games!" Within a week, the boy stopped sleeping and loudly snoring in class and, not so surprisingly, his grades dramatically improved.

Unfortunately, oftentimes, the screen effect on the child can be much more severe than just sleep deprivation. I had interviewed Dr. Chantelle Bernier, a Pediatric Occupational Therapist on the West Coast who describes seeing an epidemic rise in children with serious psychiatric issues and had also noticed the adverse effect that screens were having on these kids. She described one of her patients, a *9-year-old boy* who had been hospitalized for attempted *suicide*.

The child had been obsessed with playing *Grand Theft Auto* and had been so sleep deprived after playing the game for hours that he started hearing command voices to kill his entire family. The voices persisted until the boy grabbed a knife and tried to kill himself. The boy was hospitalized and put on antipsychotic medications which, apparently, only made things worse.

Another patient, an intelligent 17-year-old gamer whom Dr. Bernier described as quite thoughtful and sensitive, had been referred to her unit because he started having homicidal ideations—thoughts of killing others. To desensitize those thoughts, he had begun watching very violent porn. He finally went ballistic when his foster-father tried to get him off the computer; he grabbed a large hunting knife and started stabbing a large dummy that was in his room and then chased after the foster-father with the knife as the older man ran out of the house.

Adding to the problem, Dr. Bernier was flabbergasted that her hospital was giving iPads to these hospitalized kids; in addition to exacerbating their psychiatric symptoms, on a physical level, these children were developing bed cramps from just sitting in their hospital beds all day and playing video games.

She educated the staff and parents about the adverse effects of the iPads and the video games and, eventually, became successful in having the technology removed. She substituted activities like yoga, mindfulness, crafts, journaling and labyrinth walking. The children began to feel a sense of routine and self-efficacy and saw a huge improvement.

According to Dr. Dunckley, seeing ESS children who are "revved up" and prone to rages or, alternatively, depressed and apathetic has become disturbingly commonplace. Homicidal and suicidal cases are certainly the extreme cases; but most chronically irritable children are often in a state of abnormally high arousal and may seem "wired and tired." Because chronically high arousal levels impact memory and the ability to relate, these kids are also likely to struggle academically and socially.

These kids would normally be diagnosed with heavy-duty disorders such as major depression, bipolar disorder, or ADHD and be prime candidates for the prescription pad. But before the decision is made to go the medication route is where the tech fast comes in.

Dr. Dunckley is adamant in advocating for a full fast/detox rather than a tech reduction in order for the nervous system to fully reboot; in her experience, tech reductions simply don't work—the problematic dysregulation that leads to clinical symptoms does not get stabilized by that less-intense approach.

The one difference that I have with the way that "digital detoxes" or tech fasts are currently done—both by Dr. Dunckley and at tech addiction rehab facilities like reSTART—is the cold turkey approach. As an addictions expert who runs one of the most respected rehabs in the country, I think we need to borrow what we've learned from the drug addiction treatment community. That is, when we do a drug detox, we no longer make the addict go cold turkey; that's when we get explosive and aggressive episodes—as we've seen with some of the kids I've described who have been unplugged abruptly.

In the barbaric old days of drug and alcohol treatment, the alcoholic would be thrown into a dry-out tank or, worse, a psychiatric "snake pit" in an asylum. Today, when we detox addicts, we do so gradually because (a) it's more humane and (b) it eliminates any of the above-mentioned adverse behavioral effects. There is no punching, kicking or screaming when someone is gradually tapered down toward abstinence.

Similarly, when doing a "digital detox," we should slowly taper the young person down: for example, five hours of screen time should be tapered down by one hour per day. Thus, gradually over a roughly weeklong period, the child is weaned off screens. However, during this time it's critically important that alternate healthy activities be substituted. You don't just cut back the screens and have the kids sitting in their rooms twiddling their thumbs. You take them to the park, or give them creative projects to work on. Things like that.

Once the young person is down to zero screen time, then the minimum recommended period of abstinence to reset his or her adrenal clock is four weeks, although some kids need several months. Obviously, long-term tech abstinence is difficult if not close to impossible in our screen culture. Short of living a hermetic and ascetic life off the grid, most people have to inevitably intersect with screens and technology at *some point*.

After the fast, once the child's brain is reset, parents can monitor him or her to determine just how much electronics use can be tolerated without the symptoms returning. But the treatment goal after the fast-as-detox is to encourage a healthy relationship with technology and to learn to identify the difference between "digital vegetables" and "digital candy" so as to avoid the latter. Digital vegetables can be a healthy use of screens (researching a term paper), while digital candy (*Minecraft, Candy Crush*) are hyperarousing and dopamine-activating digital stimulants without any ostensible "health benefit."

Interestingly, the new *DSM-5* (*Diagnostic and Statistical Manual*) has included a new childhood diagnosis called disruptive mood dysregulation disorder (DMDD).[4] DMDD is a condition wherein a child is chronically irritable and experiences frequent, severe temper outbursts that seem grossly out of proportion to the situation at hand. These symptoms sound familiar to those of us who have worked with hyperaroused kids suffering from either screen addiction or ESS.

In addition to DMDD, many researchers and clinicians have also pointed the finger of blame at screens for the explosive increase in the ADHD epidemic. Let's take a look at some of those claims.

SCREENS AND THE ADHD EFFECT

Six million kids have been diagnosed with ADHD. That's one in ten kids.

What the hell is going on?

Some have attempted to explain away what has been called the ADHD epidemic by saying that the higher rates of diagnosis are just a function of more screening and more awareness about the disorder. Others disagree.

Earlier, in chapter one, we discussed the notion that exposing kids to hyperstimulating screen experiences conditions them to continually require stimulating screens in order to stay engaged. Sure, glowing screens may quiet little Johnny and Suzie down for a bit and make life for mom and dad a bit easier—in the short term.

As Dr. Susan Linn, author of *Consuming Kids* and a lecturer in psychiatry at Harvard Medical School, puts it: "It's true that if you provide children with a screen device when you go on car trips, take public transportation, or go for their annual physical, the periods you spend waiting may be more restful or easier to manage. But such convenience comes at a cost. It fosters dependence on screens to get through a day, and prevents children from getting in the habit of noticing, and engaging with, the world around them."

Said another way, once kids have developed a taste for *Grand Theft Auto*, sitting down to do their algebra homework just doesn't cut it anymore.

Sure enough, ample research has shown that exposure to video games and television in childhood and adolescence is a significant risk factor for subsequent attention problems. In addition to the theory that experiencing something exciting makes it difficult for a kid to downshift to something less exciting, others have hypothesized that because most TV shows or video games involve rapid changes in focus, frequent exposure to screens may compromise children's abilities to sustain focus on tasks that are not inherently as attention-grabbing—like schoolwork.

In a 2010 Iowa State University study called "Television and Video Game Exposure and the Development of Attention Problems," published in the journal *Pediatrics*, 1,323 middle-childhood participants were assessed during a 13-month period.[5] The conclusions? Viewing television and playing video games each are associated with increased subsequent attention problems in childhood; 6- to 12-year-olds who spent more than two hours a day playing video games or watching TV had trouble paying attention in school and were 1.6 to 2.1 times more likely to have attention problems. Surprise, surprise.

"The reality is that we're seeing ten times more ADHD then we were seeing twenty years ago," says Dr. Dimitri Christakis, co-author of the study and associate professor of pediatrics at the University of Washington and a longtime researcher into screen effects. "I think that the concern is that the pacing of the program, whether it's video games or TV, is overstimulating and contributes to attention problems."

The researchers consider the increased risk significant. According to study co-author Dr. Craig Anderson, "The risk is just big enough that it does warrant parents taking action." He suggests that they allow only one to two hours of screen time per day, consistent with what the American Academy of Pediatrics recommends. Dr. Christakis disagrees: "My feeling is that two hours is too much."[6]

In an earlier study, from 2004, Dr. Christakis found that the more TV a child watches between the ages of one and three, the greater the likelihood that they will develop an attention problem by age seven. In fact, the study showed that for each hour of television viewing, the risk of attention problems increased by 10 percent over that of a child who didn't stare at a screen. Thus three hours of TV time translated to a 30 percent increase in the likelihood of developing an attention problem.

Things to consider that have become known since that study was published: more recent research indicates that the attention-dampening effect is amplified by tablets and interactive media. Additionally, screen time for kids has increased exponentially since 2004. According to the Kaiser Family Foundation (2010), kids between age 8 and 18 spend a whopping 7.5 hours a day in front of a screen—computer, television or other electronic device. That time estimate does *not* count the additional 1.5 hours kids spend texting or the half-hour that they talk on their cell phones. That's the majority of a kid's waking life—in fact, that's more time than they spend sleeping.

Knowing what we do about the attention-dampening effects of hyper-stimulating and hyper-arousing screens on young brains, is it any wonder that we have an ADHD epidemic?

Dr. Christakis puts it this way: "When you condition the mind to become accustomed to high levels of input, there's a chance that reality can just become boring."

And that, in a nutshell, is what I've seen in my clinical work with the hundreds of teens I've worked with. Reality is, you know, boring. How can it compare to the surreal and larger-than-life, vivid and hyperstimulating imagery of *World of Warcraft* or the rapid-fire stimulation of hypertexting? Look at any kids' show from an earlier generation—say, *Mister Rogers' Neighborhood,* with its star's thoughtful and slow manner as he spoke, God bless him, to his young audience. Compare that to a Nickelodeon whiz-bang show of today—say, *Team Umizoomi* or even *SpongeBob SquarePants;* the scene cuts are much faster, the music is louder, the pace more frenetic. How does constantly watching something frenetic vs. something that requires *patience* to watch shape a young child?

Of course, there are those who disagree with the theory that hyper-stimulating technology causes ADHD. While acknowledging that the research clearly links screen viewing with poorer attention spans later in life, the screen deniers will use the age-old chicken-or-the-egg argument, suggesting that perhaps parents of already restless ADHD-like kids are more likely to put them in front of the TV to calm them down. As Dr. Jacquelyn

Gamino, head of ADHD research at the University of Texas, succinctly puts it: "Which causes which?"

These are valid questions from people trained in the sciences; we are taught the distinction between correlation and causation early on. To be sure, we know that attention is interest-based; children with ADHD may indeed be drawn to video games because they are stimulating enough to focus on. And the game stimulation can be self-medicating and dopamine-boosting for kids who may have a dopamine deficit.

But did the screens perhaps *cause* the ADHD thirst for stimulating fare?

I would offer several arguments to push the dial toward causation rather than correlation—meaning that screens are indeed causing disorders of attention.

First, we have brain-imaging research that shows that the frontal cortex (which controls impulsivity—a big ADHD component) gets compromised by screen exposure stimulation. The research by Dr. Wang at Indiana University School of Medicine showed that people who had been *nongamers* who then played ten hours of video games for one week showed less activation in the left inferior frontal lobe and less activation in the anterior cingulate cortex than in their baseline results and less than the control group. Those are brain regions instrumental in impulsivity and emotional regulation.[7]

"For the first time, we have found that a sample of randomly assigned young adults showed less activation in certain frontal brain regions following a week of playing violent video games at home," Dr. Wang says. "The affected brain regions are important for controlling emotion and aggressive behavior."

Beyond brain imaging, we have Dr. Dunckley's previously mentioned clinical work and my own clinical observations. By using "tech fasts," we see a significant decline in clinical symptoms, including symptoms associated with ADHD, when screens are removed from kids' lives, thus proving the old axiom that "if the cure works, you probably have the disease."

Finally, we have our own common sense and powers of observation. Based on everything that we know about how children grow and develop, does it make sense that if we hyperstimulate their fragile nervous systems and not-yet-fully-developed brains that this somehow won't lead to some problems? Do any of us who have kids—or have worked with kids—not see how easily they can get overstimulated? And then how they need to *keep* getting stimulated in order to sit still and stay engaged?

The trap that many parents fall into is in believing that when their kids are hypnotically looking at a screen, they are demonstrating a profound ability to stay focused. After all, they maintain a laserlike attention on the screen, so how can there possibly be an attention problem?

But that rapt attention to the screen actually typifies an attention problem. As NYU pediatrics professor Dr. Perri Klass wrote for the *New York Times* (May 9, 2011): "In fact, a child's ability to stay focused on a screen, though not anywhere else, is actually characteristic of attention deficit hyperactivity disorder."

She adds that the kind of concentration kids bring to video games and TV is *not* the kind that will help them thrive in school or elsewhere in their life. According to Dr. Christopher Lucas, associate professor of child psychiatry at NYU School of Medicine, that kind of concentration is problematic: "It's not sustained attention in the absence of rewards; it's sustained attention with frequent intermittent rewards."[8]

It's those frequent intermittent rewards that, as mentioned in the addiction chapter, create the addictive hook that then, in a classic vicious cycle, further perpetuates the attention problem, which in turn further compromises the child's impulse control and ability to avoid being glued to the screen. Indeed, what we have seen in the age of Glow Kids is that children raised on a high-screen diet have laser focus for screens but little patience for anything else.

Beyond just a widespread lack of interest in school, we've seen this lack of patience apply to attention-challenged kids when it comes to the sports they play. Many sports commentators have lamented the declining popularity of patience-requiring baseball, both among spectators and as an activity for American kids, as faster-paced sports like football, soccer and basketball have rapidly grown in popularity and many kids complain that baseball is just too slooooow.

New York Mets baseball legend Darryl Strawberry was interviewed several years ago and asked about why young American kids aren't playing baseball in the same numbers that they used to. He sadly replied that the game just seems to be too boring for today's kids, who are raised on action and video games. His own son, DJ Strawberry, who chose to play college basketball at the University of Maryland, said in an interview: "I liked baseball, but it was kind of boring to me. I played outfield, and just standing out there was boring. I'm more of an up-and-down [the court] kind of person. I like the action."[9]

If you really want a child to thrive and blossom, lose the screens for the first few years of their lives. During those key developmental periods, let them engage in creative play. Legos are always great, as they encourage creativity and the hand-eye coordination nurtures synaptic growth. Let them explore their surroundings and allow them opportunities to experience nature, either at a park or in the real deal. Activities like cooking and playing music also have been shown to help young children thrive developmentally. But most importantly, let them experience boredom; there is nothing healthier for a child than to learn how to use their own interior resources to work through the challenges of being bored. This then acts as the fertile ground for developing their powers of observation, cultivating patience and developing an active imagination—the most developmentally and neurosynaptically important skill that they can learn. Let them live without the glow while they're kids—they'll have plenty of time later on to deal with screens.

SCREENS AND DEPRESSION

We talked about Facebook depression in the last chapter; yet other recent clinical research is also linking depression to increased Internet use as well:

- A 2012 Missouri State University study of 216 kids showed that 30 percent of Internet users showed signs of depression and that the depressed kids were the most intense Web users.
- A 2014 study in the journal *Comprehensive Psychiatry* that looked at 2,293 seventh-graders found that Internet addiction exacerbated depression, hostility and social anxiety.
- A 2014 study done in Pakistan with 300 graduate students found that there is a positive correlation between Internet addiction and depression and anxiety: "This result shows that excessive use of Internet makes students addicted to it and consequently causes anxiety and stress among users. The more one is addicted to it the more one is psychologically depressed."

- A 2006 Korean study found a correlation with Internet addiction, depression and increased suicidal ideation. The participants were 1,573 high school students living in a city, who completed the self-reported measures of the Internet Addiction Scale, the Korean version of the Diagnostic Interview Schedule for Children–Major Depression Disorder–Simple Questionnaire and the Suicidal Ideation Questionnaire–Junior.
- An earlier 1998 Carnegie Mellon University study found that Web use over a two-year period was linked to increased depression, loneliness and the loss of "real world" friends.

SCREENS AND ELECTROMAGNETIC FIELDS (EMFS)

What is very, very often overlooked when we consider negative screen effects is the radiation emitted by phones and screens. We have all grown up in a world bathed with radio and television waves, and perhaps, like the fish who isn't aware of the existence of water, we are unaware that invisible waves course through our bodies at all times. But we are discovering that the electromagnetic fields (EMFs) emitted by screens and cell phones are a bit different from others—and more dangerous.

Let's start with phones.

After years of denying that there were any adverse effects to cell phone use, the World Health Organization (WHO) finally got on board in 2011 and declared that radiation from cell phones can possibly cause cancer. The agency now lists mobile phone use in the same "carcinogenic hazard" category as lead, engine exhaust and chloroform.[10]

Engine exhaust? Chloroform? Good Lord—ADHD and tech addiction may be the *least* of our worries regarding screens.

The type of radiation coming out of a cell phone is called non-ionizing radio frequency (RF); it's less like an X-ray than like a very low-powered microwave oven—you know, the radiation box that we nuke our burritos in—and it's having a similar effect on our brains. According to Dr. Keith Black, chairman of neurology at Cedars-Sinai Medical Center in Los Angeles: "What microwave radiation does in the most simplistic terms is similar to what happens to food in microwaves, essentially cooking the brain."[11]

It doesn't take long for our cell phones to make our brain cells go snap, crackle and pop: A 2011 study conducted by researchers at the National Institutes of Health showed that it only took 50 minutes of cell phone radiation to "increase activity" in brain cells; "increase activity" is a nice, academic way to say "cook."

Yet while our brain cells can show signs of being microwaved after only 50 minutes, it could take *years* before our microwaved brains begin to show signs of trouble: "When you look at cancer development—particularly brain cancer—[it] takes a long time to develop. I think it is a good idea to give the public some sort of warning that long-term exposure to radiation from your cell phone could possibly cause cancer," says Dr. Henry Lai, research professor in bioengineering at the University of Washington, who has studied radiation for more than 30 years.

Dr. Black echoes that sentiment: "The biggest problem we have is that we know most environmental factors take several decades of exposure before we really see the consequences." Yet Dr. Black also indicates that we may be vulnerable to radiation effects other than just cancer: "In addition to leading to a development of cancer and tumors, there could be a whole host of other effects like cognitive memory function, since the memory temporal lobes are where we hold our cell phones."

Um. Okay. Brain cancer. Tumors. Cognitive deficits. But hey, I can take a selfie!

The World Health Organization finally made the "oh yeah, by the way, cell phones can cause brain cancer" announcement after a team of 31 scientists from 14 countries, including the United States, considered peer-reviewed studies on cell phone safety. In the largest international study on cell phones and cancer that the WHO team looked at, from 2010, researchers found that participants who had used cell phones for ten years or more had *double* the rate of brain glioma, a type of tumor. They also found evidence of an increase in acoustic neuroma brain cancer for mobile phone users as well.

As a result of the WHO announcement, the European Environmental Agency has pushed for more studies, saying that cell phones could be "as big of a public health risk as smoking, asbestos and leaded gasoline."

And to all those parents who think it's a swell idea to give smartphones to your little ones, Dr. Black sheds some very sobering light on that idea:

"Children's skulls and scalps are thinner. So the radiation can penetrate deeper into the brain of children and young adults. Their cells are dividing at a faster rate, so the impact of radiation can be much larger."

This, then, begs the question: is any ostensible educational benefit or ability to "stay connected" worth getting brain cancer?

Indeed, today there is an entire movement that encourages people to use antiradiation hollow-tube headsets with their phones and to keep phones as far away from peoples' bodies as possible. Personally, I need to spend a lot of time on my phone for professional reasons and have found the hollow-tube headsets to be a godsend. My friend Dr. Caroline Fierro, a wellness M.D., encourages her clients not to have phones in their bedrooms or anywhere on their bodies; if you do have it in your bedroom, she tells them, put it in a radiation-proof lead box.

That's the advice for the adults. The advice for kids is simpler: don't give them a phone. Don't give their little brains and thinner skulls the glowing little microwave ovens to put next to their heads.

And what about EMFs with tablets and computers?

Computers generate both low-frequency (LF) and radio-frequency (RF) EMFs (the same as cell phones). Both types are potentially harmful. All computers, no matter what the technology, radiate a relatively strong EMF consisting of 5–60 Hz and higher.

The EMFs don't come only from the computer screen; the electronics inside the computer generate a powerful EMF as well. Studies have shown EMF exposure above 2 milligauss (mG) begins to harm biological organisms; prolonged exposure to higher levels, from 2 mG up, has been associated with cancer and immune system effects. How much is your typical desktop computer throwing off? At three feet away, computers typically measure from 2mG to 5mG; at four inches and closer, computers measured from 4mG all the way to 20 mG.[12]

But tablets and laptops are even worse than desktop computers.

Tablets that connect to the Internet via WiFi and cellular connectivity emit EMF radiation like the WiFi from your laptop *and* cellular transmissions from your cell phone. This means that you are now being hit from two radiating sources. There is also a third source of tablet radiation: tablets emit extremely low frequency (ELF) radiation from the components and circuitry found within them; desktops also have low frequency radiation, but we are typically not very close to it (although it can register up to 18 inches away).

The bigger problem with laptops and tablets is that unlike desktop computers, by their very design, they are carried close to the body, thus increasing the exposure to tablet radiation. Many people actually work with their laptops or tablets on their laps. This is the worst possible way to use the device, as it maximizes EMF exposure—especially to the reproductive organs. There is research about EMF causing damage to sperm and affecting male fertility; for a woman, the concern can be even greater, as damaged eggs can never be replaced.

Researchers are also exploring other EMF dangers. Research has been done at Harvard on a potential correlation between EMF exposure and autism. According to the authors, EMF is suggested as a contributing factor in the disruption of normal bioelectrical synchronization, which is believed to aggravate autism spectrum conditions.

In August 2009 researchers at Columbia University published a paper describing how EMF can interfere with and break down DNA.[13] In a Hungarian study from 2000, EMFs were documented as a cause of irreversible structural and functional changes to cells and organelles, the specialized subunits within cells that allow them to work. Perhaps more troubling, morphological signals associated with cell death were also triggered. In an Italian study from 2005, independent research corroborated the Hungarian findings; EMFs were shown to induce apoptosis, or programmed cell death, in human recombinant cells.[14]

We had always known that our screens glowed; now we are also realizing that they are making us—and our kids—glow as well. Unfortunately, it ain't a healthy glow.

———————————

We've examined some psychological, clinical, developmental and physical problems associated with glowing screens. But what about behavior? Can the content of what a child sees on a screen actually shape the way that the child behaves?

As we shall read in the next chapter, that debate has raged for decades.

SEVEN

MONKEY SEE, MONKEY DO

MASS MEDIA EFFECTS

DO THINGS THAT KIDS SEE ON SCREENS REALLY INFLUENCE THEIR behavior?

Yeah, we know commercials can get kids to ask for everything from Happy Meals to Teenage Mutant Ninja Turtle action figures and that what Katy Perry wears can influence the preteen fashions of countless young girls. But the question that many ask is: can electronic media with violent content, like certain video games and TV shows, make kids more aggressive and more violent?

Politicians and advocacy groups have certainly thought so. In 2005, after a public outcry over the explicit content in *Grand Theft Auto: San Andreas,* then–U.S. senator Hillary Clinton became so concerned about the influence of violent or sexualized video games that she introduced a bill that criminalized the selling to minors of video games that were rated "mature" or "adults only."

Arguing that those games were a "silent epidemic of desensitization," the Family Entertainment Protection Act was referred to the Senate Committee on Commerce, Science and Technology. Despite the former First Lady's best efforts, the bill expired without becoming law at the end of the 109th Congress.

Trying to criminalize, censor or label problematic media content was nothing new. A few years earlier, back in the early 1990s, right around the time when Kurt Cobain and Nirvana were still smelling like teen spirit and a pre-Monica Lewinsky Bill Clinton was the fresh new face in D.C., there was a fierce culture war going on—one that rages to this day.

In this cultural divide, you had the "family values" faction, led by Tipper Gore and the so-called values warriors of James Dobson's Focus on the Family, vs. the "coarsening of the culture" crowd led by hip hop icons—at that time, 2 Live Crew—who extolled the virtue of creative expression and free speech, while painfully contorting the definition of art and protected speech with lyrics rife with racial epithets, profanity and misogyny.

So Tipper vs. 2 Live Crew became must-see-TV for the sheer theatrics of the cultural polarities that they represented. The values warriors felt that content *mattered* and that certain language and images simply shouldn't be accepted in the media of a civilized society. After all, *kids were watching* . . . and listening . . . and, most importantly, *imitating*. Such vileness surely must be influencing their impressionable little hearts and minds, the thinking went.

Luther Campbell, aka 2 Live Crew's front man, Luke Skyywalker, wasn't having it. But 2 Live Crew was under siege by the values warriors; with songs like "Pop that Pussy" and "Me So Horny," their album *As Nasty As They Wanna Be* was viewed as pornography; the American Family Association (AFA) hired attorney Jack Thompson* to appeal to Florida governor Bob Martinez to declare their music obscene.

In 1990 County Circuit Court judge Mel Grossman found that grounds for charges of obscenity violations did indeed exist, and on March 15 of that year, a 19-year-old Sarasota, Florida, record store clerk was arrested on a felony charge after selling a copy of the album.

In June of 1990, *Nasty* became the first record to be legally ruled as "obscene"—as decided by U.S. district court Judge Jose Gonzalez—which consequently made the album illegal to sell. Record chains and independent stores stopped selling the controversial record, but Charles Freeman, a local

---

*Jack Thompson is the same attorney we'll read about in the next chapter, involving the 2003 *Grand Theft Auto* murder trial—and subsequent Sony lawsuit—of Devin Moore, the Alabama teenager who was convicted of killing three police officers.

Florida retailer, was arrested two days after the ruling for selling a copy to an undercover cop. This was followed by the arrests of three members of 2 Live Crew after they performed songs from their album at Club Futura in Hollywood, Florida.

Campbell, aka Skyywalker, didn't understand why he and his music were under attack, saying that people should focus on more important things like "poverty and hunger." He decided to fight back; hoping to prevent additional obscenity arrests and reverse the pornographic stigma attached to the album, Campbell's attorney filed suit on March 16, 1990, in Federal District Court in Fort Lauderdale, seeking to declare that the record was *not* obscene.

In a 1990 interview with the *Los Angeles Times,* Campbell said that his music is "adult comedy, not pornography" and that his many critics simply didn't understand it. "These people act like I invented the idea of sexually explicit material," Campbell said. "Haven't they ever heard of Richard Pryor or Andrew Dice Clay? . . . Why, all of a sudden, is everybody picking on me?" Campbell went on to say: "The way I feel about it, 2 Live Crew is no different from sculptors who carve naked statues. We're not sex fiends. In our minds, we're artists."

But Florida's governor and the U.S. District Court didn't share Campbell's sense of humor or outlook on art. And Campbell and his music continued to get eviscerated by media watchdog groups like Focus on the Family and the Reverend Donald Wildmon's Family Association for being "pornographic." Meanwhile, the national media was eating it up, with the *Los Angeles Times* saying that the 2 Live Crew legal battle had "the blow by blow intensity of a prize fight."

If it were a boxing match, we might say that the Crew got off the canvas and staged a furious 15th-round comeback, as the U.S. Court of Appeals for the 11th Circuit overturned the obscenity ruling of Judge Gonzalez in 1992. During the trial, Harvard professor Henry Louis Gates, Jr., testified in defense of the group's lyrics, arguing that the material that the county alleged to be profane actually had important roots in African-American vernacular, games and literary traditions and should be protected.

The court agreed. Aided by all of the controversy, *As Nasty As They Wanna Be* went on to sell more than two million records.

Tipper Gore and her Parents Music Resource Center (PMRC) had a victory of sorts as well. In 1990 the Recording Industry Association of America (RIAA), in order to alert parents to potentially unsuitable material, agreed to put a black-and-white warning label reading "Parental Advisory: Explicit Lyrics" on records deemed to have excessive profanity or inappropriate references. So 2 Live Crew was allowed to sing their songs, but their records—and all others with questionable content released since then—got that big "Parental Advisory" sticker slapped on the cover.*

Even though 2 Live Crew had won the legal battle, the question remained: was their music so vulgar that it was negatively influencing the youth of America? After all, the idea that words, lyrics and images could be impacting the young and impressionable was not a new one; mass media boogey-men had been scaring parents for decades, from *Reefer Madness* to Joe Camel; from rock and roll to Marilyn Monroe; from Elvis's hips to *Steal this Book.*

Even our beloved comic books were once upon a time in the media crosshairs (no first-person-shooter pun intended)—in the 1950s, when they were the subject of a Senate hearing investigating their role in juvenile delinquency. At that hearing, the forensic scientist Frederic Wertham decried the "endless stream of brutality" in comic books, denouncing one title in particular as embodying sadistic fantasies that would be "particularly injurious to the ethical development of children."

Just what was the sadistic and brutal comic book that Wertham warned the Senate about? Clue: He wears a red cape and has the letter "S" on his chest. Yes, that's right, our beloved Superman was once suspected of corrupting the youth of this country and contributing to their misconduct.

In the 1960s, the film industry came under similar scrutiny when controversial movies like *Who's Afraid of Virginia Woolf*—with its sexual themes and profanity—led the Motion Picture Association of America (MPAA) to abandon the old system of self-censorship and adopt the film rating system

---

*Over 20 years later, a more circumspect Luther Campbell said during a 2014 interview that if he had it to do all over again, 2 Live Crew wouldn't have been so extreme. "Some of the things that were said I wouldn't have allowed to be said," he explained. "In some of the cases, some of the guys went overboard."

that's still in use today. Even though that Mike Nichols film was one of the top-grossing movies of 1966 and received critical acclaim and 13 Oscar nominations, there was a public backlash that certain content needed to be labeled with an adult-content rating as a tool for parents.

In 1975 the television industry—which had long used censors to monitor questionable content—created the short-lived "family viewing hour," a policy that was established by the Federal Communications Commission (FCC), according to which each network had a responsibility to air "family-friendly" programming during the first hour of prime time. After litigation, the policy was overturned in court in 1977.

While the FCC had federally mandated it, the impetus for the family viewing hour had been a public groundswell in 1974 regarding the amount of sex and violence on TV, with one television scene in particular causing the bulk of the backlash: a lesbian gang-rape scene in *Born Innocent*, the notorious 1974 NBC television movie starring Linda Blair; a disturbing scene that had featured a plunger handle was even briefly shown in daytime commercials for the film.

Reflecting the idea that the media can influence real-life behavior, the scene was pulled from the movie after it was blamed for the rape of a nine-year-old girl with a glass soda bottle by some of her peers. The California Supreme Court in *Olivia v. National Broadcasting Company* (1981) declared that the film wasn't obscene and that NBC wasn't liable for the actions of the kids who had committed the crime.

Yet while NBC was found legally not liable by the judicial system, the field of psychology has been able to demonstrate that the media can influence people's behavior. Not counting obvious examples such as TV commercials' shaping people's shopping or eating habits, there is a significant amount of research that shows that television violence can increase viewer aggression.

In a 2014 meta-analysis of 217 studies published between 1957 and 1990, psychologists Dr. George Comstock and Dr. Haejung Paik found that the short-term effect of exposure to television violence on actual physical violence against a person was moderate to large in strength. Their results, published in the journal *Communication Research,* showed a "positive and significant correlation between television violence and aggressive behavior."[1]

Dr. Comstock is no lightweight when it comes to understanding the media's effects; having earned his Ph.D. at Stanford, he's currently the S. I. Newhouse Professor at the School of Public Communications at Syracuse and is the author of *Television and the American Child* as well as the former science advisor and senior research coordinator of the U.S. Surgeon General's Scientific Advisory Committee on Television and Social Behavior.

Supporting Dr. Comstock's study is an earlier (2005) comprehensive review of the research on media and violence that was published in *The Lancet* by Dr. Kevin D. Browne from the University of Nottingham Medical School and Dr. Catherine Hamilton-Giachristis from the University of Birmingham.[2]

Their conclusions?

The weight of the studies reviewed supports the position that exposure to media violence leads to aggression, desensitization with regard to violence and lack of sympathy for victims of violence, particularly in children. According to Drs. Browne and Hamilton-Giachristis: "There is consistent evidence that violent imagery in television, film and video, and computer games has substantial short-term effects on arousal, thoughts, and emotions, increasing the likelihood of aggressive or fearful behaviour in younger children, especially in boys."

Yet many people give an eye roll when media effects on behavior are mentioned. "I watched a lot of murders on TV and I haven't killed anyone!" is a typical response that I hear.

When Jim Carrey tweeted that he was distancing himself from his film *Kick-Ass 2* because he felt uncomfortable with its violent content in the wake of the Newtown school shootings, Mark Millar, a creator of the *Kick-Ass* comic book series and one of the movie's executive producers, responded in an August 23, 2013, *New York Times* article that he has "never quite bought the notion that violence in fiction leads to violence in real life any more than Harry Potter casting a spell creates more boy wizards in real life."

Cute quote. But in addition to being nonsensical, it's simply not accurate.

Because the research *does* correlate violent content with increased aggression. Indeed, at the Congressional Public Health Summit in July of 2000, the respected heads of the country's six leading public health groups (the American Medical Association, the American Psychiatric Association, the American Academy of Pediatrics, the American Psychological Association, the American Academy of Family Physicians and the American Academy of Child and Adolescent Psychiatry) ALL signed a "Joint Statement on the Impact of Entertainment Violence on Children":

"At this time, well over 1,000 studies—including reports from the Surgeon General's office, the National Institute of Mental Health, and numerous studies conducted by leading figures within our medical and public health organizations—our own members—point overwhelmingly to a causal connection between media violence and aggressive behavior in some children. The conclusion of the public health community, based on over 30 years of research, is that viewing entertainment violence can lead to increases in aggressive attitudes, values and behavior, particularly in children."

The strongly worded statement went on to say, "Its effects are measurable and long-lasting. Moreover, prolonged viewing of media violence can lead to emotional desensitization toward violence in real life. . . . Viewing violence may lead to real life violence. Children exposed to violent programming at a young age have a higher tendency for violent and aggressive behavior later in life than children who are not so exposed."

This illustrious group charged with safeguarding our public health also took a shot at the naysayers in the entertainment industry who have, for *decades,* tried to dispute the harmful influence of violent media on children:

"There are some in the entertainment industry who maintain that 1) violent programming is harmless because no studies exist that prove a connection between violent entertainment and aggressive behavior in children, and 2) young people know that television, movies, and video games are simply fantasy. Unfortunately, they are wrong on both counts."

The statement concluded by pointing a finger toward the potency of interactive media (i.e., video games): "Although less research has been done on the impact of violent interactive entertainment (video games and other interactive media) on young people, preliminary studies indicate that the negative impact may be significantly more severe than that wrought by television, movies, or music."[3]

Keep in mind that that report, indicating the nascent state of interactive media research and warning about the "significantly more severe" effects of video games, was written 16 years ago; since then, hundreds of peer-reviewed studies have been done that confirm the link between violent video games and increased aggression.

Also in 2000, the FBI released a report on shootings in schools that stated that media violence is indeed a risk factor in such shootings.[4] In 2003 a panel of media violence experts convened by the National Institute of Mental Health, at the request of the U.S. surgeon general, published its comprehensive report on the effects of media violence on youth and affirmed that media violence is a "significant causal factor in aggression and violence."[5]

In 2007, the Federal Communications Commission (FCC) released its own report on violent TV programming and its effects on children and agreed with the surgeon general that there is "strong evidence" that exposing kids to violent media can increase their aggressive behavior.[6] Most recently, in 2009, our friends at the American Academy of Pediatrics published a comprehensive report on media violence in the journal *Pediatrics* that stated: "Exposure to violence in media, including television, movies, music and video games represents a significant risk to the health of children and adolescents."[7]

For good measure, the report added: "The weight of scientific evidence has been convincing to pediatricians, with more than 98% of pediatricians . . . expressing the personal belief that media violence affects children's aggression. Yet, the entertainment industry, the American public, politicians, and parents all have been reluctant to accept these findings and to take action. The debate should be over."

I think we all get why the entertainment industry, including video game manufacturers, may want to keep these studies on the down-low—after all, there are billions of dollars at stake. But why are the parents late to the dance? It is mind-boggling, in light of all of the research that exists, that there are *still* parents who fail to see that letting their kid play *Call of Duty* for hours on end may not be a good thing.

Of course, this is not to say that someone who watched Kojak shoot a bad guy on TV or any kid who plays *Call of Duty* will go out and fire off a few rounds at someone. It simply means that, as we know from Social Learning Theory, we *learn* by watching things; we are influenced and *shaped* by behavioral models, both in the real world and in the media. The extent to which those media models and shaping influences impact us is largely determined by other mediating factors (psychiatric/emotional factors, IQ, environment and other countervailing influences, etc.).

This idea that video games are just *one* possible risk factor amongst many in increasing aggression and violence is echoed in the Congressional Public Health Summit Joint Statement: "We in no way mean to imply that entertainment violence is the sole, or even necessarily the most important factor contributing to youth aggression, anti-social attitudes, and violence . . . numerous other factors may all contribute to these problems."

As Ohio State University professor Dr. Brad Bushman, one of the most prolific researchers on the media's role in aggressive behavior, puts it: "No researcher I know would say violence in the media is the only risk factor for aggression or violence or that it's the most important factor. It's usually a culmination of factors." According to Dr. Bushman, while video games aren't the only risk factor for violence, they can be viewed as an "amplifier."

Dr. David Walsh, a child psychologist who co-authored one of the studies connecting violent video games to aggression, explains the multiple-factors perspective this way: "Not every kid [who] plays a violent video game is gonna turn to violence. And that's because they don't have . . . other risk factors going on. It's a combination of risk factors. . . ."

If we can begin to understand exposure to violent video games as a contributing risk factor toward acting violently or, using Dr. Bushman's term, as an amplifier, we then have to also understand that such aggression amplification would, based on other factors, affect different kids in different ways, just as any aggression amplifier may affect any adult differently.

For example, let's say that we have three random adults who all drink two cups of their beloved Starbucks mocha latte every morning. We know from research—and some of you may know this experientially—that caffeine, as a stimulant, can also lead to increased aggression and can be an aggression *amplifier.*

Now that's not to say that Starbucks devotees are homicidal maniacs; it merely means that a person's caffeine consumption can amplify or increase his or her aggression level. So let's say that our three random and amped-up Starbucks fans get into their cars to drive to work and all three get cut off by rude drivers. All three have potentially had their aggression amplified by the caffeine, but that doesn't mean that all three will react or act aggressively or violently, because other factors also come into play.

Two of our coffee-wired participants may just bite their tongues and grip their steering wheels a bit tighter as they continue their drive to work. Yet our third driver might have had an argument with his or her spouse that morning—another aggression amplifier—and, let's say, has also been worried and stressed about possible job loss. And perhaps driver number three has poor coping skills and is temperamentally predisposed toward aggressive reactions because of being wired with a short fuse.

Thus the caffeine, the stress of the job and the argument that morning all act as *aggression amplifiers* for an already aggressively predisposed person, pushing that person over the edge into a fit of full-blown road rage.

Yet the other drivers had coffee—and increased aggression—but without going after the drivers who had cut them off; can we then conclude that coffee *didn't* play a role in the third driver's road rage? No, we can't; in fact, it most likely was a factor, but we certainly can't say that it was the *sole* factor, or even the most important factor—and it certainly wasn't the caffeine's "fault," just as we can't say that the domestic argument or the job stress "caused" the road rage incident. But were they all contributing factors in the driver's tipping point? Obviously.

Researcher Dr. Walsh also points to the developmental vulnerabilities that teenagers have that makes them more susceptible to certain risk factors: "The impulse control center of the brain, the part of the brain that enables us to think ahead, consider consequences, manage urges—that's the part of the brain right behind our forehead called the prefrontal cortex. That's under construction during the teenage years. In fact, the wiring on that is not completed until the early twenties."

Walsh further explains that this diminished impulse control is heightened when a person has additional risk factors such as being from a troubled household, having emotional issues and/or being unduly stressed: "And so when a young man with a developing brain, already angry, spends hours

and hours rehearsing violent acts and then he's put in this situation of emotional stress, there's a likelihood that he will literally go to that familiar
pattern that's been wired repeatedly, perhaps thousands and thousands of
times."

When it comes to gaming effects, repetition matters. And, sure enough,
there have been studies that show that aggression increases the longer a person sits and plays a violent game.[8]

This repetitive aspect of video gaming is a key dynamic in increased
aggression. According to Dr. Russell Heusmann, a psychologist at the University of Michigan: "The important thing is repetition. I think any child can
play *Grand Theft Auto* or a first-person shooter a few times, and it's not going
to have much effect. But if they play day in and day out, over a period of
years, any psychologist who understands the power of observational learning
is going to find it hard to believe that it's not going to have a major effect on
increasing risk."

Yet while most researchers tend to agree that there is indeed a strong correlation between violent gaming and increased aggression, some researchers,
like Dr. Chris Ferguson, feel that "increased aggression" is not only an im-
precise concept but one that's difficult to quantify.

Dr. Ferguson is a Stetson University professor and media-effects researcher who has been the most vocal critic of the increased-aggression studies. Having written a pro-gaming piece for the December 7, 2011, issue of
Time magazine ("Video Games Don't Make Kids Violent") and having been
quoted in dozens of pro–video game articles and blogs, Ferguson has become
the darling of video gamers everywhere. In fact, odds are that if you see a
headline saying something like "No Link Between Video Games and Real
Life Violence," Chris Ferguson's name will be close by.

According to Ferguson, studies that show increased aggression have no
practical utility: "Let's imagine you played a violent video game and it made
you one-half of a percent more aggressive (as one study showed)—would you
notice that? I don't think you would. To put it into context, if tomorrow
you're one-half of a percent more happy than you are today, what does that
really mean? It's a very tiny effect. . . . If my son was one-half a percent more
aggressive today than he was yesterday, I'd never notice that."

But as we've already noted, the research shows that the aggression effect increases with time and repetition. The studies that Ferguson points to, which indicate a half-percent increase, were those in which participants played a violent video game for 15 to 30 minutes and then were assessed for aggression immediately thereafter (more later about how that's done). We wouldn't expect to see whole-cloth personality changes in 15 to 30 minutes. But what about the kid immersed in gaming—the kid playing hour after hour in a virtual bunker?

If we understand aggression to be on a continuum that's affected by repetition and time played, where might we say that the proverbial tipping point to violence is? Where on that continuum does an angry kid get violent or an already unstable Adam Lanza—who fatally shot 20 children in Newtown, Connecticut, in 2012—go from being "just" more aggressive to being homicidal and violent?

While Iowa State University professor Doug Gentile echoes the multiple-risk-factor perspective, he also very appropriately suggests that we be careful about not reflexively pointing the finger of blame to just one cause—especially after tragedies like Newtown:

"Once we have a horrible tragedy like this, it really distorts the way we think about the issue . . . we have what I call a culprit mentality. 'What's the cause of this?' Well, it's never *the* cause. There's never one reason for anything like this. There's never one reason. Humans are complex."

Dr. Gentile is right. Post-Newtown-style rushes to judgment, in which video games are *blamed* for tragedies, shouldn't happen; yet nor should we discount their impact as contributing factors in a larger, complex dynamic.

Interestingly, physician and epidemiologist Dr. Gary Slutkin views the spread of real-life violence as being analogous to an infectious disease—and violent video gaming as a risk factor in contracting that disease.

As the founder of Cure Violence (www.cureviolence.org), an innovative organization that has successfully reduced gun violence in major cities and countries throughout the world, Dr. Slutkin employs the Cure Violence Health Model, which applies the same methods that he learned fighting infectious diseases to eradicating violence. In keeping with the infectious-disease analogy, first-person-shooter games weaken the psychological immune system and change the odds of whether violence (the disease) takes root within the person or not.

While we can argue about the *degree* to which the media influences people, we have to, if we are to be honest as we look at the research, acknowledge that the media—while not all-powerful—certainly does have an impact as a potential contributing factor in increasing aggressive behavior.

But, as the Congressional Public Health Summit statement indicated, not all media are created equal in their abilities to shape and impact. That's essentially the entire premise of this book; that the new *virtual* media— primarily because of its ubiquity, interactive nature, realism and intensity— has an even bigger impact, an even larger shaping influence, than the mass media that preceded it. And within the new virtual media realm, video games have specifically been targeted for research on electronic media and increased aggression over the past 15 years.

Indeed, the first major violent video game study took place even further back than that, way back in 1984—the year made famous by George Orwell. Published in the *Journal of Communication*, that study looked at the rather quaint idea of violent *video arcade* games, surveying 250 high school students (110 boys; 140 girls) who were quizzed about their video game–playing habits, violent TV–viewing habits and aggressive behavior with a series of questions such as, "Somebody picks a fight with you on the way home from school. What do you do?"[9]

Students who watched violent TV tended to also play violent video games; those students "were significantly related to manifest physical aggression." In the end, the researcher's conclusions were somewhat ambiguous: "The data indicate that video game playing is neither the menace that many of its critics have portrayed it to be, nor necessarily without possible negative consequences."

But 1984 *arcade* video games are qualitatively an entirely different animal from today's first-person-shooter games. Since that early study, we now have the benefit of hundreds of others with tens of thousands of participants, with the vast majority of that research attempting to explore whether exposure to violent media increases aggression.

EIGHT

VIDEO GAMES AND AGGRESSION

THE RESEARCH

CAN WATCHING VIOLENT VIDEO GAMES MAKE A KID MORE LIKELY to act more physically aggressive over the course of a school year?

That was the question that Iowa State University Distinguished Professor of Psychology Craig Anderson wanted to answer in 2008. Dr. Anderson, the director of the school's Center for the Study of Violence, is a well-known pioneer and leading researcher in video game effects. Since earning his Ph.D. from Stanford in 1980, he has spent the bulk of his professional career trying to research the impact that violent video games have on kids, even testifying before the U.S. Senate on the subject.

The study that he and his research associates conducted in 2008 examined the "longitudinal effects of violent video games in Japan and the United States." Publishing their work in the journal *Pediatrics,* the official journal of the American Academy of Pediatrics, Anderson and his team set out to see if violent video game exposure had an adverse effect on kids and teens over time, hypothesizing that exposure to violent video games early in a school year would predict physical aggressiveness later in the school year.[1]

They were right.

Using three different sample groups (364 U.S. third- to fifth-graders; 1,050 Japanese students aged 13 to 18; and a third sample consisting of 180 Japanese students aged 12 to 15), the researchers found that habitual violent video game playing earlier in the year predicted aggression when measured later in the school year (three to six months later)—even after statistically controlling for gender and previous physical aggressiveness.

Results from each sample group yielded "statistically reliable positive correlations" between HVGV (habitual video game violence) exposure and aggressive acts several months later "of a magnitude that falls in the medium to large range for longitudinal predictors of physical aggression and violence." In research parlance, this is a "robust" effect—not something that happens just by chance.

The study noted that American children were playing (as of 2008, the time of the study) over four times more video games every week than they were in the 1980s (16–18 hours vs. 4 hours) and that previous research (Anderson et al., 2004; Dill et al., 1998) had shown a link between violent video gaming and aggressive behavior.

The researchers defined "aggression" as behavior that's intended to harm another person and is *not* just an emotion, thought or intention; rather, "aggression," for the purposes of the study, had to be an actual harmful act, such as kicking, punching, getting into fights, etc. For the Japanese students in the study, these behaviors were self-reported; for the American students, aggressive behavior was an index of teacher, peer and student self-reports of physical aggression.

Not only did the researchers conclude that "habitually playing violent video games leads to increases in physical aggression . . . relative to those who do not play violent video games," but that those impacts were roughly the same in the American students and the Japanese students, even though the United States is considered an individualistic culture that has high levels of societal aggression and violence while Japan is considered a collectivist society with low levels of aggression and violence. Yet the gaming-and-increased-violence effect was the same in both, albeit more pronounced in the younger children, both in the United States and Japan.

The researchers concluded that this cross-cultural consistency of the increased-violence effect of gaming "illustrates the power of violent video games to affect children's developmental trajectory in a harmful way." The fact that the findings of a gaming-and-aggression link were so uniform also led the researchers to conclude: "These findings also contradict another popular alternative hypothesis: that only highly aggressive children (either by nature, culture or other socialization factors) will become more aggressive if repeatedly exposed to violent video games."

In other words, it wasn't just the already aggressive kids who were affected—*all* kids who were exposed to violent games became more aggressive. The researchers hypothesized that the underlying psychological mechanism of this increased aggression was "exposure to violent models, in either the real world or in entertainment media," which "teaches a host of aggression-enhancing behavioral scripts, attitudes and beliefs."

The fact that people—and especially children—learn new behaviors by observing "models" in, as the researchers point out, "either the real world or in entertainment media" is a key precept in Social Learning Theory. But the researchers hypothesize that this monkey-see, monkey-do phenomenon is increased by the "interactive nature of video games . . . [and] their immersive qualities, the fact that the user is an enactor as well as an observer of aggression."

To that I would also add the visual intensity and graphic realism of the latest generation of video games, coupled with, as I mentioned in chapter three, the frequent "reward schedule" and repetition of something as highly dopaminergic as video gaming, only further intensifies the strong shaping and "modeling" potential effect of violent video games.

Some more research:

A 2014 study titled "The Effect of Online Violent Video Games on Levels of Aggression" by Dr. Jack Hollingdale, University of Sussex, United Kingdom, and Dr. Tobias Greitemeyer, University of Innsbruck in Austria, found that participants who played violent video games showed more aggression than those who played neutral video games.[2]

The researchers randomly divided 101 students into violent gaming and nonviolent gaming groups. The violent gaming group played *Call of Duty: Modern Warfare* for 30 minutes while the nonviolent group played *Little Big Planet 2* for 30 minutes. *Call of Duty: Modern Warfare* is an ultraviolent military first-person-shooter game set in both Middle Eastern and Russian combat zones, with the player being either a U.S. marine or a British commando. The game involves realistic shooting and killing of enemy soldiers. In contrast, *Little Big Planet 2* is an innocuous, cartoon-like puzzle platform game that features the lovable Sackboy as the primary character.

After the participants played their respective video games, their levels of aggression were measured surreptitiously, using the "chili sauce paradigm," a method that has been successfully used in other studies to measure aggression.

What's the chili sauce paradigm, you might ask? After their 30 minutes of video gaming, the students were asked to participate in a bogus marketing survey, ostensibly to investigate a new hot chili sauce recipe. The students were not made aware that the chili survey was fake or that it had anything to do with their just-completed gaming experience.

The students were asked to season food with the chili sauce in question—a very spicy recipe that they were told was "3 out of 3" in "hotness"—for a taste tester who, the students were told, "couldn't stand hot chili sauce" but was participating in exchange for good pay.

The students were also told that they themselves weren't required to taste the seasoned food. After the students left the room, the researchers were able to measure the amount, in grams, of hot sauce that the participants had added with the idea that the amount of hot sauce added for an anonymous taste-tester represented the participants' animus or aggression level.

The researchers found that those students who had just played *Call of Duty* added significantly more hot sauce during the chili sauce paradigm. Now, does this mean that adding more hot chili sauce means that they're also more likely to shoot up a school? Of course not. But it does indicate that playing violent games raises one's aggression. And, as we've already noted, that can be especially problematic for those with underlying psychiatric vulnerabilities.

A similar conclusion was reached by Kansas State University researcher C. Barlett in a 2007 study published in the journal *Aggressive Behavior*.[3] In his research paper, entitled "Longer You Play, the More Hostile You Feel: Examination of First Person Shooter Video Games and Aggression During Video Game Play," Barlett's team measured physiological arousal and how aggressively participants would respond to three hypothetical scenarios after playing the first-person-shooter-game *Time Crisis 3* for 15 minutes over two separate trials.

Their conclusion?

"This study adds to the existing literature on video games and aggression by showing that increased play of a violent first person shooter video game can significantly increase aggression from baseline."

Interestingly, aggression researchers have identified frustration and the presence of blood and gore as "aggression eliciting factors." Indeed, in a fascinating 1996 study by Ballard and Wiest, published in the *Journal of Applied Social Psychology,* the researchers made a discovery about *Mortal Kombat II,* a competitive martial arts–style video game in which competitors can fight each other to the death.[4] In earlier versions of the game, players were able to turn off the digital blood, which spilled copiously; participants who played with the "blood function" turned on had a significant increase in hostility as compared with those who had disabled the blood function.

We can hypothesize that seeing blood—even video game blood—triggers something primordial in our ancient reptilian brain, where the fight-or-flight response lives. For eons, blood equaled violence and danger, which is not an association that a twenty-first-century gamer can choose to shut off.

This notion that seeing more graphically violent imagery can make a person more aggressive was also echoed by Dr. Russell G. Geen, a professor at the University of Missouri and the author of *Human Aggression* (1990). He theorizes that seeing (or visualizing) violent depictions can "prime" an individual to act upon aggressive thoughts or emotions.

An illuminating 2011 study published in the journal *Psychological Science* by Dr. Tobias Greitemeyer, from the University of Innsbruck in Austria, and Dr. Neil McLatchie, from Lancaster University in the United Kingdom, concluded that playing violent video games "increased dehumanization, which in turn evoked aggressive behavior. Thus, it appears that video-game-induced aggressive behavior is triggered when victimizers perceive the victim to be less than human."[5]

We know from history that when people are dehumainized—as Jews were in Nazi Germany or blacks were during slavery—it becomes easier to inflict violence on them. According to Dr. Greitemeyer's research, playing violent video games desensitizes the player to the basic humanity of all people; it dehumanizes them, thus making them easier to hurt.

Dr. Greitemeyer also published another study in the *Journal of Applied Social Psychology* in 2013, titled "The Changing Face of Aggression: The Effect of Personalized Avatars in a Violent Video Game on Levels of Aggressive Behavior."[6] His study concluded that gamers who had designed their own avatars were significantly more aggressive than those who played nonviolent games and even more aggressive that those who played violent video games but used generic avatars. There seems to be an empowering effect when a person "creates" his or her own digital persona; one can only imagine the potentially adverse and violent aspect of that empowering effect on the troubled, alienated kids of the world, like Newtown's Adam Lanza.

Now let's take a look at a brain-imaging study. Brain-imaging studies are particularly wonderful in that they offer very clear evidence of any adverse neurophysiological effects as a result of video gaming.

Recall that in chapter three, we discussed Dr. Yang Wang's work at the Indiana University School of Medicine in 2011. His brain-imaging research was the first of its kind that clearly showed a direct relationship between playing violent video games and measurable brain changes that included "less activation in certain frontal brain regions (regions that control aggression, self-control and emotion) following *one week* of playing violent video games."[7]

According to Dr. Wang: "These findings indicate that violent video game play has a long-term effect on brain functioning. These effects may translate into behavioral changes over longer periods of game play. . . . The affected brain regions are important for controlling emotion and aggressive behavior . . ."

Thus people with compromised frontal brain regions tend to be much more impulsive and potentially aggressive; this, in turn, helps us to understand from a neurological perspective what those aggression studies were showing. Since Dr. Wang's research showed frontal lobe effects after just *one week* of violent gaming, the question then becomes: what might happen to kids after *years* of violent video gaming?

Finally, in a masterful summary of years' worth of research, Iowa State University's Dr. Craig Anderson, in the most comprehensive meta-study review ever conducted in this area, exhaustively analyzed 130 research studies with more than 130,000 participants worldwide. The result, he found, "proves conclusively that exposure to violent video games makes more aggressive, less caring kids—regardless of their age, sex or culture." Published in 2010 in the APA journal *Psychological Bulletin,* the study concluded that violent games are not just a correlation, but a *causal* risk factor for increased aggressive thoughts and behavior.[8]

Dr. Anderson had more to say about his conclusions:

"We can now say with utmost confidence that regardless of research method—that is experimental, correlational, or longitudinal—and regardless of the cultures tested in this study [East and West], you get the same effects. And the effects are that exposure to violent video games increases the likelihood of aggressive behavior in both short-term and long-term contexts."

I know that when I speak to my gaming clients, they tell me that if they've been playing a violent game all weekend they are more prone to be aggressive. "I'm definitely more amped and would get into a fight if someone bumped into me or mouthed off" was how one of my gamers put it.

Another young man, "Sam," who, after playing *Call of Duty* all weekend, came into my office the following Monday and proudly proclaimed: "I did it! I signed up for the marines! Now I can go kill for real!" When I asked him what he was talking about, he said that he had been so pumped up after playing the game all weekend that he wanted the chance to do the real thing. When I reminded him that *Call of Duty* is a game that can be turned off, and that the Iraq War is real and has no off button, he just grinned and said, "Yeah, I know!"

Dr. Anderson, who has spent the bulk of his professional research career studying video games' effects on aggression, believes that the debate over whether or not video games increase aggressive behavior is now over: "From a public policy standpoint, it's time to get off the question of, 'Are there real and serious effects?' That's been answered and answered repeatedly. It's now time to move on to a more constructive question like, 'How do we make it easier for parents—within the limits of culture, society and law—to provide a healthier childhood for their kids?'"

Dr. Brad Bushman, one of the researchers who most strongly asserts the link between video games and aggression, has this to say about making the leap from aggression to actual physical violence: "On average, the research shows that exposure to violent video games increases aggressive thoughts, it increases angry feelings, it increases physiological arousal such as heart rate and blood pressure, which may explain why it also increases aggressive behavior. . . . Are they more likely to stab someone? I dunno. Are they more likely to shoot someone? I dunno. Are they more likely to rape someone? Beats me. Those are very rare events and we can't study them ethically . . . we can't give our participants knives and guns and see what they do with them. . . . But we know that there is a link between playing violent video games and more common forms of aggressive behavior—such as getting in fights."

But not everyone agrees with that. As mentioned, Dr. Ferguson disputes the notion that violent video games are problematic and has been very critical of the aggression research. The only problem is that his critiques of the voluminous aggression research are, at best, faulty arguments. And Dr. Ferguson's own headline-making 2014 research study—which inspired literally dozens of news stories and blogs that breathlessly screamed: "Long Term Study Finds Zero Link Between Violence in Video Games and Real Life Violence" (an actual headline)—was, as I'll explain, fatally flawed in its assumptions and conclusions.[9]

But that didn't matter—it made for great headlines and guilt-free gaming; one gaming blog, using Ferguson's "no link" study as its headline, opened with the reassuring line: "Go ahead and keep playing *Grand Theft Auto*." Game on!

So what did Dr. Ferguson, who, interestingly, is the author of the fictional thriller *Suicide Kings* (2013), about a Luciferian death cult, actually research in his study to draw the "no link" conclusions?

He used as his two experimental variables rates of media violence (both in television and in video games) and national youth crime rate statistics to see if there was any connection between the two. Feeling that previous studies in "laboratory" settings were too artificial to gather good data—although several longitudinal aggression studies collected their data over time from the "real world"—Ferguson decided that culling youth crime stats and comparing them with analyses of violent video game playing would answer the old does-media-cause-violence question.

Before we even look at his results, what might we think is a problem with the way that Ferguson's study is constructed? Unfortunately, Ferguson didn't just look at a particular sample group of gamers and monitor their violent episodes or violent behaviors over time; instead, he considered the *entire* youth population, among which gaming usage had significantly increased, and then looked at national statistics for youth crime.

When he did that, Ferguson saw an inverse relationship: video gaming had gone up while youth crime rates had gone down. Cue the screaming headlines: *No Link Between Violent Video Games and Real Life Violence!*

But what about the intervening variables? Usually, when trying to see if one experimental variable is impacting another experimental variable—in this case, violent video games and actual player violence—experimenters try to create studies that minimize or account for any other "intervening variables," or variables that could also be impacting the results.

We know that crime rates *as a whole* have decreased from the 1990s to the present. This has been variously credited to: better policing practices, youth gang intervention programs, youth drug and alcohol treatment programs. These crime rate interventions have proven to be effective because we know that the vast majority of violent crime is gang- or drug-related.

In fact, according to the FBI Web site, 48 percent of violent crime is gang-related (2011), while an *ABC News* report stretches that number to 80 percent, saying that "as many as one million gang members are believed to be responsible for as much as 80% of crime in America."[10] These gang-related crime statistics have nothing to do with video games and everything to do with gang culture and violent drug trafficking.

Yet, oddly, the fact that national crime-reducing programs have been effective is being hailed as "data" that violent video games don't increase gamer aggression. That's a bizarre conclusion. Unfortunately, Ferguson didn't study a more targeted sample group of, say, extreme gamers (who play

25 hours a week or more) in order to measure how their aggression levels were affected across time; instead, he looked at misleading overall national youth crime stats.

The other problem with relying on crime stats as the barometer of gamer aggression is that most aggressive or violent acts are not reported as crimes; if I kick my sister, odds are that a police report won't be filed, but it is, nonetheless, an aggressive and violent act.

Thankfully, even though Dr. Ferguson's head-scratcher of a study found a "strong correlation" between violent video game consumption and *declines* in youth crime stats, he conceded that this downward correlation was likely related to "chance" and "should not be taken as an indication that playing violent video games can lead to a safer world."

Unfortunately, this flawed study with its untenable conclusions gets a significant amount of news ink. In spite of the misleading nature of his own work, the ubiquitous Dr. Ferguson is very critical of other aggression studies. When pointing out methodological flaws, he cites the fact that many of the studies have used college students and not children, arguing that college students are more prone to give researchers the responses they want to hear, a type of response bias known in the research world as "demand characteristics": "Of course most of these college students probably have heard theories about media violence and aggression, because they're in college and taking these classes. . . . [A] typical college student can draw that link of what they're supposed to do, basically." College students are more likely than kids to show evidence of aggression, Ferguson speculates, because "these college students are guessing what they're supposed to do and doing it, in order to get their extra credit."

But Dr. Ferguson's tortured explanation doesn't make sense; in studies in which students participate for extra credit, that credit is not contingent on the nature of their responses, one way or another. In other studies, middle and high school children were used rather than college students. Dr. Ferguson's dismissal, on those rather speculative grounds, of research—which, he acknowledges, demonstrates increased aggression—doesn't hold water.

Other critics and video game enthusiasts have attempted to dispute some of the increased-aggression findings by suggesting that, perhaps, more-aggressive kids are gravitating to violent games—so that, in chicken-or-the-egg fashion, the aggression that's being measured in frequent gamers was a preexisting condition, as it were.

But that's refuted by both Dr. Anderson's and Dr. Wang's studies; in Dr. Anderson's study, a baseline for aggression was determined, and the aggressive acts came later in the year; additionally, the same effects were shown in "low-aggression" Japanese students. In Dr. Wang's study, the brain imaging was done before and after the exposure to the violent games, which clearly showed that the measurable brain changes were a byproduct of the exposure to the game.

Dr. Ferguson has also suggested that perhaps what's being measured in some of the studies as increased aggression is actually *frustration* that participants experience when they're asked to stop playing the game after 15 or 30 minutes.

Here Dr. Ferguson and I agree, although probably for different reasons. Given the addictive potential of hyperarousing games, a gamer can indeed become *very* frustrated—and angry—if a game is taken away.

According to Dr. Michael Fraser, a professor at Weil Cornell Medical College and a clinical psychologist who treats kids and teenagers with Internet addiction, it's not just the violent *content* of games but, as with any addict, the *threat* of having the object of obsession taken away that can lead to impulsive aggressiveness and even physical violence: "Kids can become physically and verbally abusive. Most parents have trouble imagining this—that their 12-year-old boy would push his mother when she tries to unplug the game."[11]

Dr. Kimberly Ross, a psychologist and the founder of the Center for On-line and Internet Addiction, agrees: "There definitely seems to be a correlation between violent game use and aggressive behavior. Kids throw things, they'll hit their parents, they'll start becoming violent at school. Parents say, 'He was a good boy; he didn't act like this before.'" Indeed, I've also worked with several families who have been attacked by their kids, some mentioned already in this book, when the kids' devices were taken away.

Odds are that most of the abovementioned types of increased aggression and violence never make it to national crime stats that Dr. Ferguson uses as data. Yet according to Dr. Young and Dr. Fraser, while the Adam Lanza–type cases are exceedingly rare, increased "everyday" aggression—like kids' shoving or pushing parents who attempt to take away their games—is becoming increasingly more common.

The extreme cases that do make the news—like many of the "ripped from the headlines" stories that we'll explore in the next chapter—share similarities to and parallels with drug addiction and the violent way that addicts can react when their drugs are taken away.

Indeed, there's an old saying in the drug addiction recovery community: "Never get in between a drug addict and their drugs." In the next chapter, we'll see just how explosively violent gaming addicts can be when their drug of choice is taken away.

A CLINICAL SNAPSHOT:
A PARENT'S DISTRESS

"Can you help my son?"

The mother on the other end of the phone told a fairly typical story in today's teenage landscape: a once-social 15-year-old who had played soccer and been a good student had been swallowed up by his video gaming addiction and was now failing all of his classes and unwilling to attend school.

I asked her to tell me when she first realized there was a problem. Her answer was a bit more atypical: "When he was ten years old . . . he was hospitalized . . . in a psych hospital." Her voice became more nervous, perhaps from embarrassment, as she tried to normalize something that no parent should have to endure: "He was fine . . . I mean, it was just to make sure that he was okay."

"Why was he hospitalized? And how long was he there for?"

"He's a good kid—really. I don't want you to think he's crazy or anything. He's not. He's just . . . just gotten into some bad habits. When he started playing it was like something came over him . . . like he was someone else. He was hospitalized for a month. My husband and I were scared. . . . He started isolating more and more and would only play that horrible game. So we took it away from him. We took the game away, we took his Xbox away . . . we took it all away."

Then she added, wistfully, "He used to love to be outdoors all the time . . . soccer . . . and he would love to be on the water—sailing, boogie-boarding. . . . I have photos of when he was eight or nine—"

"Why was he hospitalized?" I asked again.

"He came after me with a butcher knife . . . I . . . I don't think he was going to hurt me, but when we took away his game . . ." As she dissolved in tears, she repeated again, "I don't think he would have hurt me . . ."

NINE

RIPPED FROM THE HEADLINES

REAL CASES OF VIDEO GAME–INFLUENCED VIOLENCE*

DANIEL PETRIC KILLED MOTHER, SHOT FATHER BECAUSE THEY
TOOK *HALO 3* VIDEO GAME, PROSECUTORS SAY[1]

Wellington, Ohio, is a classic American small town; quaint and picturesque, it's located about 50 minutes southwest of Cleveland. With just under 5,000 residents, Wellington is a vestige of a rapidly disappearing America: a small town where everyone knows everyone else.

But back in 2007, sleepy Wellington made national news. It became Ground Zero in the violent-video-game debate thanks to Dan Petric, a 16-year-old Wellington boy who had inexplicably shot both of his parents, killing his mother while his father survived a gunshot wound to his face.

What made national headlines was the motive: police indicated that Dan had shot his parents because they had taken away his *Halo 3*,† a violent

---

*The headlines in this chapter are actual headlines from various newspapers or magazines with the sources cited in the notes at the end of this book. The accounts written in this chapter have been written by the author using those various news stories as a primary source.

†*Halo* is one of the most popular first-person-shooter violent video games; it is based on a military/science fiction theme. The Halo franchise has, as of 2014, sold over 60

video game to which he had become compulsively addicted. What made the case especially compelling was that Dan Petric, by all accounts and as clichéd as it may sound, was a normal kid raised by loving, caring parents.

Here are the details of the crime as presented during Dan's trial:

According to his sister Heidi's testimony, Dan had never played the game *Halo* until he got into a snowboarding accident and developed a staph infection, which caused him to miss school for almost a year. During that time, he discovered Xbox and *Halo* while playing at a friend's house, eventually becoming so compulsively addicted that he would often play up to 18 hours a day without taking a break.

Dan's father, Marc, a minister with the New Life Assembly of God, testified that he became so concerned about his son's video game habits, especially in light of the violent nature of the game, that he forbade him from purchasing it. He went on to testify that his son snuck out of the house one evening and bought the game anyway. When Dan returned home, his parents caught him with the game, took it away from him, and put it in a lockbox they kept in a closet—the same lockbox where his father also kept a 9mm handgun.

About a week after his game was taken away, Dan used his father's key to unlock the lock box and take his game out—along with the handgun. Daniel then went up behind his parents as they were relaxing on their couch in the living room and said, "Would you close your eyes, I have a surprise for you." Dan proceeded to shoot both of his parents; his father said that "his head went numb and he saw blood pouring down from his skull" as Dan's mother died from shots to the head, arms and chest.

A few minutes after the shooting, Dan's sister and her husband, Heidi and Andrew Archer, came over to watch the Cleveland Indians baseball game; Dan tried to shoo them away at the front door by telling them that their parents had been arguing, but his sister and husband heard groaning and pushed their way past Dan to find the bloody scene in the living room.

Dan's sister called the police, but before they could get there, Dan ran out of the house and fled in the family van. He was caught by Wellington police a short time later—with his beloved *Halo 3* riding shotgun on the front seat.

---

million units and grossed over \$3.4 billion for Microsoft.

During the trial, Dan's attorney argued that he wasn't in the right state of mind to understand the finality of shooting his parents—that he'd been playing the game for so long that he didn't comprehend the fact that death was real and permanent. Because of his age, Dan was not eligible for the death penalty but could have received life without parole.

Instead, Judge James Burge found him guilty of murder but gave him a lesser sentence of life in prison with the possibility of parole after 23 years, saying that Dan had been so obsessed with the game that he may have believed that, as with the characters in the game, death wasn't real.

Dan had showed little emotion throughout the trial; indeed, he maintained a detached, almost bored expression—except when his mother's autopsy photos were flashed on a large screen. That was when he bowed his head and stared at his hands for about 20 minutes while the photos were discussed.

Since the trial, Dan's father has forgiven him, saying that his son apologized:

"Dad, I'm so sorry for what I did to Mom, to you and to the family . . .
I'm so glad you're alive."

"You're my son," Marc Petric responded. "You're my boy."

Five years later, in a 2013 jailhouse interview with ABC News, when asked if he had realized during the shootings that he was killing his parents, a more reflective and game-free 22-year-old Dan Petric responded: "I'm used to playing these video games and at the end of every round, everything just resets . . . everyone is still there."

When asked if he blames the video games, he answers, "No, I've always taken responsibility . . . I know that it's nobody's fault but my own. But did it [the game] play a part? Yes. It did. It was the catalyst behind the mindset that caused the murder."

NATHON BROOKS, TEEN WHO ALLEGEDLY SHOT PARENTS OVER VIDEO GAMES, CHARGED WITH ATTEMPTED MURDER[2]

Fourteen-year-old Nathon Brooks loved playing basketball. Known throughout his small town of Moses Lake, Washington, as an avid baller, he was considered an all-American kid. But on Friday March 8, 2013, just before 10:00 p.m., Nathon quietly crept into his parents' bedroom as they slept and aimed a .22 caliber pistol at the back of his father's head.

According to the police report filed by Moses Lake police sergeant Mike Williams, the Washington State teen then " . . . shot his dad first, [and] then he shot his mom, [and] then shot again at his dad when [his father] rolled out of bed. Nathon said that when he was firing at his mom, she tried to get up, so he fired at her twice more and she stopped moving."

Why would a clean-cut kid like Nathon try to kill his parents? The police report indicated that Nathon was upset that he'd recently been grounded for two weeks from using electronic devices—including playing video games. Nathon told police that he'd been obsessed with video games; as Sgt. Williams wrote in his report: "I asked him how much he played video games, and he told me '24/7,' up until he got his electronics taken away."

Police believe the boy pried open a gun safe to retrieve his father's pistol and then went to his room and listened to music for an hour and a half as he tried to decide whether or not he should shoot his parents: "He said he was rethinking it, but said ultimately the voice telling him to do it was louder than the one telling him not to," Sgt. Williams wrote. "He said he just heard over and over in his head that he would be able to do whatever he wanted if he killed his parents."

After about 90 minutes, his radio batteries went dead; as he plugged the radio into a wall charger, he decided that he would go into his parents' bedroom and kill them. He then slowly and quietly entered their darkened room and began firing.

When the gun was empty, Nathon went back downstairs to reload; he became scared when he heard his father, Jonathon—who, unbeknownst to Nathon, had survived the shooting—yelling and saying he was getting his .40 caliber pistol. That prompted Nathon to drop the bullets he was carrying and run out the back door, where he threw the reloaded gun into the family's swimming pool.

Bloodied and wounded, his father was able to dial 911 and, not realizing that his son had been the shooter, told the operator that an intruder had shot both him and his wife.

When officers arrived on the scene, they were greeted by young Nathon at the front door; the investigation report noted that the two officers recognized Nathon because he played basketball on teams with the officers' sons. Police discovered that both parents were still alive. Jonathan Brooks had been shot at least once in the head, and his wife had been shot at least twice, once in the left side of the face and once in the hand.

Nathon's story about an intruder came undone when police reviewed a surveillance video from inside the house, which clearly showed Nathon walking through the living room while carrying a gun. The jig was up, and Nathon soon confessed. The entire community was shocked. Nathon's neighbors indicated that he seemed like a normal kid: "He played basketball and threw hoops out here a lot," said Arnold Valdez. "I never seen any trouble with him at all."

Nathon faced up to 30 years in prison for attempted murder; in February 2015 he was sentenced to 15 years in prison after the court refused to sentence him as a juvenile offender.

"GRAND THEFT AUTO" COP KILLER FOUND GUILTY[3]

In 2003 15-year-old Devin Moore was brought into an Alabama police station to be booked for grand theft auto after he had been found sleeping in a stolen car. Devin, who had no prior criminal history, had initially cooperated with Officer Arnold Strickland. But once inside the police station, he suddenly snapped when Officer Strickland told him that he might have to spend a few years in jail if he were found guilty of grand theft auto. He lunged at the officer, grabbed Strickland's .40 caliber Glock and shot him twice, once fatally in the head. Hearing the commotion, Officer James Crump, who had been in another part of the station house, started running toward the gunfire. He was met by Devin in the hallway and was shot three times, also once fatally in the head.

Devin kept walking down the hallway, toward the door of the emergency dispatcher. There, he fired five shots into dispatcher Ace Mealer, killing him as well. Devin then grabbed a set of car keys and sped away in a police cruiser.

Three officers were dead. It all took less than a minute.

Devin was captured several hours later in Mississippi, where he told the arresting officers: "Life is a video game. Everybody's got to die sometime." During his trial for capital murder, his attorney argued that PTSD from severe childhood physical abuse and the repeated playing of *Grand Theft Auto*** caused him to dissociate from reality when stressed. His attorney discovered that Devin had played *Grand Theft Auto* for hundreds of hours and, shockingly, that there is a vivid depiction in the game of a player doing exactly what Devin did: escaping a police station by shooting officers and fleeing in a squad car. But the judge didn't allow expert witnesses to testify regarding the video game defense, and the attorney was thus unable to present an insanity plea. Devin was found guilty and sentenced to death by lethal injection.

In February 2005 attorney Jack Thompson, a longtime media crusader, filed a civil lawsuit against Sony, Walmart and GameStop on behalf of the three police victims' families, alleging under Alabama's manufacturers' liability and wrongful death statutes that *Grand Theft Auto* had resulted in "copycat violence" that caused the deaths of the three officers.

According to Thompson in a 2005 *60 Minutes* story about the case: "What we're saying is that Devin Moore was, in effect, trained to do what he did. He was given a murder simulator." Thompson went on to explain: "The video game industry gave him a cranial menu that popped up in the blink of an eye, in that police station. And that menu offered him the split-second decision to kill the officers, shoot them in the head, flee in a police car, just as the game itself trained them to do."

Child psychologist Dr. David Walsh agreed: "When a young man with a developing brain, already angry, spends hours and hours rehearsing violent acts, and then, he's put in this situation of emotional stress, there's a likelihood that he will literally go to that familiar pattern that's been wired repeatedly, perhaps thousands and thousands of times."

Steve Strickland, a Methodist minister and the brother of slain officer Arnold Strickland, was convinced that violent video games and the

---

*The *Grand Theft Auto* video franchise is the granddaddy of violent video games. Players are aspiring gangsters in grimy inner cities who have to commit a series of violent crimes in order to advance. There are vivid depictions of shootings and of beatings of prostitutes with baseball bats; *Grand Theft Auto V* even has a "rape mod" that allows players to simulate raping female victims.

cop-killing scenes in *Grand Theft Auto* had played a role in his brother's death: "Why does it have to come to a point where somebody's life has to be taken before they realize that these games have repercussions to them? Why does it have to be to where my brother's not here anymore?"

On July 29, 2009, the court granted summary judgment to Sony/Take Two; Devin Moore is still on death row.

Admittedly, some of the cases of video game violence described above can be tough to read—and to believe—but they are merely a sampling of the dozen or so cases of gaming-influenced murder or matricide/patricide that have occurred in the United States. But can that be possible? Can gamers become such addicts that they actually kill people in order to get their virtual fixes, just like strung-out heroin addicts might? Apparently so.

In addition to the violent rage of a drug-deprived addict and the research that we've already read about, which indicates that video games can make kids more aggressive, there is another factor to consider in the gaming-violence dynamic: the repetitive simulation of violent acts is actually "training" kids to shoot and kill.

Lt. Col. David Grossman, a former West Point psychology professor and author of *Stop Teaching Our Kids to Kill* (1999), uses the term "murder simulator" to describe first-person-shooter games that he believes train children in the use of weapons and, even more importantly, emotionally desensitizes them to murder. Grossman, a former special forces officer who specializes in "killology"—the psychology of killing—places the blame for this shooter-training and violence-generating effect directly with video game manufacturers.

Unfortunately, the government moves at a glacial pace when it comes to keeping up with the scientific consensus about an issue—just ask the climate-change crowd.

Thus it wasn't until 2013, *after* the Newtown, Connecticut, massacre, that Senate Commerce Committee chairman Jay Rockefeller (D-WV) introduced a bill to have the National Academy of Sciences study the link between violent video games and violent acts by children. Also in 2013, President Barack Obama asked Congress to set aside $10 million for the Centers for Disease Control and Prevention to study the ties between violent images in the media—specifically mentioning "the effects violent video games have on young minds" and violent crime.

Yet, as we saw in the previous chapter, there's already a plethora of studies supporting that link—over *two decades'* worth of research.

We have just looked at cases in which addicted gamers acted like violent, crazed drug addicts when their games are taken away. In other instances, it appears that the penetrating screen imagery's blurred reality—as we have discussed with regard to Game Transfer Phenomenon—can lead to delusional or psychotic violent behavior. In still other instances, addictive gaming has seemed to amplify the gamers' sense of isolation and depression.

A TROUBLED GAMING ADDICT TAKES HIS LIFE[4]

In 2002, 21-year-old Wisconsin native Shawn Woolley committed suicide on Thanksgiving after having become addicted to the virtual reality game *EverQuest;* his body was found in a rocking chair in front of his computer, still facing the screen of the online game that had become his obsession.

Police found his body in a filthy apartment with dozens of empty pizza boxes, dirty clothes and chicken bones haphazardly thrown on the floor. Based on the few scribbled names and *EverQuest* terms found in his suicide note, his mother, Liz Woolley believes that his suicide was fueled by a rejection or betrayal in the game: "That damn game. Shawn was worse than any junkie I've ever seen. After he started playing the game, he just didn't enjoy life anymore."

Shawn's younger brother, Tony, says that Shawn changed once he discovered the game; they no longer hung out together, going bowling and riding go-karts as they used to. Obsessed, he'd lock himself in his room for endless hours. Hopelessly addicted, he stole his mother's credit card and used it to pay for the game. Desperate, his mother tried taking his keyboard to work with her.

Eventually he moved out and quit his job as the game became his entire life. His mother found his body Thanksgiving morning after pounding on his door and windows for two days; she had to cut through his chain lock to get into his apartment that terrible morning.

"If you're an alcoholic or addicted to drugs, there's places you can go for help," she told a local reporter, tears running down her face. "But there was no one there for him—no one who knew how to help." That's why Liz Woolley started an organization called Online Gamers Anonymous and a Web site to help people like Shawn.

"I can't just sit here," she says. "I cannot let him die in vain."

POLICE: 8-YEAR-OLD SHOOTS, KILLS ELDERLY CAREGIVER AFTER PLAYING VIDEO GAME[5]

An eight-year-old boy living in a trailer park in the unfortunately named town of Slaughter, Louisiana, shot his 87-year-old grandmother in the back of the head as she watched television.

She died instantly.

Investigators believe that the shooting was intentional, pointing to the child's having played the hyperviolent video game *Grand Theft Auto IV* just before the time of the shooting.

According to the local sheriff's department: "Investigators have learned that the juvenile suspect was playing a video game on the Play Station III *Grand Theft Auto IV,* a realistic game that has been associated with encouraging violence and awards points to players for killing people, just minutes before the homicide occurred."

The boy won't face charges; under Louisiana law, a child younger than ten is exempt from criminal responsibility. He now resides with his parents.

THE GIRLS WHO TRIED TO KILL FOR SLENDER MAN[6]

Slender who? That was the reaction of most of the adults who read about the "Slender Man stabbings," which made national headlines in 2014.

In the shocking case, 12-year-olds Morgan Geyser and Anissa Weier were charged with first-degree attempted murder in Wisconsin after they had lured a classmate into the woods and stabbed her 19 times, almost killing the girl. As Morgan and Anissa told police, they believed that by murdering someone, they could be elevated to the realm where virtual phantasm Slender Man lives and become his "proxies"; they had first learned about Slender Man on the horror Web site Creepypasta.com.

Most adults had heard of neither Slender Man nor Creepypasta.com. Thus many were shocked to learn that a large percentage of kids and teens know all about the site and the legend behind Slender Man. When I asked a random sampling of the teenagers I work with, the majority nodded their heads and went on to give me their own takes on the site and the eerie, tall fellow without a face.

While not a video game per se, Slender Man was a very psychologically penetrating virtual image that the girls discovered after they were given iPads in school. Video-influenced violence is often thought to be the purview of boys. And, to be sure, violent first-person-shooter games are predominantly played by boys (although girls do play as well).

In this case, we have a different sort of obsession that led to violence—not the desensitizing and aggressive amping-up of shooter games. Instead, the Wisconsin girls became seduced by a virtual urban legend, so much so that they almost killed their friend in order to be with him. It was a teen heartthrob scenario, with virtual reality and a dash of reality-blurring psychosis thrown in.

Indeed, Morgan told detectives that Slender Man communicated to her telepathically and "appeared in my dreams"—classic Game Transfer Phenomenon. But Morgan and Anissa were not the only ones; there are several "Slenderblogs" as well as a number of support sites that help other young people to purge the virtual Slender Man from their infected dreams.

Morgan and Anissa had seemed like any other 12-year-old girls before their creepy obsession. According to one of Anissa's classmates, "It's really scary because she seemed so normal. We were like, in a group project together and, you know, she seemed completely normal. She was really nice . . ." And Anissa's brother William said: "If you looked at my younger sister you'd see a happy normal 12-year-old. She loved Creepy Pasta and Slender Man . . . but I don't see why it changed from dream to reality."

Both girls were found competent to stand trial in November 2014 and are charged with attempted murder. If convicted, they face up to 65 years in state prison. At the time this book went to press, the question of whether they should be tried as adults was still pending on appeal.

A further sampling of gaming-induced psychotic behavior from around the world:

- On December 27, 2004, after playing *World of Warcraft* for 36 straight hours, and before jumping to his death from a tall building, a 13-year-old boy in China named Xioyi left a suicide note saying that he wanted "to join the heroes of the game he worshipped." His parents sued the Chinese distributors of the game for $12,500.

- In 2007 a boy in Beijing, after losing a schoolyard fight, poured gasoline on a classmate and set him on fire, burning the other boy over 55 percent of his body. When asked by a reporter why he did it, he responded that he had lost himself in *World of Warcraft* and believed that he had become a "fire mage." The boy has been sentenced to eight years in prison and ordered to pay the victim and his family a restitution of 760,000 RMB (approximately $103,140).

- A young South Korean couple was arrested after their three-month-old baby had starved to death. According to reports, the baby had been neglected and malnourished as the parents had become addicted to playing *Prius Online*, a game similar to *Second Life*, in which players work virtual jobs and raise virtual families. In the game, the parents had been nurturing a virtual baby—while their real baby was left to die. After their arrest, the couple admitted to feeding their baby rotten milk and spanking it numerous times when it cried, while their virtual baby was well-maintained and perfectly healthy.

- In China in 2005, Qiu Chenwei stabbed Zhu Caoyuan to death after Caoyuan had sold Chenwei's virtual sword in the game *Legend of Mir 3*. Caoyuan had offered the money to Chenwei, but Chenwei lost his temper and reportedly stabbed Caoyuan while he slept. While China has no laws to deal with the theft of virtual property, some countries (such as South Korea) have a section of their police force that investigates in-game crime.

Finally, in the next chapter, I will examine one very well-known and disturbing case that I am now convinced is an example of homicidal video game psychosis.

TEN

THE NEWTOWN MASSACRE

VIDEO GAME PSYCHOSIS

AS I SAT AT MY DESK WRITING THIS CHAPTER AND REFLECTING on the impact that violent imagery can have on a psychiatrically vulnerable teen, I thought of "Tom," a 15-year-old client whom I worked with almost ten years ago. While Tom did *not* have a video game problem—indeed, I worked with him before I had even become aware of tech addiction—his case can be helpful in illuminating the interplay between mental illness and violent imagery.

When Tom first walked into my office, there was nothing memorable or noteworthy about his appearance: he had that awkward facial hair that many 15-year-old boys have—not quite a shave-worthy beard, just scattered clusters of hair on his cheeks and chin with a loose array of upper-lip hair masquerading as a mustache. To complete his work-in-progress look, he wore a yellowed white T-shirt and had a small, unimposing stature.

He'd been diagnosed and was struggling with a nasty case of obsessive compulsive disorder (OCD). OCD can have many variations and expressions. In some cases it can look more like a "thought disorder" consisting of mental obsessions (as in not being able to get certain thoughts out of one's head); in other cases, troubling thoughts or underlying anxieties and/or fears lead to problematic and oftentimes ritualistic and compulsive *behaviors*. Tom had the obsessive, intrusive thought variety of OCD. More specifically, his mind was constantly bombarded by violent, horrific images of dismemberments and bloody mutilations. It would be fair to say that the landscape of Tom's mind was not a pretty place.

Belying his intrapsychic demons, the scruffy boy in the yellowing T-shirt presented as a fairly nice kid—polite, soft-spoken, with stable and supportive parents. Yet he was obviously a young man with a turbulent mind. I recognized the look of a person with intrusive thoughts: the tendency to stare down or off into space during a conversation as the uninvited thoughts marched disruptively through his head; delays in his responses, as he had to shake himself out of his fantasy-thought world and get back into the reality of the moment.

Tom had been away at a special school for children with psychiatric disorders and had just returned to a mainstream school setting. As I got to know him better, I discovered that, while he had suffered from persistent and obsessive thoughts since he was a child, his thoughts had become graphically violent only *after* he'd been exposed to such imagery in the sadistic *Saw* movies, the progenitors of what critics have come to call "torture porn" films.

Unfortunately for Tom, because of his OCD, once those images became seared into his mind's eye, they became a permanent part of his mental furniture. Worse still, Tom didn't just constantly remember those scenes—they fed his fantasies as he used them as fodder for his own torture imagery.

Tom had also been working with Dr. Fred Penzel, the man who literally wrote the book on OCD, *Obsessive Compulsive Disorders* (2000). Dr. Penzel had encouraged our obsessed client to journal his fantasies as a means of expelling some of the power of those thoughts, or what I liked to call "loosening the valve of the pressure cooker and dispelling the steam—before the cooker blows." While this horror-journaling presented a challenge to his frightened English teachers, who chanced upon some of his entries, it did seem to keep him in check.

But I'll admit that I was concerned. As he'd go into detail about his torture fantasies (again, a recommended treatment approach—bottling up or pushing away the troubling thoughts can give them more intrapsychic power), I would find myself wondering if the young man had the potential to act on those fantasies.

Indeed, I found myself putting away the pictures of my wife that I kept on my desk before I'd meet with Tom. I started doing this after one unnerving session, during which I found Tom staring intensely—as if in a trance—at my wife's picture for several long moments. He had just been sharing with me the difficulties he was having in controlling his violent fantasies of torturing and dismembering women when he just happened to look over at her picture and went silent, staring at it. You could see on his face that his mind was in the land of his obsessions; unnerved, I had to repeat his name two or three times to shake him out of his trance.

Yet Dr. Penzel would assure me that "these types of clients NEVER act out violently." When I incredulously responded, "Dr. Penzel . . . never? That's a rather absolute statement," he countered, "Well, almost never."

It was that "almost never" that worried me, since it implied that there were cases—admittedly outliers—in which the mental tipping point would be reached and thought would spill over into action. After all, the whole basis of cognitive behavioral therapy—the most popular and evidence-based form of psychotherapy—is that thoughts (cognitions) shape our behaviors. But what if a person suffers from underlying mental disorders—like OCD—that make it extremely difficult for a person to effectively control, reframe or manage the content of thoughts?

About a year later, a shocking and gruesome murder on Long Island in nearby Glen Cove confirmed that Dr. Penzel should never say never regarding the possibility that those consumed by deviant obsessive thoughts might act out violently. In a crime that sickened our local area, 31-year-old Evan Marshall dismembered and decapitated his neighbor, 57-year-old special education teacher Denice Fox, who had lived across the street from him. Police found sexual fetish drawings of dismembered women—similar to the drawings that my client Tom had—along with a collection of torture porn which is said to have fueled his violent fantasies.

My client Tom did not go on to hurt anyone; he was helped immensely by psychotropic medications and psychotherapy, and his life went on to follow a somewhat more normalized trajectory. Not having directed specific threats toward any one person, he didn't reach that critical point at which he needed to be reported to law enforcement authorities. Indeed, psychotherapists often work with clients who have troubling thoughts; we can't—and don't—report every client who has a violent fantasy, but we *are* compelled by law to report those clients who we believe are in *imminent* danger of hurting themselves or hurting someone else.

But the mental health field is not an exact science; there are no crystal balls when it comes to human behavior; assessing when violent thoughts cross over into the "acute" and "imminent risk" realm can be a tricky and subjective business.

Unfortunately, there are several high-profile cases of mentally ill young men who had been on the psychiatric radar yet who were still able to commit violent crimes: Jared Lee Loughner, who shot Arizona congresswoman Gabrielle Gifford and killed six others; "Batman" shooter James Holmes, who killed 12 at an Aurora, Colorado, movie theater; Virginia Tech shooter Seung Hui-Cho, who killed 32. All of these young men had either been psychiatrically evaluated, received psychiatric care or been referred for psychiatric evaluation.

Years later, as I began to work more in the area of video gaming effects, I would think: how would my severely OCD client Tom have behaved if he were constantly bombarded by graphic video game violence? He saw violent imagery only every couple of months in a movie theater, and that was enough to entirely preoccupy his mind. What if he had played *Grand Theft Auto* for 18 hours a day, as some kids do; might he have become one of those outliers whose thoughts spill over into violent behavior?

My professional opinion is: very possibly. The research—which we've already examined—is showing us that violent video games do increase aggressive behavior in children *without* underlying disorders. That then begs the question: how can it not be more impactful to the psychiatrically vulnerable? And, unfortunately, that's what we're seeing: violent outlier behavior in kids with underlying mental health issues.

In order to crystalize this point, I would like to examine the case that I think most powerfully—and disturbingly—illustrates that point.

SHOOTING IN NEWTOWN, CONNECTICUT SCHOOL LEAVES 28 DEAD

LANZA'S DESCENT TO MADNESS AND MURDER: SANDY HOOK SHOOTER
NOTCHED UP 83,000 ONLINE KILLS INCLUDING 22,000 "HEAD SHOTS"
USING VIOLENT GAMES TO TRAIN HIMSELF FOR HIS MASSACRE[1]

Newtown, Connecticut. Sandy Hook Elementary. Adam Lanza.

This is perhaps the most powerful—and controversial—example of what we are discussing, representing the worst, most horrific possible outcome of the intersection of mental illness and developmental issues with violent and graphic video game imagery. It's difficult to even write about the Newtown massacre without a feeling of overwhelming grief . . . of sadness . . . of anger . . . but mostly of the senselessness of the loss of innocent life that morning on December 14, 2012.

There are tragic events that occur in a society that scar the collective consciousness: 9/11 . . . the *Challenger* space shuttle explosion . . . and the Newtown massacre. We are not used to the slaughter of children, and hopefully we will never become accustomed to that. So when we read about a child who is murdered, we, as a civilized society, grieve.

But when we read—and see—the methodical slaughter by semiautomatic weapons of *20* children who were innocently attending elementary school that fateful, sunny morning, something deeper happens: it undermines our sense of an orderly world—innocent kids are *not* supposed to be butchered in their classrooms. That's not the way things are supposed to be.

Those with faith are forced to question it, and those without faith are also left unraveled. When kids die in car accidents or in natural disasters, our collective soul is left scarred, because children represent our purity and innocence; but as horrible as those so-called "acts of God" may be, we, on some level, understand that accidents, earthquakes and tsunamis happen.

But how do we reconcile a sentient being, strapped with semiautomatic weaponry, walking into a crowded elementary school and shooting small children with high-powered ammo like so many fish in a barrel? Didn't the 20-year-old shooter—barely an adult himself—feel any compassion, any empathy, for the little ones as his bullets pierced their skin and mortally wounded them? Didn't he have any remorse or inclination to stop when he heard the blood-curdling screams as the children ran for their lives? Apparently not. Because Adam Lanza kept shooting and shooting until he took his own life.

And now, postmortem, we, as a grieving society, are left with a horror puzzle: what went wrong with Adam Lanza that he was able to do such a thing? Yes, we know; there have been crazy murderers and serial killers since time immemorial; but this young man—this deranged murderer—had some shaping influences different from those of the usual Ted Bundys or John Wayne Gacys . . . this young man had a profile that we should—that we *must*—look at. The gun debate justifiably rages, but what *shapes* the mind of a killer, allowing that person to use such a weapon? What went into creating a monster who could shoot bullets into the backs of kindergarteners?

Strangely, when you look at Adam Lanza's bug-eyed picture, you don't see evil. You see an awkward, lost kid. Gacy was evil. Bundy was evil. They were cunning and intelligent men who relished torture and human suffering. Adam Lanza, meanwhile, looks like so many video game–playing geeks, lost in a first-person-shooter fantasy world. I've never met Adam Lanza. But looking at his face, I see the expression I've seen many times before. Not necessarily evil; just lost in a violent dream of virtual bullets and the crackle of video gunfire.

While we can never really know what was going on inside the mind of Adam Lanza, we now have several very important clues from Matthew Lysiak's shocking and recently published investigative book *Newtown: An American Tragedy*[2] and two recently released reports from the state of Connecticut that chronicle his all-consuming violent video gaming habits and his macabre obsession with mass killers. (He assigned them points for kills.) This information points to the conclusion that he just may have been psychotically playing out a first-person-shooter video game fantasy.

The facts:

We know that long before the shooting, Adam had shown signs of being a troubled kid; an exhaustive 114-page investigative report released in November of 2014 by the Connecticut Office of the Child Advocate[3] indicates that several medical professionals at the Yale Child Study Center had, several years *before* the shootings, recommended that Adam be treated for psychological issues. Unfortunately, those recommendations went largely un-heeded by Adam's mother, Nancy.

The Connecticut report was painstakingly put together by state officials as well as psychiatric experts in order to help shed light on what led to the shooting. It remains the most detailed publicly available document chroni-cling Adam's life, giving us a window into his childhood and psychological development.

According to the report, his problems in his early teens were belied by a relatively normal early childhood. Adam's father told the investigators that Adam seemed to enjoy being a kid when he was eight or nine years old; that he took part in school activities, including a school play, and attended Boy Scout meetings. His father also said that Adam played baseball for two seasons.

Yet also included in the Connecticut report was Adam's preoccupation with violence, which went back to at least the fifth grade, when he co-authored "The Big Book of Granny," a class project that was filled with narrative and images of child murder, cannibalization and taxidermy. In it, there is also a prophetic depiction of a boy shooting his mother in the head—just as Adam would shoot his own mother in the head ten years later.

According to the experts who authored the Connecticut report, a major red flag was missed with Adam's horrific fifth-grade writing project: "Mental health professionals contributing to this report determined that the content of 'The Big Book of Granny' can only be described as extremely abhorrent and, if it had been carefully reviewed by school staff, it would have suggested the need for a referral to a child psychiatrist or other mental health profes-sional for evaluation."

Also in the report: concerned about his son's mental state, Adam's father took him to the Yale Child Study Center in 2006, when the boy was a ninth-grader, via his company's Employee Assistance Program; Adam had also been seeing a community psychiatrist at the same time. He was diagnosed with severe anxiety and Asperger's syndrome. Adam told one of the center's psychiatrists that he didn't want to have more friends and that he didn't even really understand what a friend was.

Kathleen A. Koenig, a nurse at the Yale Child Studies Center, indicated that Adam also presented with symptoms of OCD, because he frequently washed his hands and changed his socks up to 20 times a day, to the point where his mother did three daily loads of laundry. In addition, he would sometimes go through a box of tissues in a day because he couldn't touch a doorknob with his bare hand.

The authors of the Connecticut report did stress that those with autism spectrum disorder and the other psychiatric problems that Adam had rarely engage in outward violence and are far more likely to internalize their issues: "Individuals with those mental health or developmental disorders are more likely to internalize (that is, to feel distressed emotionally or to be confused, socially inappropriate or inept, and sometimes to harm themselves inadvertently or intentionally) than to externalize (that is, to act out aggressively)."

Nonetheless, the psychiatrist who evaluated Adam indicated that Adam's constructed social and educational world *was* a matter of concern and prescribed him anti-anxiety medication, which Adam refused. The psychiatrist went on to note that creating a "prosthetic environment" for Adam posed significant risk and that those around Adam should work to help him overcome social difficulties instead of forming a "bubble." He also noted that the family needed "tons of parental guidance . . ."

According to the report, an advanced practice registered nurse (APRN) also told Adam that he had psychological disorders that could be helped with medication, indicating that Adam was living in a box that was only going to get smaller over time if he didn't get treatment. Adam did briefly go on anti-depressants and anti-anxiety medications in 2007, but his mother took him off them, saying that he was experiencing adverse side effects.

In 2008, when he was 16, Adam's "box" did indeed become smaller when his mother pulled him out of Newtown High School in order to home-school him, indicating that she'd been unhappy with the public school system's plans for her son. Between receiving home instruction and taking some classes at Western Connecticut State University, he acquired enough credits to graduate a year early.

After graduation Adam would sometimes play the arcade music video game *Dance Dance Revolution* with his brother and his one friend; that one friend indicated that he had a somewhat normal friendship with Adam, telling investigators that he and Adam would talk about a number of topics, including "computers, chimp society, human nature, morality, prejudice and occasionally . . . family members." That sole friend said that Adam was capable of showing emotion and would laugh, smile and make jokes, though he did also say that Adam wasn't very expressive.

But not having a structured social setting like school was an increasing problem for Adam. While a public school setting—where he had been an honor student, joined the tech club and been described as "intelligent, but nervous and fidgety" by those who knew him—may not have been the *perfect* place for Adam, he at least had a semblance of normalcy and social interaction.

But now that the social tether of school had been cut, Adam withdrew further into his virtual fantasy world. He had first shown signs of an abnormal video obsession the prior year when, at age 15, he discovered *World of Warcraft,* a game in which, as previously discussed, players live in an alternate universe of mythical monsters and must heroically vanquish competitors in order to move ahead.

As time wore on and Adam continued to play alone for hours on end in his mother's bunkerlike basement, his obsession with *World of Warcraft* quickly morphed into an obsession with *Combat Arms,* a multiplayer first-person-shooter game. The object of the game, as with most first-person-shooter games, is to kill the most enemy combatants.

By September 2009 Adam had become a fixture in the online community for *Combat Arms* and was accepted into a "cluster," a group of other online *Combat Arms* players, among whom gaming strategy discussions were mixed with small talk and banter. By all accounts, Adam fit in this virtual world much more comfortably than he did among the face-to-face interactions of the nonvirtual realm.

But according to the mental health experts who authored the Connecticut Office of the Child Advocate report, replacing real-world social interactions with a virtual group of peers was a problem for a boy with Adam's issues: "Unlike normalizing influences and positive community peer groups, his cyber group would have had little willingness or ability to stop his dangerous trajectory or to offer cautioning feedback to him about his impulses."

Since he was unable to fit into the real world, the virtual realm—with its myriad of avatar games—allowed this meek, socially awkward boy to reinvent himself; in *Combat Arms,* Adam was able to create a powerful anti-Adam avatar. As author and investigative journalist Matthew Lysiak describes it in *Newtown: An American Tragedy* (2013): "Alone and in the darkness, with the illuminated screen his only light, Adam had found a level of comfort in his world of computers and video games that he could rarely attain in the outside world. . . . Adam was able to show a bravado and confidence that was unfamiliar to classmates and family who only knew him as an awkward and meek teenager. . . . In his alternative online universe, the skinny and frail teenager chose to create an imposing bulky muscle-bound soldier dressed in desert camouflage and also a light vest, goggles, and a black beret. He chose equally imposing weapons for his missions: the M16A3, a military variant of the Bushmaster AR-15 assault rifle, and the G23 pistol, which strongly resembles a Glock 10-millimeter handgun."

By the time Adam had turned 17, in 2009, he had logged over 500 hours in the darkness of his sequestered fantasy world. According to his online profile, Adam-as-lethal-warrior had tallied 83,496 kills, including 22,725 "head shots."

At an age when most kids were planning for college, Adam was deep in the virtual bunker; using an online persona, "Kaynbred," he demonstrated an ever-growing fixation with violence as he began frequenting Internet chat rooms that focused on violent video games, weapons and mass killers.

His obsession with mass killers was very troubling. As his real world continued to shrink—he stopped communicating with his father in 2010, had stopped speaking with his only friend over the summer of 2012 after a dispute involving a movie, and, while *living in the same house with her,* would communicate with his mother only via email—his obsessions with violence deepened.

Between August 2009 and February 2010, using his Kaynbred alias, Adam spent countless hours going over entries about mass killers on Wikipedia, obsessively correcting small details of the killers' lives or the types of firearms that they used. According to the Connecticut report: "AL [Adam Lanza] increasingly lived in an alternate universe in which ruminations about mass shootings were his central preoccupation."

But Adam's mass killer obsession went beyond just correcting the minutiae of Wikipedia pages or collecting mass-murder fun facts. Indeed, after a forensic review of his computer usage, the FBI Behavioral Analysis Unit indicated that Adam's obsession and attention to detail with mass killings was "unprecedented."

In a detailed investigative report[4] released by Stephen J. Sendensky, Connecticut's state attorney, on November 13, 2013—roughly one year after the murders—investigators indicated that they had also found among Adam's possessions a news clipping from the *New York Times* regarding the February 18, 2008, shooting at Northern Illinois University; photocopies of newspaper articles from 1891 regarding the shooting of schoolchildren; a book on the 2006 mass shooting of children at an Amish school in Lancaster County, Pennsylvania; a spreadsheet listing mass killings over the years; and other "electronic evidence or digital media that appeared to belong to the shooter [that] revealed that the shooter had a preoccupation with mass shootings, in particular the Columbine shootings."

According to a March 17, 2013, *New York Daily News* story by Mike Lupica, the mass killing "spreadsheet" that was mentioned in the Connecticut attorney's report was *not* just a spreadsheet meant to compile murder data; instead, the macabre seven-foot-by-four-foot sheet of paper was a murder *score sheet* that had been obsessively filled in in nine-point font with the names of hundreds of murderers, along with their death tallies and the names of weapons they used.[5]

Lupica had interviewed veteran cops who had gathered at the annual conference for the International Association of Police Chiefs and Colonels in New Orleans three months after the Newtown massacre; at that conference, Connecticut State Police colonel Danny Stebbins, one of the speakers, told his fellow officers what had been found at Adam Lanza's house.

As one veteran cop told Lupica, the Connecticut State Police believe with regard to the score sheet that it was Adam's "intent to put his own name at the very top of that list. They believe that he picked an elementary school because he felt it was a point of least resistance, where he could rack up the greatest number of kills."

The veteran cop told Lupica that the spreadsheet was so comprehensive that "it sounded like a doctoral thesis, that was the quality of the research," and he speculated that it had to have taken Adam years to put together.

Based on Adam's dual obsessions with real-life murderers and virtual-world violence, is it possible that the two became blurred in his mind and that he believed the flesh-and-blood murders he was committing on that horrible day in 2012 were all part of some game? It appears that this slow-yet-steady blurring of reality for Adam—a blurring in which the *real* mass killers on his spreadsheet were just so many first-person shooters on his glowing computer screen—continued as he fell deeper and deeper into the darkness of his gaming bunker.

But do gamers shoot civilians—and children, no less? We may have some more clues from Adam's actual online profile, which tells us the games that he immersed himself in: by 2011, 19-year-old Adam had stopped playing *Combat Arms* and moved on to *Call of Duty* and *Call of Duty: Modern Warfare 2,* both violent, first-person-shooter games in which, as with *Combat Arms,* players compete to rack up the most number of kills.

But in *Call of Duty: Modern Warfare 2,* in a foreshadowing of the murders at Newtown, the shooting victims *are* civilians, including women and children. In this shocking game, Adam became an undercover CIA agent who joined a group of Russian terrorists at an airport to massacre unarmed civilians; in order to keep his cover and fulfill the mission's objective, he had to shoot and kill women and children. Unbelievably, just as in Newtown, the shot and injured civilians in the game would crawl away, leaving a trail of smeared blood, while those who had initially survived would make attempts to help others—only to be shot dead. Just as in Newtown.

According to the Connecticut attorney's report, Adam is said to have also had an obscure game called *School Shooter** on his hard drive; in that first-person-shooter game, the player goes from classroom to classroom targeting children and teachers before taking his own life—just as Adam did in Newtown.

But didn't *anybody* see the red flags of his deepening problems? Indeed, Adam was such a sick and addicted video gamer that, like that of drug addicts, his physical health also deteriorated as he pursued his obsession. The

---

* *School Shooter* isn't the first game to exploit tragedy; in *Super Columbine Massacre RPG,* released in 2005, players assume the roles of the Columbine murderers. In 2013 *Boston Marathon 2013: Terror in the Streets* featured players dodging pressure-cooker bombs. In 2004 *JFK: Reloaded* allowed players to see President Kennedy's limousine through the crosshairs of a rifle scope as the player attempted to recreate the lethal headshot.

Connecticut report indicated that Adam had "profound anorexia" at the time of his death, weighing just 112 pounds despite being six feet tall.

Unfortunately, during Adam's downward spiral into madness, his mother, Nancy, became an eager enabler. It was Nancy who thought it would be a good idea to expose her troubled, video game–obsessed son to the world of real guns, misguidedly believing that she was engendering some healthy mother-son bonding at shooting ranges; it was Nancy who pulled her autistic and socially awkward son out of school, thus practically ensuring the lonely and isolated existence that led to his virtually enabled psychotic solitude; and it was she who, in oblivious denial, told a friend who had expressed concerns about Adam's increasing isolation, "He's fine. Just so long as he has his computer and video games, he can keep himself occupied."

Adam certainly was occupied—and obsessed. The basement, which Adam's mother had originally remodeled into a game room for him, had taken on the look of a military bunker, with nearly every inch of the walls covered by posters of weapons and military equipment. In a former exercise room, Adam created a quasi–indoor shooting range; there, he would dress in head-to-toe military gear and shoot his pellet gun at cardboard targets he'd set up on a clothesline. In his bedroom, every inch of window was covered in plastic, so as not to let in one ray of outside light.

At some point, even Adam's clueless mother began to become somewhat concerned, telling a friend that she had begun to notice that her son rarely ventured outside and was "like a zombie in front of the screen." Adam, she revealed, sat and played his games well into the night and slept most of the day.

She finally became concerned enough that she secretly went into his room one day to look around. She found several drawings, hidden underneath his nightstand, that depicted mutilated corpses; another drawing she found was of a bloodied woman clutching a rosary as bullets ripped through her spine; yet another depicted a grassy field lined with the corpses of young children.

In that gruesome sketch, the faces of the children were severely mutilated and couldn't be recognized. Still another sketch appeared to be a self-portrait of a younger Adam with blood gushing from a large hole in his forehead and his arms stretched toward the sky in a posture of triumph.

It's important to remember that these games and violent images were Adam's entire world. For a young man who had shown signs of OCD, they were just so much kerosene to throw onto his already burning, obsessive and turbulent mind. As the veteran cop told Mike Lupica at the law enforcement conference: "In the end, it was just a perfect storm: These guns, one of them an AR-15, in the hands of a violent, insane gamer. It was like porn to a rapist. They feed on it until they go out and say, enough of the video screen. Now I'm actually going to be a hunter."

The cop went on to say that according to the theory of the Connecticut State Police, Adam thought that going to the school "was the way to pick up the easiest points. It's why he didn't want to be killed by law enforcement. In the code of a gamer, even a deranged gamer like this little bastard, if some-body else kills you, they get your points. They believe that's why he killed himself."

There are two things that investigators theorize may have pushed Adam from virtual violence into real-world violence: according to Lysiak, just a few days before the shootings, Adam's mother told Dennis Durant, a bartender friend, that she had recently told her son that his "medical" conditions precluded him from ever becoming a real soldier. Nancy told Durant, "I told Adam, in as gentle terms as possible, that he will never be a marine, that he's just not cut out for it and that life has something different planned for him."

According to Nancy, he did not take her news well.

The other blow that Adam received: Adam's mother had hinted that she might be planning to move, either to Washington State or North Caro-lina. She had told a friend that if she moved to Washington she would en-roll Adam in a "special school." According to the Connecticut Office of the Child Advocate report, the idea of moving from Newtown had made Adam increasingly despondent and anxious in the months preceding the shootings. The report went on to say: "The looming prospect of moving from Newtown may have increased AL's anxiety, as he may have worried about where he would go or live, and the loss of the sanctuary he had developed in his home. This was quite possibly an important factor leading to the shootings."

However, the report does also clearly state that Adam didn't just "snap"— that the shootings were planned out. The report cites the facts that he had visited the school's Web site on numerous occasions, viewed the student handbook and familiarized himself with the school's security procedures.

The notion that Adam didn't just snap was also echoed by the veteran cop whom Mike Lupica had interviewed: "He didn't snap that day, he wasn't one of those guys who was mad as hell and wasn't going to take it anymore. . . . He had been planning this thing forever. They have pictures from two years before, with the guy all strapped with weapons, posing with a pistol to his head. That's the thing you have to understand: He had this laid out for years before."

Extreme social isolation. OCD. Increasing exposure to violent games. A tenuous grasp on reality mixed with total immersion in virtual violence. Access to guns. Was Adam a psychologically vulnerable youth who crossed over into a form of gaming-induced psychosis that was triggered by his fear of moving—and the fear of having to leave the safety of his virtual bunker?

The question that I asked at the beginning of this chapter remains: what role did video games play in Adam's "perfect storm" of violent insanity? We can never truly know, but we can draw psychological postmortem inferences based on the evidence that we have.

As the veteran cop had told Lupica, the violent games were like porn to a rapist. He went on to say: "It really was like he was lost in one of his own sick games. That's what we heard. That he learned something from his game that you learn in [police] school, about how if you're moving from room to room—the way he was in that school—you have to reload before you get to the next room. Maybe he has a 30-round magazine clip, and he's only used half of it. But he's willing to dump 15 rounds and have a new clip before he arrives in the next room."

According to Lupica, the veteran cop's voice started to shake as he continued: "They believe he learned the principles of this—the tactical reload—from his game. Reload before you're completely out. Keep going. When the strap broke on his first weapon [the AR-15], he went to his handgun at the end. Classic police training. Or something you learn playing kill games."

Was Adam Lanza's act the by-product of what Lt. Col. David Grossman had earlier called a "murder simulator?" Was he psychotically playing out a shooter game? We had read earlier about the research into Game Transfer Phenomenon—through which compulsive gamers can blur the game with reality. Or was Adam just an angry teen who had reached a violent breaking point because he feared that life as he knew it in Newtown was about to end?

In the end, we can never really know for sure. But what seems certain is that violent video games played a key role in his insane perfect storm—either as the reality-blurring mechanism of a psychotic break or as the virtual training ground wherein an angry kid became desensitized to violence and honed his skills to shoot defenseless children.

Either way, I think it's fair to say that first-person-shooter games were an instrumental part of the Newtown massacre equation.

As I've already stated, the previously mentioned cases from the last two chapters are the extreme outliers. I don't mean to suggest that every kid who plays a video game will shoot up a school, just as not every person who drinks a beer will become an alcoholic.

But *all* kids exposed to the hyperarousing and hyperstimulating glowing screens will be impacted on some level; kids whose brains are exposed to the hypnotic flashing lights of electronic media during key developmental windows will have their ability to focus and concentrate adversely impacted, leaving them open to the possibility of virtual addiction. And according to all of the aggression research that was cited, kids exposed to violent games *will be* more aggressive.

At this point we have to ask ourselves: how did this happen? How did our entire society shift so quickly that children have gone from being normal kids to being screen-obsessed Glow Kids?

ELEVEN

ETAN PATZ AND THE END OF INNOCENCE— AND OUTDOOR PLAY

MAY 25, 1979, BROUGHT THE END OF INNOCENCE. ON THAT DAY, A sweet six-year-old boy named Etan Patz disappeared. He certainly wasn't the first child ever to be abducted and murdered. Yet somehow his disappearance profoundly affected an entire generation—and changed the way that we parent.

Born in New York City on October 9, 1972, Etan Patz grew up in Manhattan, in a loft building near the corner of Prince Street and West Broadway. Etan was nearing the end of his first year of kindergarten when his parents decided that he could walk by himself—*for the first time*—to the school bus stop located just two blocks away from his home.

They never saw him again.

Immediately after Etan's disappearance, his father, a photographer, posted photos of his son throughout New York City, and police initiated a weeks-long search. Etan's case would captivate America and garner national media attention as the whole country asked, "What happened to Etan?"

For any parent, this is the worst horror that could ever happen. His parents never stopped looking for him, and his disappearance helped to create the missing-children movement, including new legislation and new methods for tracking down missing kids, such as the milk-carton campaigns of the mid-1980s. Little Etan was the first missing child to be pictured on the side of a milk carton.

Many sociologists and psychologists point to the Etan Patz kidnapping as a turning point in our society. It was the beginning of a new age of worry for parents, and many of the "kid freedoms" that people from an earlier generation remember are now a thing of the past.

Before Etan, it wasn't unusual for young children to walk to school without an adult—or at least to walk to the bus stop. I have friends who remember taking the subway alone or with other kids when they were nine or ten years old. That would almost *never* happen today—it would almost certainly prompt a CPS call.

Although they were not the first, the high-profile kidnapping-murders of young children in the late 1970s and early 1980s, including Adam Walsh and Johnny Gosch, had a very significant effect on American life. The FBI had been involved in child-abduction cases since 1932, when legendary aviator Charles Lindbergh's baby was kidnapped and murdered, and child murderers like Albert Fish had been around since the 1920s. But it wasn't until 1984, after Etan, Adam Walsh and a handful of other kids went missing, that the National Center for Missing and Exploited Children was authorized by Congress.

Parents became more afraid after the 1970s and 1980s. Was it the increased media saturation that heightened everyone's fear? Increased news cycles and awareness via the milk-carton campaign aside, abductions and murders of children have always been and continue to be exceedingly rare events.

The vast majority of the 800,000 reported annual cases of abducted and missing children end with the return of the children within hours. More than 200,000 of those children are victims of family abduction, often involving parents in custody disputes. Of the 58,000 "nonfamily" abductions, most involve abductors who know the children or families, and more than 99 percent of those children are returned alive.[1]

Now, to be clear, that's not to say that those cases don't send shivers down the spines of parents. But they fall into a different category than the stranger-as-bogeyman abductions. Those types of abductions—the Etan Patz–like cases, in which a child is kidnapped by a stranger and held for ransom, or with the intent to harm or keep the child—occur approximately

115 times a year, with a nearly 60 percent survival rate and about a 4 percent rate of going unsolved. That means that roughly 45 kids get abducted and killed every year by strangers-as-real-life-monsters.

This number hasn't increased since the 1980s, and, in fact, there is some evidence that it may have actually decreased along with national crime rates as a whole. Indeed, crime specialists seem to agree that this is probably the safest time in history to be an American child.

But a sociological shift was also occurring around the time of Etan Patz's disappearance—one that gave people a sense that they might be able to "control" the uncontrollable. Erika Christakis, an educator at the Yale Child Study Center, wrote in an article, "Did Etan Patz Mark the End of Carefree Parenting?," which appeared in the April 24, 2012, issue of *Time* magazine: "Once, people viewed car crashes, electrocution, fires, head injuries and the like as tragic and inevitable, perhaps even 'acts of God.' But when epidemiologists began observing that most accidents had clear, predictable causes, they were more accurately relabeled as preventable injuries. This led to bicycle helmets, car seats, food safety and 'baby proofing.' Soon, it seemed, everything 'accidental' could be prevented. Sudden infant death syndrome. Asthma. Drowning. Burns. Broken bones. Allergic reactions. Concussions."

As Christakis notes, this way of thinking was soon applied to parents' sense of responsibility: "It was a huge shift in perception, and with it came a heightened responsibility—and anxiety—about keeping children safe. If bad outcomes were now in a parent's control, then a parent who didn't take these preventive steps was a slacker at best, and criminally negligent at worst."

The perceived social pressure on parents was on—and helicopter parenting and the overprotected child were born.

The term "helicopter parenting" was first used in 1969, in the book *Between Parent and Teenager*. The author, psychologist Haim G. Ginott, quoted his intensely (s)mothered teen patient: "Mother hovers over me like a helicopter and I'm fed up with her noise and hot air. . . . I'm entitled to sneeze without explanation." The term became part of the language after former school principal Jim Fay and psychiatrist Foster W. Cline used it in their 1990 book, *Parenting with Love and Logic*. Now it's part of our culture.

In her 2014 *Atlantic* article "The Overprotected Kid," Hanna Rosin also describes this shift of parenting styles: "It's hard to absorb how much childhood norms have shifted in just one generation. Actions that would have been considered paranoid in the '70s—walking third-graders to school, forbidding your kid to play ball in the street, going down the slide with your child in your lap—are now routine. In fact, they are the markers of good, responsible parenting. One very thorough study of 'children's independent mobility,' conducted in urban, suburban, and rural neighborhoods in the U.K., shows that in 1971, 80 percent of third-graders walked to school alone. By 1990, that measure had dropped to 9 percent, and now it's even lower."[2]

Rosin's parents used to let her roam around unsupervised without ever scheduling things like play dates and swimming lessons. Rosin realized that she is a very different kind of mom: "I, on the other hand, might easily spend every waking Saturday hour with one if not all three of my children, taking one to a soccer game, the second to a theater program, the third to a friend's house, or just hanging out with them at home. When my daughter was about 10, my husband suddenly realized that in her whole life, she had probably not spent more than 10 minutes unsupervised by an adult. Not 10 minutes in 10 years."

Why are so many parents today so much more obsessed with their kids' lives? I have seen it hundreds of times in my clinical practice and feel that tendency in my own life as a parent (and need to consciously resist that tendency). Parents today seem much more enmeshed with their children—that is, parents' and children's identities seem fused in ways that they weren't in earlier generations. Being close to your child is one thing, but when children seem to become extensions of the parents—and of their parents' hopes, dreams and expectations—the result can be unhealthy micromanaging, aka helicoptering.

It seems that many people of my parents' generation were too busy working and trying to make ends meet to be hyperfocused on play dates, violin lessons and soccer camps. My generation played sports and did things; I just don't remember our parents hovering every step of the way. And that helped foster a sense of resilience and agency within me and my friends. "We can do this" was our mantra. Now many kids can't even carry their own backpacks to school; I see many moms walking to my kids' elementary school weighted down like pack mules as they carry their kids' bags. Why?

It's that fine line between helping and enabling. My pediatrician friend Dr. Michael Schessel told me that his seven-year-old demanded that his father untie the knot in his shoelaces. As Dr. Schessel bent down to ac-commodate the child's request, he realized, "Wait a minute. You can do this. Learn to untie your own knot!" It's as Erika Christakis writes: there is now social pressure to be hypervilgilant and endlessly supportive lest we be shamed as bad parents.

I think much of this dynamic has its roots in the case of poor little Etan Patz's disappearance. The title of a May 6, 2015, piece by Michael Wilson about Etan Patz in the *New York Times* sums it up: "The Legacy of Etan Patz: Wary Children Who Became Watchful Parents."[3] Those of us who were kids at the time of Etan's disappearance were profoundly shaped by it. We are the ones who then pulled the leash tighter on our kids and became the dreaded HPs—helicopter parents.

Wilson talked to several people who were kids at the time and who give various versions of how things changed after Etan's disappearance. Eddie Spaedh, who grew up in Brooklyn and was a boy at the time, talked about how "the whole neighborhood changed. We went from having to go in when the lights went on, to parents looking out the window and out on the streets, always watching us."

As the Etan Patz generation grew up and became the overprotective helicopter generation, something else also happened: kids were encouraged to stay indoors, where it was thought to be safer. After all, there are no bogey-men kidnappers—usually, at least—inside the house. And so a shift began: kids who had once been encouraged to go outside and play from sunup until sundown—and maybe even a little after that—were now encouraged to stay indoors.

And what's a healthy boy or girl to do inside? Computer time! Enter the Glow Kids.

Yes, the Etan Patz tragedy, which led to an entire generation of scared and hypervigilant helicopter parents, was a major factor in the emergence of the Glow Kids generation. Add to that the competitive social pressure that many parents exert on each other, and you have a misguided "my child will out-tech your child," scenario, a screen-based version of keeping up with the Joneses: You got your child an Xbox? I got mine an Oculus Rift virtual reality headset! What, your child has an iPad and iPhone in second grade? Mine has his in kindergarten—no—in pre-K! God bless them, they mean well—but this screen competition amongst parents is a huge part of the Glow Kids problem.

At the other end of the spectrum, we have a new countervailing force— the "free range kids" movement, started by Lenore Skenazy. A mother and journalist from Queens, New York, Skenazy believes in giving kids freedom and autonomy. Meanwhile, the media demonized her, dubbing Skenazy "America's Worst Mom" in 2008 for letting her then-nine-year old son take the New York City subway home alone from Bloomingdale's.

The following year she published the book *Free Range Kids: How to Raise Safe, Self-Reliant Children,* in which she advocates for a "commonsense approach to parenting" in these "overprotective times."[4] She, too, points to the legacy of Etan Patz as creating a culture of hypervigilant, fearful parents but believes that this mind-set can be changed if mothers and fathers consciously reject this worst-case-scenario or "worst first" thinking.

"Sometimes it feels as if this constant dread is natural. As if it's just the way parents are 'programmed to worry.' But it is cultural, it is specific. We can almost pinpoint when it began," Skenazy writes in her blog. In 2015 Skenazy's Free-Range Kids Project declared May 9 as "Take Our Children to the Park . . . and Let Them Walk Home By Themselves Day." This was a direct response to the case of a Maryland couple who were accused of neglect for letting their two children, ages ten and six, walk home alone from the park.

Regardless of where on the parenting continuum a parent may fall— from helicopter to free-range—the healthy recommendation is to allow children time outdoors away from screen devices.

But there's a problem.

Even if a parent chooses to raise a screen-free kid, he or she faces one very, very major hurdle. The informed parent may begin to understand that hyperarousing screens are a digital drug, but the places where our children spend the bulk of their day—schools—haven't gotten the memo yet that screens can be a significant problem and must be used judiciously and only when age-appropriate.

Welcome to the screen-obsessed Educational Industrial Complex.

TWELVE

FOLLOW THE MONEY

SCREENS AND THE EDUCATIONAL INDUSTRIAL COMPLEX

THERE IS A NEW WILD, WILD WEST IN EDUCATION: EDUCATION technology, predicted to become a $60 billion industry by 2018.[1] Yes, that includes things such as smart boards and data systems . . . but the real gold rush, which has attracted the deep pockets of entrepreneurs and tech companies alike, is the tablet—more specifically, the idea of a tablet for *every* student in America—and the expensive educational software and annual licensing fees that go with it.

To be sure, there is a place for technology in education—and for screens in the classroom. But most education experts agree that tech alone is not the cure to what ails education. And we must be very careful with how and, most importantly, at what *age* and *grade level* the screens are rolled out.

Unfortunately, for some just looking to cash out, that hasn't mattered. As with any gold rush, some of the speculators are more unsavory than others.

The story of technology in the classroom is a fascinating one.

As a *story*, it has all of the elements of a real page-turner: greed, corruption, betrayal. However, it's more than just a story—it's the real-life betrayal of our children by a combination of greed, incompetence, hubris and ego.

In that sense, the story of tech in the classroom reads more like a Greek tragedy.

Let me set the stage before we meet our dramatis personae.

There are educational reformers—also known as edupreneurs—who are selling the false narrative that the current educational system is so broken that only their technology snake oil can fix it. Some of these edupreneurs are driven strictly by a desire for profit; others are driven by ego—the misguided, messianic fervor that they can be "the ones" who can transform education, research and reality be damned.

This mix of ego and greed is driving the education technology juggernaut at the top of its food chain. In the midlevels are school principals and superintendents. Alas, this is an "emperor's new clothes" phenomenon, in which many who actually know better—who realize that education can't be fixed by gadgets—stay silent to save their careers. No one likes a dissenting voice.

What, the emperor has no clothes? You mean the millions that we've spent on worthless and ineffective devices that are being hacked by students or are sitting in storage rooms have been a total waste? Be silent or be reassigned!

Others are driven by an effort to keep up with neighboring districts in a misguided tech arms race. Westhampton has tablets K-12? Quickly—tablets for everyone in this district! Or, worse yet, some clueless administrators have bought the tech companies' pitch hook, line and sinker and are blinded by the glow of the shiny new devices. Do they work? Do they help kids become better students? Who cares? Just look at how shiny they are!

When speaking to school administrators in the course of giving presentations at tech-effects workshops, I've encountered various versions of all of the above. A select few seem to genuinely get it and are even prepared to halt—or at least slow down—the march of screens into the younger and younger grades. Others, not so much.

My sense is that parents must speak up in a unified voice and ask more questions like: does all of this tech in the classroom actually help my child learn? And, more importantly, can some of these tablets even be hurting my child developmentally and psychologically? Until parents begin to speak up to protect their children, school administrators will be led by tech company Pied Pipers.

And now, I present Act I of Greed in Education.

AN UNHOLY ALLIANCE:
RUPERT MURDOCH AND JOEL KLEIN

Joel Klein, former New York City schools chancellor, has become the leading voice in "transforming" our broken educational system via technology. He sees the solution as being a tablet for every student in America, K-12—the digital equivalent of a chicken in every pot—a plan that, conveniently, his education tech company Amplify is ready, willing and able to carry out for every school district in the nation.

Yet for years Klein has been dogged by conflict-of-interest allegations and has been accused of using misleading and erroneous information to claim that the current educational system is more broken than it actually is.[2]

But just who is Joel Klein? We should know, because this man could very well shape the educational landscape for generations to come—as he becomes a very, very rich man.

Klein had never taught in a classroom or studied education. Before being appointed as chancellor by Mayor Michael Bloomberg in 2002, Klein had been a Harvard-educated lawyer.

He was in private practice before founding his own law firm; then, in the 1990s, before being appointed as Assistant Attorney General in charge of the Anti-Trust division, he served in the White House Counsel's office in the administration of Bill Clinton before being appointed as a U.S. assistant attorney general in the Department of Justice. After leaving the Justice Department, he became legal counsel to Bertelsmann, an international media group.

There was not a whiff of any educational bona fides in Klein's career before he was handpicked to oversee the education of New York City's 1.1 million students. During his tenure, he spearheaded a series of initiatives, including breaking up larger schools and working with the Gates Foundation to open a series of 43 small high schools. After some initial accolades regarding improved graduation rates, he was accused by New York University professor and education policy analyst Diane Ravitch, among others, of cooking the books in order to obtain those positive outcomes.[3] According to the journalist Bob Herbert, Bill Gates later admitted that breaking up those schools was a mistake: "Simply breaking up existing schools into smaller units often did not generate the gains we were hoping for."[4]

Klein's other major accomplishment as chancellor was spending $95 million of New York City taxpayers' money on a tech albatross: in 2007 Klein oversaw the implementation of ARIS (Achievement Reporting and Innovation System), a data collection and student tracking computer system. ARIS immediately got blasted by critics, teachers and parents as being slow, clunky and largely unutilized. Klein then awarded Internet start-up Wireless Generation a $12 million annual contract to fix and maintain his broken and expensive clunker.

Now this is where it gets good, but you have to follow along closely, as the muddy ethics make the waters a little murky. In 2011 Klein stepped down from his $225,000-a-year position. And why not? He had a better offer; he took a $2 million-a-year job offer from Rupert Murdoch—complete with a $1 million signing bonus—in order to head up Amplify.[5] And what is Amplify, you might ask? Amplify is the ed tech company that used to be Wireless Generation—yes, the same company that had gotten the $12 million contract from Klein while he was schools chancellor to fix his broken ARIS data albatross.

That's right, Klein gave a private company a lucrative public contract to fix a disaster that he created, and then he went to work for—correction: he went to *run*—that private company, making almost ten times what he had made toiling for the board of ed. But Klein wasn't paid all that money by Murdoch just to muck around with ARIS and data collection; Murdoch had invested almost a billion dollars in Amplify in pursuit of the educational holy grail—an Amplify tablet (for only $199!) in the hands of every student in America.

A public sector employee cashing out in the private sector? Happens all the time in politics: poor public-servant-as-congressman cashes out as a lobbyist; move along, nothing to see here. Some might even say, God bless him—this is America. Who are we to begrudge a man a chance to reach for the gold? But in education, selling out to the private sector can be problematic. The question that needs to be asked is: is he cashing out at the expense of our kids' learning and, even more problematically, their well-being?

We know Rupert Murdoch's motives. Never one to be confused with a saint or a person with unshakable ethics, Murdoch has been known to bend and even break the law in pursuit of profit. Executives at his now-defunct tabloid newspaper *News of the World* were accused of phone hacking and police bribery. In the ensuing criminal investigation, it was revealed that not only were the phones of celebrities, politicians and members of the British Royal Family hacked, but so were those of murdered schoolgirl Milly Dowler, relatives of deceased British soldiers, and victims of the July 7, 2005, London bombings—all to sell more newspapers.

This paragon of virtue and ethics was now Klein's new boss in an effort to transform American education. Entrepreneurial rascal that he is, Murdoch had always been keen to exploit new media opportunities, and he had been attempting to cash in on ed tech for some time. Wireless Generation presented the perfect opportunity. Larry Berger had started Wireless Generation in 2000, and by the time Murdoch purchased it in 2010, for $360 million, it had turned into a thriving, 400-employee company that focused on analytics, data and assessment.

But Murdoch wasn't interested in analytics and data assessment. He saw Amplify as a firm through which he could replace the lucrative textbook market with shiny new tablets—fully loaded with expensive educational software.

This was now possible because a couple of key changes in the education world were making it very attractive for entrepreneurial gunslingers. In the old days, McGraw-Hill, Houghton Mifflin Harcourt, and Pearson ruled the $7.8 billion textbook and curriculum development market. But textbooks and curricula had to be customized to meet individual state standards—a very expensive and time-consuming endeavor.

Then, in 2010, came the development that would change everything—and make the whole education field finger-licking good for profit-motivated, ethically challenged entrepreneurs like Murdoch: the Common Core of Standards, aka the Common Core.

The Common Core created a set of curriculum and textbook standards that were adopted by 45 states. There was no need to muck around with different standards for smaller markets like, say, Alabama. Now, a company that could create K-12 curricula that adhered to the Common Core requirements could sell its materials across the country. Better yet, a company that could create a tablet that could be programmed with all of this new Common Core goodness would make textbooks obsolete—and all with annual licensing fees. Ka-ching!

But Murdoch needed a good front man; the King of Fleet Street couldn't very well be seen as the man who could transform American education. Along came Klein—a bargain at only $2 million a year. By rebranding Wireless Generation as Amplify and hiring Klein, Murdoch had found the high-profile "education expert" he needed to shill his new tablet-based education company.

The company was divided into three divisions: Amplify Learning, which was to develop and provide Common Core–based curricula for K-12; Amplify Insight, which was to provide analytics and data assessment; and Amplify Access, which was to sell a customized Android tablet with a 10-inch Gorilla Glass screen.

But with Klein at the helm, things got off to a rough start.

The poor, taken-advantage-of New York City Department of Education (DoE) had finally had enough and decided to cut their losses and scrap the whole $95 million ARIS disaster. According to a DOE spokesperson: "The Education Department has decided to end our contract with Amplify as a result of the extremely high cost of the ARIS system, its limited functionality, and the lack of demand from parents and staff."

A letter from the office of Thomas P. DiNapoli, the New York State comptroller, also pointed toward Murdoch and the phone-hacking scandal as part of the reason to shed Amplify: "In light of the significant ongoing investigations and continuing revelations with respect to News Corporation, we are retuning the contract with Wireless Generation unapproved."

"Good news they're junking it," said Arthur Goldstein, an English teacher at Francis Lewis High School in Queens, in an interview with the *New York Daily News*. "They spent $95 million on that thing and my kids are in trailers. What they did with that money is criminal." Sure, the kids, parents, teachers and taxpayers had to take a hit, but Klein got to keep his $2 million salary and set his eyes on the bigger prize: tablets for all.

Amplify went to work hiring hundreds of the best twenty-somethings to develop their tablets and software. Let's not forget that kids simply cannot pay attention to something unless it's a video game, so hundreds of video game designers were hired to "game" the educational software—game points for everybody! Meanwhile, dozens of "product tester" kids were hired (and paid weekly in $100 Amazon.com Gift Cards) to test drive the new edu-games.

The Amplify mission statement was, "Amplify is reimagining the way teachers teach and students learn." They sure were. But not everyone was crazy about a videogame classroom.

Douglas Clark, an associate professor at Vanderbilt University's Peabody College, one of the top schools of education in the country, was bothered by this gaming approach; as he told Travis Andrews for the Web site *Mashable:* "Points are extrinsic motivations, and 'when [kids] get bored with extrinsic, they stop.'"

Even more problematically, as we explored earlier in this book, video games can be dopaminergic and addicting, and as with educational tools like *The Oregon Trail,* the child tends to focus on the points-accumulation aspect rather than the educational content.

But beyond video games, the bigger question was: does any of this even work? Is there any research that any of these expensive new screen gadgets are educationally beneficial? Some supporters will point to studies that indicate increased pattern recognition and spatial awareness as well as some increased word retention with the use of iPads and tablets, but many other education researchers believe that those positive outcomes are greatly overstated. But even if we cede that there may be a beneficial pattern-recognition increase or word-retention effect, do those effects lead to better educational outcomes—do they lead to students' becoming better learners?

The more comprehensive research doesn't bear that out.

In fact, the research on technology is clear: an exhaustive 2012 meta-analysis, which systematically reviewed 48 studies that examined technology's impact on learning, found that "technology-based interventions tend to produce just slightly *lower* levels of improvement when compared with other researched interventions and approaches [emphasis mine]."[6]

Whatever minimal gains were shown couldn't be causally linked to tech. Instead, the study concluded that technology can be a useful tool in already effective schools with effective teachers—but, in and of itself, tech was not the educational panacea.

"[I]t is not whether technology is used (or not) which makes the difference, but how well the technology is used to support teaching and learning." the researchers wrote, concluding: "Taken together, the correlational and experimental evidence does not offer a convincing case for the general impact of digital technology on learning outcomes."

That idea is echoed by Greg Anrig, author of *Beyond the Education Wars* (2013): "None of these studies identify technology as decisive." Anrig also points to the importance of good teachers collaborating with students and administrators as key to successful student outcomes.

Dr. Kentaro Toyama, an associate professor at the University of Michigan's School of Information and a fellow of the Dalai Lama Center of Ethics and Transformation Values at MIT, came to a similar conclusion. No Luddite, he had received his Ph.D. in computer science from Yale and had moved to India in 2004 to help found a new research lab for Microsoft. While there, he became interested in how computers, mobile phones, and other tech could help educate India's billion-plus population and aid in learning.

While he had been hopeful to find that tech could solve many of education's problems, he came to understand what he began to think of as technology's "Law of Amplification"; unlike Klein's Amplify, Dr. Toyamo saw that technology "amplified," all right—but not always in a good way. He found that technology *can* help education where it's already doing well, but it does little for mediocre educational systems, and, worse, in dysfunctional schools it "can cause outright harm."

The main problem, according to Dr. Toyamo, is that technology does not address fundamental issues of student motivation. Without that key human ingredient, all the shiny tech is meaningless.

As Dr. Toyama writes in his commentary, "Why Technology Will Never Fix Education," which appeared in the May 19, 2015, issue of the *Chronicle of Higher Education:* "One problem is a widespread impression that Silicon Valley innovations are good for society. We confuse business success with social value, though the two often differ." He adds: "Any idea that more technology in and of itself cures social ills is obviously flawed. . . . Unfortunately, there is no technological fix, and that is perhaps the hardest lesson of amplification. More technology only magnifies socioeconomic disparities, and the only way to avoid that is non-technological."

Even as far back as 1983, educators understood that teaching was more important than the medium. In a sort of inverse corollary to Marshall McLuhan's "the medium is the message," research by Richard Clark showed that pedagogy—and not the method of delivery—was all-important. He said that instructional media that delivered the educational content were "mere vehicles that deliver instruction but do not influence student achievement any more than the truck that delivers our groceries causes changes in our nutrition."[7]

The well-respected Alliance for Childhood, a consortium of some of the nation's top educators and professors, put out a report back in 2000, "Fool's Gold: A Critical Look at Computers in Childhood," that also shared a skeptical view of technology in the classroom. They concluded: "School reform is a social challenge, not a technological problem . . . a high-tech agenda for children seems likely to erode our most precious long-term intellectual reserves—our children's minds."

Dr. Patricia Greenfield, distinguished professor of psychology at UCLA, agrees. A January 2009 article for *UCLA Newsroom*, "Is Technology Producing a Decline in Critical Thinking and Analysis?," states that Greenfield analyzed more than 50 studies on learning and concluded that "technology is not a panacea in education, because of the skills that are being lost." She points out that reading for pleasure among young people has decreased in recent decades, which is problematic because "studies show that reading develops imagination, induction, reflection and critical thinking, as well as vocabulary . . . in a way that visual media such as video games and television do not."

She is also opposed to Internet-wired classrooms, citing one study in which students who were given access to the Internet during class and were encouraged to use it during lectures subsequently did not process what the speaker said as well as those students who did not have Internet access. Indeed, the Internet-connected students did more poorly on tests after the class lecture. Dr. Greenfield concludes by unequivocally stating, "Wiring classrooms for Internet access does not enhance learning."

There has also been some surprising research out of Canada counter-ing the narrative that kids prefer e-learning over traditional education.[8] A study conducted by the Canadian Higher Education Strategy Associates on 1,289 college undergraduates found that students actually had a preference for "ordinary, real-life lessons" rather than e-learning or the use of technol-ogy. Those results surprised the researchers: "It is not the portrait that we ex-pected, whereby students would embrace anything that happens on a more highly technological level. On the contrary—they really seem to like access to human interaction, a smart person at the front of the classroom."

Imagine that. Is it possible that we are actually projecting our own infat-uation with shiny tech and gadgetry and just assuming that our little digital natives—little Johnny and Suzy—would prefer to learn that way when they actually crave human contact and teaching? The Canadian study would seem to bear that out.

Teaching preferences aside, we are also left with the educational con-sensus that the high-tech classroom simply isn't producing better student outcomes. Leonie Haimson, executive director of Class Size Matters, a non-profit advocating smaller class sizes, puts it more bluntly: "There's absolutely no evidence showing online learning works, especially K through 12."

In fact, she thinks it's actually detrimental. "This trend is likely to under-mine education," she says. "Somehow, [people believe] the idea that putting kids on tablets or computers and giving them software programs to work on is personalizing learning rather than depersonalizing it." She also points to the profit motive: "Murdoch wants to make money off of public education, so it's no surprise that Amplify is pushing forward with no evidence that this works. My concern is this is taking money away from proven reforms."

There was also one other very important concern raised about Rupert Murdoch's ownership of a company that sought to create all of the educa-tional content that an entire generation of students would use: would his po-litical ideology shape or influence academic curricula?

As the owner of conservative media outlets such as FOX News, Murdoch is famous in part for his political leanings. In an article in *Forbes* magazine titled "Conflict of Interest Behind News Corp Tablet" (2013), technology commentator Roger Kay speculated that Murdoch could potentially use ed tech as another media market to spread his political gospel to kids:

"From my point of view, the problem with [Murdoch's] News Corp. being in this business is that it creates a channel to our youngest, most vulnerable minds for a guy with extreme politics and highly questionable ethics."

Yes, curricula would have to adhere to Common Core guidelines, but as most news readers know, "objective" news isn't always "fair and balanced." News—and academic content—can be shaped by editorial bias.

Kay concludes by saying: "I don't know about you, but I don't want those guys anywhere near the controls of a conduit that funnels 'learning materials' to my kids. . . . School systems should be very wary of buying anything from this source."

All of the concerns that I've just cited are the views of education researchers, educators, education experts and even technology experts.

But none of that deterred Murdoch's lawyer-for-hire, Joel Klein. Like a modern-day P. T. Barnum, he went on a media barnstorming campaign, carnival barking in his shrillest voice about how his magic tablets would "transform" the broken educational system.

In a 2013 *New York Times* interview ("No Child Left Untableted"), Klein repeats this mantra, glowingly talking about the marvels of Amplify's tablets and saying that education is "ripe for disruption." Meanwhile, the article's author, Carlo Rotella, director of American Studies at Boston College, wryly notes: "Entrepreneurs sound boldly unconventional when they talk about disrupting an industry, but they also sound as if they're willing to break something in order to fix it—or just profit from it."

Klein then goes on to make several sweeping statements about the dire state of American education. He needs to make this point convincingly before he can persuade the public to buy his cure. As Richard Rothstein, former national education columnist for the *New York Times*, says in an article he wrote to rebut Klein: "The assertion by school reformers—that their treatments are necessary because the patient is dying" is central to "a belief that public education needs to be transformed by the technology he is selling."

So the first part is to convince everyone that education is on life support, and the second part *should* be: my cure *works*. Klein misses on both counts; that's not to say that public education can't be improved, but it's not as broken as Klein claims. And like many experimental "cures," this one just might kill the patient. At the very least, it will only widen the achievement gap, because, as we have seen in the London School of Economics cell phone study and Dr. Toyama's Law of Amplification, marginalized students and poor schools suffer the most when distracting technology is allowed in the classroom.

So is the patient dying?

They are, according to Klein. In a September 2013 *New York Times Magazine* interview, Klein says: "K-12 isn't working . . . and we have to change the way we do it . . . Between 1970 and 2010 we doubled the amount of money we spent on education and the number of adults in the schools, but the results are just not there. Any system that poured in as much money as we did and made as little progress has a real problem. We keep trying to fix it by doing the same thing, only a little different and better. This [tablet-based instruction] is about a *lot* different and better. . . . We've spent so much on things that haven't worked." He then made a list of failed solutions, including underused computers, obsolete textbooks, useless layers of bureaucracy and smaller class sizes.

Richard Rothstein counters these exaggerated or misleading claims in the *Washington Post*. Yes, money spent on education has doubled since 1970, but half that amount has gone to providing education services to disabled and special needs children—kids who in 1970 were not acknowledged as being entitled to free public education. Rothstein claims: "It is foolish, as Mr. Klein in effect does, to claim that because we are now spending so much money on children with disabilities, schools must be failing because the spending has not caused the achievement of regular students to improve."

Even more importantly, Rothstein claims that Klein is wrong that achievement hasn't improved since 1970: "Our only sources of information about trends in academic achievement are two sampled tests sponsored by the federal government, the National Assessment of Educational Progress. One . . . shows that academic achievement for black children has improved so much that black fourth graders nationwide now have average basic skills proficiency in math that is greater than that of white fourth graders in 1970.

"The other, a test requiring original computations and written answers, shows the average academic achievement of black fourth graders to be greater than that of white fourth graders in 1990. Improvements have also been substantial in reading, and for eighth graders. White students have improved as well, so the black-white test score gap has not changed very much, narrowing only to the extent that black achievement has been rising faster than white achievement."

Rothstein also points out that there has been improvement at the high school level as well, noting that in the last four decades, the share of young adults who graduate from both high school and college has doubled.

With regard to "failed" interventions such as smaller class sizes, Rothstein says: "This, too, is only the incantation of conventional wisdom, but is not what the research shows. The only scientifically credible study of class size reduction, an experiment conducted in Tennessee 20 years ago, found that smaller classes were of particular benefit to disadvantaged children in the early grades . . ."

He concludes by saying: "Of course, like any institution, public education should be improved. We should be able to do much better. But some, perhaps many of the things American schools have been doing have turned out to be quite successful. By making a blanket charge of failure and proposing to overturn the entire enterprise, whether in favor of tablet-based instruction, charter schools . . . or private school vouchers, the reformers may well be destroying much of what has worked in favor of untested fads."

Interestingly, Klein often brings up his own overstated biography of a poor-kid-from-Queens-housing-projects-makes-good-thanks-to-great-teachers as further "evidence" that things are broken in New York City public schools. According to Klein, great public school teachers were responsible for his path to success. Yet he implies that today's disadvantaged kids fail because those opportunities no longer exist, as that once-glorious public school system full of wonderful teachers has crumbled and now exists only in memory.

The solution? A tablet in every pot.

Aside from the claims of several people that Klein has exaggerated the conditions of an essentially middle-class upbringing (assertions I agree with, having grown up less than ten blocks from where he was raised), the New York City public education system that was good enough to get him into Columbia and then Harvard has not changed that radically.

Eighteen years after he did, I also made it from New York City public school to Ivy League campus. Today, 30 years later, thousands of kids pull off that same trick every year. Yes, of course it's an imperfect system that needs plenty of work. But Klein needs us to believe that the entire system is broken beyond repair—that it's "ripe for disruption"—in order to sell us his digital cure.

But the Amplify story does not end there—there is an interesting epilogue.

Amplify failed. The company, never able to sell as many tablets as it envisioned, subsequently bled money. After losing over $371 million in 2015 alone—not to mention the $1 billion that he had invested since 2010—Murdoch decided to cut his losses and put the whole thing up for sale.

Finally, after laying off two-thirds of its staff—approximately 800 employees—the sputtering entity was sold in October 2015 to 11 Amplify executives, including Joel Klein. The terms of the sale were not disclosed.[9]

But in an interesting restructuring, original Wireless Generation founder Larry Berger took over as CEO, and Joel Klein was kicked upstairs to the board of directors. They're getting back to basics: they are retaining the curriculum (Amplify Learning) and the analytics and data assessment (Amplify Insight) arms of the business. And the tablet? In the garbage. The failed Amplify Access has been discontinued.

As educational tech consultant Doug Levin said in *Education Week*, Murdoch and Klein's foray into the K-12 marketplace "was another example in a long history of education entrepreneurs who have crashed on the rocks because the market was not what they thought it would be."

And now, I present Act II of Greed in Education—the West Coast Version.

THE LOS ANGELES SCHOOL DISTRICT AND
THE $1.3 BILLION IPAD FIASCO

While the largest school district in the United States did its best to fend off Joel Klein, Rupert Murdoch and the invasion of the glowing screens, the second-largest district didn't fare so well. It succumbed to the glow—to the tune of 1.3 billion wasted dollars.

This West Coast Version of Greed in Education has served as a cautionary tale throughout the land. It even led to this colorful headline on *Mashable:* "L.A.'s 'iPad for Every Student Program' is a Complete Sh*t Show" (April 17, 2015).

Where to begin?

Superintendent John Deasy thought that it would be a great idea to have every single student in Los Angeles Unified School District—all 650,000—get an iPad loaded with educational software goodies from Pearson, one of the country's biggest educational publishers. All for the low, low cost of $1.3 billion.

School officials and tech advocates who pushed for this framed the debate, obscenely, as a civil rights issue—using those actual words: "This is a civil rights issue. My goal is to provide youth in poverty with tools that heretofore only rich kids have had. And I'd like to do that as quickly as possible." Superintendent Deasy said in a promotional video that he made, interestingly, for Apple in 2011.

Move over, Rosa Parks—an iPad needs to sit next to you.

With messianic fervor, Deasy said that the tablets would lead to "huge leaps in what's possible for students" and would "phenomenally . . . change the landscape of education."

Deasy wasn't alone in embracing this misguided idea that student access to the Internet had somehow become a right as inalienable as the right to life, liberty and the pursuit of happiness. In a June 2010 *Boston Globe* article, the writer Rebecca Tuhus-Dubrow not only discussed Internet access as a basic human right, but even suggested what the government's role should be in securing that "right":

"Increasingly, activists, analysts, and government officials are arguing that Internet access has become so essential to participation in society—to finding jobs and housing, to civic engagement, even to health—that it should be seen as a right, a basic prerogative of all citizens. And in cases where people don't have access, whether because they can't afford it or the infrastructure is not in place, the government should have the power—and perhaps the duty—to fix that."

Predictably, media executives who may have had a financial interest in proclaiming Internet access a human right were quick to agree: "Access to the internet is akin to a civil rights issue for the twenty-first century. It's that access that enables people in poorer areas to equalize access to a quality education, quality health care and vocational opportunities," was the noble social-justice perspective of Comcast senior vice president David Cohen.

One man who does *not* think that access to the Internet is a civil right is the man who invented it. No, I'm not talking about Al Gore. I'm talking about Dr. Vinton G. Cerf, a legendary engineering pioneer widely known as one of the "fathers of the Internet." Cerf was the co-designer of the TCP/IP protocols and architecture of the Internet; in December 1997 President Bill Clinton presented him with the U.S. National Medal of Technology, and in 2005 he was given the Presidential Medal of Freedom by President George W. Bush for his work in helping to create the Internet.

In a January 4, 2012, *New York Times* op-ed article titled "Internet Access Is Not a Human Right," Cerf had this to say on whether or not access to his progeny—his invention—was indeed a right:

"That argument, however well meaning, misses a larger point: technology is an enabler of rights, not a right itself. There is a high bar for something to be considered a human right. Loosely put, it must be among the things we humans need in order to lead healthy, meaningful lives like freedom from torture or freedom of conscience. It is a mistake to place any particular technology in this exalted category, since over time we will wind up valuing the wrong things. For example, at one time if you didn't have a horse, it was hard to make a living. But the important right in that case was the right to make a living, not the right to a horse."

His point is well taken. "Things," like tablets, cars or, as he wryly notes, horses, are not human or civil rights. No technology is.

But Superintendent Deasy was very passionate about the "right" to have an iPad and spread his zeal to an agreeable school board, which voted for the plan to give every student an iPad. The district had estimated that it would cost about $500 million to obtain more than 600,000 tablets and the accompanying software and an additional $800 million to install wireless Internet and other infrastructure at more than 1,000 schools and offices. Unfortunately, the cash-strapped district didn't have that kind of money lying around—so it had to sell public bonds in order to raise the money.

In hindsight, the board members think that they may have voted too hastily. A September 4, 2014, *Los Angeles Times* article quoted several board members as saying that they should have asked tougher questions early on and were too quick to defer to their "crusading superintendent" and an ongoing mission they also strongly believe in—closing the technological gap between Los Angeles' poor students and their wealthier peers.

"The notion of the constantly ticking inequity clock" fueled the fervor of iPads for all, school board member Steve Zimmer said. "It's my job to balance that urgency with scrutiny. And never have I failed more at that balance."

So how does this story end?

With an FBI investigation and $1.3 billion spent on a dysfunctional disaster. The Pearson platform had an incomplete curriculum that was essentially worthless, and the tablets themselves were easily hacked within weeks by students who bypassed the feeble security restrictions and were able to freely surf the Internet—video games and porn for everyone!

The whole deal was killed in December 2014—the day *after* the FBI seized 20 boxes of documents from the district's business office as part of its investigation into the contract with Apple.

Under scrutiny were the bidding process and the relationship between Superintendent John Deasy—who resigned abruptly under pressure in October 2014—and his close relationship with Apple and Pearson executives, the beneficiaries of the mammoth contract. The deal is also being currently investigated by a federal grand jury.[10]

Where did this all go wrong?

To answer that, we need to go to back to the beginning.

John Deasy was hired as superintendent in 2011 and was determined to make a difference. By most accounts, he was passionate and sincere about his desire to make the Los Angeles school district better and to help level the student playing field, given what he had perceived as an achievement gap.

To be sure, the district he inherited was in crisis: thousands of teachers, counselors and librarians had lost their jobs during the recession; fewer than half of the students were reading at grade level, and more than 10,000 students were dropping out of high school annually.

Deasy made no apologies—and ruffled some feathers—as a reformer who was going to fix a very complicated mess in order to make things better for students: "I'm not going to be interested in looking at third graders and saying, 'Sorry, this is the year you don't learn to read,' or to juniors and saying, 'You don't get to graduate," he told Los Angeles Public Radio station KPCC in 2012. "So the pace needs to be quick, and we make no apologies for that."[11]

He was clearly a man on a mission. Unfortunately, he picked the *wrong* mission.

I asked my friend Dr. Pedro Noguera, who knew Deasy professionally, what he thought of him. Pedro is one of the most respected voices in American education; he's been tenured at Berkeley, Harvard and NYU and is currently Distinguished Professor of Education at UCLA. He is one of the most thoughtful, caring people and educators you will ever meet. Pedro told me: "John Deasy is a good man—he tried to make a positive difference; the teachers union wasn't thrilled with him because he had no patience for the union. But he tried to do what he thought was best for the kids."

Unlike Joel Klein and Amplify in New York, Deasy hadn't sold out to corporate overlords. Nonetheless, as is clear when the emails exchanged by Deasy, Pearson and Apple are examined, Deasy was enthralled by the prospect of working with the tech giants; they, in turn, seemed only too eager to financially exploit his enthusiasm. But there has been no accusation or insinuation that Deasy personally profited from the deal. What is apparent is that Deasy was a zealot who believed in tech as the cure and in himself as "the one" who would transform the broken Los Angeles public school system—and that he would go to any lengths to realize his vision.

The essence of the FBI investigation is that dozens of meetings, conversations and email exchanges with Pearson and Apple had occurred beginning nearly a year before Los Angeles Unified officially put the project out to bid. Eventually, 19 other bids were also submitted. Apple and Pearson, although not initially the lowest bidders (as finalists, they were allowed to rejigger and lower their bid), won the lucrative contract on June 24, 2013.

And the epilogue?

Nearly two years later, the program is dead. Deasy has resigned amid scandal. The FBI investigation is ongoing. And the Securities and Exchange Commission (SEC) has gotten involved, having recently questioned school district officials as part of an informal inquiry into whether they properly used bond funds for the disastrous $1.3 billion project.

The sad reality is that companies like Apple and Pearson are profit-driven entities whose mission statement is to increase the bottom line. I think we all understand that this is America, and that companies should be allowed to make profits, but they shouldn't do so at the expense of children's well-being. There should be extra scrutiny and vetting before schools get in bed with for-profit companies, because, unfortunately, those companies don't always have the best interests of the kids in mind.

An example: two executives of Houghton Mifflin Harcourt—one of the Big Three in educational publishing—were recently recorded on hidden camera by conservative activist James O'Keefe of Project Veritas, a nonprofit that investigates public- and private-sector misconduct and fraud. In the hidden-cam videos, the cynical executives are caught discussing the Common Core and their concern—or lack thereof—for what's best for kids.[12]

"You don't think that the educational publishing companies are in it for education, do you? No. They're in it for the money," Dianne Barrow, the West Coast accounts manager for Houghton Mifflin Harcourt, was caught on camera as saying. After explaining that Common Core is overwhelmingly profit-driven, Barrow went on to say, "I hate kids. I'm in it to sell books. Don't even kid yourself for a heartbeat," she says as she starts to laugh hysterically.

Another cynical Houghton Mifflin executive, Strategic Account Manager Amelia Petties, had this to say to the hidden camera about the Common Core: "Common Core is not new. We're calling it Common Core, woo hoo! Call it Common Core . . . there's always money in it because kids are great but it's not always about the kids." She pauses, then says, "It's *never* about the kids," as she, too, breaks out into loud, cackling laughter.

Petties even suggests that the name Common Core should be changed, because that could increase new sales and marketing opportunities: "Slapping a new name on it, which in my case I hope they do . . . then I could sell a shit ton of training around whatever you're calling it."

Regardless of whether you find these comments shocking or business-as-usual, would you want your children's educational experience manipulated by private, profit-driven companies that demonstrate such contempt for kids and their education?

Meanwhile, back in Los Angeles, they want their money back. Los Angeles Unified general counsel David Holmquist sent a letter to Apple demanding that it stop any delivery of Pearson software and vowed to seek reimbursement for math and reading materials students have been unable to use. The vast majority of students still can't access Pearson material on their iPads, Holmquist said.

Ah, but the little rascals can play *Call of Duty* and *Grand Theft Auto* on their security-bypassed iPads until the cows come home—the tablet-as-civil-rights movement in action.

Critics claim that the move toward tablets and tech should have been implemented more slowly, with a smaller rollout. Perhaps. Meanwhile, back in Silicon Valley, Google and Apple engineers continue to send their little ones to local no-tech, no-tablet Waldorf schools.

Go figure.

EDUCATIONAL LESSONS FROM DOWN UNDER

Sydney Grammar is one of Australia's top performing schools. Founded in 1854, its over 1,100 male students from pre-K through 12 are the sons of Sydney's business and political elite and routinely place in the top 1 percent of Australian students in university entry scores each year. Boasting three former prime ministers as alumni, the historic school is well funded, with an annual tuition of over $34,000, and boasts some of the finest educators and administrators in all of Australia.

And, shockingly to some, this standard-bearer of elite education has decided to scrap technology and has done away with laptops in the classroom. According to its headmaster Dr. John Vallance, the devices "distract" from teaching, and he described the billions of dollars spent on computers in Australian schools over the past seven years as a "scandalous waste of money."[13]

Dr. Vallance is no education slouch; he's a Cambridge scholar, a trustee of the State Library of NSW Foundation, a director of the National Art School and has been headmaster of Sydney Grammar for 18 years. Indeed, in 2014 the Coalition government appointed him as a special reviewer of the national arts curriculum.

This seasoned educator has taken a decidedly sour outlook on the role of technology in the classroom: "I've seen so many schools with limited budgets spending a disproportionate amount of their money on technology that doesn't really bring any measurable, or non-measurable, benefits," he said. "Schools have spent hundreds and hundreds of millions of dollars on interactive whiteboards, digital projectors, and now they're all being jettisoned."

Further, Dr. Vallance said in a March 26, 2016, interview in *The Australian,* the $2.4 billion spent by the Australian government on the "Digital Education Revolution," which used taxpayer monies to buy laptops for high school students, "didn't really do anything except enrich Microsoft and Hewlett Packard and Apple," adding, "they've got very powerful lobby influence in the educational community."

Thus Sydney Grammar has banned students from bringing laptops to school and requires them to handwrite assignments and essays until Year 10. The students have access to computers in the school computer lab, but Dr. Vallance regards laptops in the classroom as a distraction: "We find that having laptops or iPads in the classroom inhibits conversation—it's distracting."

Dr. Vallance believes that "if you're lucky enough to have a good teacher and a motivating group of classmates, it would seem a waste to introduce anything that's going to be a distraction from the benefits that kind of social context will give you." He added, "We see teaching as fundamentally a social activity. It's about interaction between people, about discussion, about conversation," and he thinks that computers in the classroom have robbed children of the chance to debate and discuss ideas with their teacher.

He also feels that laptops have led to less rigor in the classroom and have taken away from teacher preparation, indicating that laptops "introduced a great deal of slackness" in teaching and "made it much easier of giving the illusion of having prepared a lesson."

He also inherently believes in the educational benefit of learning to write by hand: "Allowing children to lose that capacity to express themselves by writing is a very dangerous thing." He said that Sydney Grammar had been studying the difference between handwritten and computer-typed tasks among boys in Year 3 and Year 5. "In creative writing tasks, they find it much easier to write by hand, to put their ideas down on a piece of paper, than they do with a keyboard."

Aware that he'd be criticized as out of step and anti-technology, Dr. Vallance said he was sure people would call him a "dinosaur," but responded by saying, "I'm in no way anti-technology. I love gadgets. It's partly because we all love gadgets so much that we have these rules, otherwise we'd all just muck about. Technology is a servant, not a master. You can't end up allowing the tail to wag the dog, which I think it is at the moment."

Dr. Vallance said it was a "really scandalous situation" that Australia was "spending more on education than ever before and the results are gradually getting worse and worse" and said he preferred to spend on teaching staff than on technology. "They end up being massive lines in the budgets of schools which at the same time have leaky toilets and roofs and ramshackle buildings. If I had a choice between filling a classroom with laptops or hiring another teacher, I'd take the other teacher every day of the week."

The internationally respected Organization for Economic Co-operation and Development (OECD) has also chimed in and questioned the growing reliance on technology in schools. In a 2015 report, it said schools must give students a solid foundation in reading, writing and math before introducing computers. Indeed, it found that heavy users of computers in the classroom "do a lot worse in most learning outcomes," and concluded by saying: "In the end, technology can amplify great teaching, but great technology cannot replace poor teaching."

Dr. Vallance takes an even more cynical view: "I think when people come to write the history of this period in education . . . this investment in classroom technology is going to be seen as a huge fraud."

READING EFFECTS: SCREENS VS. PAPER

As far as education and screens in the classroom go, there is also the issue of the comprehension differences between reading something on a radiant screen rather than on paper.

In a study called "Reading Linear Texts on Paper Versus Computer Screen: Effects on Reading Comprehension," published in January 2013 in the *International Journal of Educational Research*, Professor Anne Mangen of the University of Stavanger in Norway found that students who read text on computers performed worse on comprehension tests than students who read the same text on paper.[14]

Mangen and her colleagues had asked 72 tenth-grade students of similar reading ability to study one narrative and one expository text, each about 1,500 words in length. Half the students read the texts on paper and the other half read them in pdf files on computer screens. Afterward, students completed reading-comprehension tests consisting of multiple-choice and short-answer questions, during which they had access to the texts.

While Joseph Chilton Pearce has attributed the decreased-comprehension effects of screens to the problematic way that the brain processes radiant light, Mangen thinks that students reading on computer screens had a more difficult time finding particular information when referencing the texts because they could only scroll or click through the pdfs one section at a time. The students reading on paper, by contrast, could hold the whole text in their hands and switch between different pages.

Mangen surmised: "The ease with which you can find out the beginning, end and everything in between and the constant connection to your path, your progress in the text, might be some way of making it less taxing cognitively, so you have more free capacity for comprehension."

This notion that reading, far from being a static affair, is instead a journey over a word landscape is echoed in a 2013 *Scientific American* article called "The Reading Brain in the Digital Age: The Science of Paper Versus Screens."[15]

"There is physicality in reading," developmental psychologist and cognitive scientist Maryanne Wolf of Tufts University is quoted as saying in the article, "maybe even more than we want to think about as we lurch into digital reading—as we move forward perhaps with too little reflection."

From an evolutionary perspective, writing is a relatively new phenomenon. Thus, as far as our brains are concerned, text is a tangible part of our physical world. Indeed, early writing, such as Sumerian cuneiform or Egyptian hieroglyphics, began as pictorial representations shaped like the objects they represented. Even in our modern alphabet, we see traces of these pictorial roots: C as crescent moon, S as snake.

The article points out that beyond just treating individual letters as physical objects, the human brain may also perceive a text, as Mangen suggests, in its entirety as a kind of physical landscape. In that sense, paper books present a more obvious landscape, with a much more pronounced topography, than onscreen texts.

An open book presents two clearly defined domains—the left and right pages—and a total of eight corners with which readers can orient themselves. In addition, the book traveler can physically see where the book begins and ends and where a particular page is in relation to those points. Finally, the reader can gauge by the thickness of the pages how much has been read/traveled and how much of the journey remains. These are reassuring physical markers that can help the reader form a coherent mental map.

In contrast, most screens lack all of that and thus inhibit people from mapping the journey in their minds. A reader of screen text might scroll through a stream of words, but it is extremely difficult to see any one passage in the context of the entire text. Even though e-readers like the Kindle and tablets like the iPad can re-create pagination, the screen only displays a single page at a time—the rest of the word landscape remains out of view and out of physical touch.

And that matters.

"The implicit feel of where you are in a physical book turns out to be more important than we realized," says Abigail Sellen of Microsoft Research Cambridge, in England, and co-author of *The Myth of the Paperless Office*. "Only when you get an e-book do you start to miss it. I don't think e-book manufacturers have thought enough about how you might visualize where you are in a book."

MORE SCREENS, LESS EYE CONTACT

Apart from screens and reading deficits, other education experts also point out the potential adverse social effects: "Major concerns are focused on the impact of computers on the children's social and emotional development."

According to a report by Colleen Cordes and Edward Miller (2000): "Children between the ages of 10 and 17 today will experience nearly one-third fewer face-to-face interactions with other people throughout their lifetimes as a result of their increasingly electronic culture, at home and in school."[16] Keep in mind that the one-third estimate is from 16 years ago; what might it be today?

Whatever happened to eye contact? It's gone way down, thanks to our screen culture. A *Wall Street Journal* article published in May 2013, "Just Look Me in the Eye Already," examined the way that technology use has affected our eye contact—and the negative effect that is having on our relationships.

According to Quantified Impressions, a Texas-based communications analytics company, an adult now makes eye contact between only 30 and 60 percent of the time in a typical conversation, but emotional connection is built when eye contact is made during 60 to 70 percent of the conversation. In other words, the less eye contact, the less a connection is made.

Our screens and screen culture have normalized the experience of having conversations with little or no eye contact. We've seen it in adults, and we all have certainly seen it in kids. Unfortunately, we are losing something vital and inherently human.

"Eye contact, although it occurs over a gap of yards, is not a metaphor," psychiatrists Thomas Lewis, Fari Amini and Richard Lannon write in the book *A General Theory of Love*. "When we meet the gaze of another, two nervous systems achieve a palpable and intimate apposition."

Adults lament that kids no longer make eye contact, but parents are often guilty of providing the model for that behavior, in what has been called "Distracted Parent Syndrome."

As Carolyn Gregoire writes in "How Technology is Killing Eye Contact," the September 28, 2013, entry of her column in *The Huffington Post*: "Many parents are concerned about what their own digital multitasking and lack of eye contact might be communicating to their children."

Blogger Rachel Marie Martin wrote in a recent post, "20 Things I Will Regret Not Doing with My Kids": "I want my kids to remember that there were times when their mother looked them in the eye and smiled. And for me this often means shutting my laptop, putting down my phone, stopping my list, and just giving them time."

SCREENS IN THE CLASSROOM?
THINK FIRST—SCREENS LATER

As Dr. Toyama discovered with his theory of technology's Law of Amplification, technology *can* help education where it's already doing well, but it does little for mediocre educational systems and, worse, in dysfunctional schools it "can cause outright harm." In my research for this book and in conversations with various education experts, that seemed to be the consensus—but with an additional proviso: that technology can only help when a child or student is developmentally ready to handle powerful and hypnotic screens.

Technology can certainly be helpful in a well-supported and thoughtful high school curriculum. Perhaps even in middle school, some limited exposure to computer learning can be helpful. But the notion of sticking a radiant screen in the hands of a kindergartener or a child in elementary school is not only not helpful educationally, but, as we have read, could be neurologically and clinically harmful—especially for already vulnerable children.

Even Joel Klein, Rupert Murdoch's dark prince, of all people, supports that view. Speaking to Carlo Rotella for the September 12, 2013, issue of the *New York Times Magazine*, he responded to tech-in-the-classroom criticisms from Sherry Turkle, MIT professor and author of *Alone Together,* by saying that he wouldn't put fourth-graders in a MOOC—massive open online course—and that he would exercise "great restraint" in introducing technology into a kindergarten classroom.[17] Thank goodness for small favors.

Maybe we should follow the lead of the tech engineers and Waldorf schools wait until our kids are beyond third or fourth grade—some suggest they should be at least ten years old—before interactive tablets are introduced.

In a 1999 interview, Joseph Chilton Pearce discussed a four-day symposium in Berkeley that he attended, where 21 education experts from around the world discussed computers in education: "At that . . . symposium at Berkeley we concluded that everything hinges on age appropriateness. One professor from MIT made the passionate plea that we must encourage children to develop the ability to think first, and then give them the computer. After that, the sky's the limit. But if you introduce the computer before the child's thought processes are worked out, then you have a disaster in the making. This is because, as Piaget pointed out, the first twelve years of life are spent putting into place the structures of knowledge that enable young people to grasp abstract, metaphoric, symbolic types of information. . . . The danger here is that the computer . . . will interrupt that development."[18]

In "Computer Integration into the Early Childhood Curriculum," published in *Education* (Fall 2012), authors Mona and Heyam Mohammad also frame the issue in developmental terms: "Piaget's theory, known also as the constructivist perspective, says that learners benefit most from 'concrete' experiences or hands-on activities that allow the learner to manipulate his/her environment in order to construct knowledge based on interaction with the world."[19]

Translation: Lego, not *Minecraft*.

As previously mentioned, Pearce attributes a large part of the adverse effect of screens on young children to the radiant light and the fact that children can go "catatonic" in front of a screen: "This has to do with the way that that the brain reacts to radiant light, which is the light source of TV and computer monitors, and reflected light, which is what brings us the rest of our visual experience . . . the brain tends to close down in response to radiant light sources. We've all seen how children get when they watch television for any length of time."

In that interview, Pearce goes on to describe how the television industry started introducing "startle effects" into kids' programming in order to snap kids out of their trance so that they could pay attention again. But over time, like any hypnotic drug, desensitization occurs to the point where the attention-grabbing startle effects had to become bigger and bigger.

Still, as Pearce explains, while the child's neocortex *may* realize that the increasingly shocking images aren't real, the "reptilian" brain does not, and the child goes into perpetual cortisol-releasing fight-or-flight response. This massive overstimulation is "causing the brain to maladapt in ways previously thought impossible. It is literally breaking down on all levels of neural development." Pearce was presciently forecasting some of the neurological and clinical issues that we discussed regarding Dr. Dunckley's work with electronic screen syndrome.

Wouldn't it just be a better idea to leave the screens out of the classroom—at least through elementary school? As Pearce says: "We must encourage children to develop the ability to think first, and then give them the computer. After that, the sky's the limit."

Unfortunately, that might be easier said than done today. In our new digital landscape, it will become increasingly difficult to insulate a child during his key developmental years from the advances in our Brave New e-World.

These are indeed strange times we live in. The divide between the real and the digital is increasingly blurring as our society is becoming more and more virtual. The thought-provoking movie *The Matrix* hints at the mind-bending that may await us just over the horizon.

In the meantime, let's take a look at the farther reaches of the digital landscape today.

THIRTEEN

IT'S AN E-WORLD

A PARABLE FROM *STAR TREK*

In the two-part *Star Trek* episode "The Menagerie" (1965)—which incorporated the series' pilot episode, "The Cage"—a badly burned and wheelchair-
bound Captain Pike, Captain Kirk's predecessor, is given the opportunity to
live out his life on a planet called Talos IV.

The Talosians are able to manipulate reality and create very pleasing
illusions—in fact, entire worlds of exciting and tempting virtual realities.
On the planet the crew meets a beautiful young Earth woman named Vina,
who they think is a captive. They find out that Vina is there willingly; she
was once an old and very badly injured survivor of a space ship crash. The
Talosians gave her the chance to live in the illusion of youth and health. In
today's digital terms, we might call this illusory Vina an avatar.

Interestingly, this species, which has the power to control illusions, is
dying. They refuse the offer of help from the *Enterprise* because they fear that
the Earthlings would learn the power of illusion and also fall victim to it, like
Talos's own illusion-obsessed civilization.

In the end, Captain Pike has a choice: live a miserable existence as a
quadriplegic burn victim who can't even speak, or be young again and live
the life of his dreams. Granted, option number two is not real—but it *feels* real.

Which would you choose?

Pike chooses to live life in a virtual reality (VR) as a young and healthy Pike avatar with the illusion-enhanced Vina. At the end of the pilot episode, the head Talosian philosophically says to the departing Earthlings, when referring to Vina and her beautiful avatar, "She has an illusion and you have reality. May you find your way as pleasant."

Today, hundreds of thousands of people are embracing the idea that the illusion may indeed be more "pleasant" and better than reality, as avatar-based "synthetic communities" are exploding.

AVATARS AND *SECOND LIFE*

Let's say you hate your life; maybe you don't have it as bad as Captain Pike, but you don't like who you are or how you live. Would you escape from that life if you could?

Many have.

With one million active users, *Second Life* is a thriving virtual community with its own shops, currency, concerts, relationships and, well, everything else that the real world has, only on a screen. Technically, you're supposed to be 18 or older, but if you're 13 or older you can use *Second Life* with some restrictions. If you're 16 to 17 years old, you can access regions and search results that have a "General" maturity rating.

Around since 2003, *Second Life* is getting a new boost with the integration of immersive VR technology. With the technology still in development but now being beta-tested, soon *Second Life* denizens will no longer have to be limited to 2-D; they can laugh, talk, play music—and have sex—in immersive and much more realistic VR 3-D with their virtual Project Sansar platform. And, make no mistake, immersive VR is where all of this is headed. Virtual and augmented reality will be a $150 billion market by 2020, according to Digi-Capital.

Wait a minute, people can actually have sex in *Second Life?* Yes indeed. This is what one *Second Life* user posted as a helpful how-to for a sexually curious newbie, including how to search for a virtual sexual organ:

Social details:
1. Find a willing partner

2. Find a private place or a designated public sex area. DO NOT do sex in public, ESPECIALLY in PG areas.

3. For the gentleman: You'll need an attachment. Search for "penis." There are a number of freebies available. DON'T wear it in public! It will stick through your pants.

Technical details:

There are lots of ways to animate your avatar. One way to kiss and hug is with an attachment called a "hugger." There are free huggers available. Many pieces of furniture (especially beds) are scripted to provide you and your partner with a menu of animations. Touch the piece of furniture to call up the menu. A pair of "poseballs," one pink and one blue, will appear above the bed. Sit on them . . . girl on the pink, guy on the blue. Touch the bed again to get the menu and change positions.

Or you may find pairs of poseballs just [lying] about. You can use those, too.

To get the most out of cyber-sex, you need to be able to "chat emote," to fill in the details that the animations don't provide. Next time you're in world, try typing this, without quotes: "/me leans close to you, brushing your lips with hers." Most sexual talk is done in private IM, rather than in open chat. Not everyone around you wants to "hear" you moaning and panting.

Like I said, these are strange times we live in.

FUTURE TECH NOW

In the future, the digital world will evolve beyond screens.

And that future is now.

From talking forks to smart clothes, new tech, according to MIT Media Lab scientist David Rose, is about making the computer more personal. Rose argues in his new book, *Enchanted Objects: Design, Human Desire and the Internet of Things* (2015), that people desire direct interaction with technology: "Screens fall short because they don't improve our relationship with computing," he writes. "The devices are passive, without personality. The machine sits on idle waiting for your orders."[1]

Yet wearable tech like Google Glass and the iWatch have not lived up to the hype and the sales that were hoped for. Virtual reality technology, on the other hand, seems to be exploding. From Oculus Rift to the do-it-yourself and affordable Google Cardboard (starting at $3 without the smartphone), VR is on the rise.

And now, the next wave of blurred reality: the hologram and "augmented reality."

Unlike VR, which immerses us in a new reality, holograms create three-dimensional objects in our real-life world. And now the Microsoft HoloLens has combined the two: both virtual reality and augmented reality in an immersive holographic experience, a device so futuristic that it makes 2-D Google Glass seem as outdated and primitive as the View-Master.

According to tech reviewer Abhijit in the blog Informatic Cool Stuff (ICS): "The 'MICROSOFT HOLOLENS' takes you to a forbidden world. As you move around in a space, like your living room, the Holographic app moves with you. That means you could have a Skype call that follows you as you walk through your house. You can also pin your favorite apps to the physical walls in your space or rest them on a table, so that every time you walk into that room, that app appears in the HoloLens. If an app is pinned to a wall, you can say 'follow me' to un-pin it and have it move with you again. You can also resize those apps, making videos take up an entire wall, or shrinking a website."[2]

And, of course, the ubiquitous porn industry is cashing in as well, taking full advantage of the new tech. In a *Mashable* story titled "VR Porn is Here and It's Scary How Real It Is," journalist Raymond Wong gushes, "I found myself transported into a bedroom. Kneeling before me was a female porn star who was seductively talking dirty to me. I looked down and saw some guy's muscular body. Well, that's not mine, I thought to myself. I was confused. Whose body was this? Then I realized, *I* was now this guy."

THE END OF REALITY

The futuristic HoloLens was developed by Alex Kipman. A stringy-haired Microsoft designer who looks the part of hipster visionary, he held a mind-blowing TED talk in February 2016 in Vancouver.[3] Decidedly anti-screens because of their archaic two-dimensional limitations, the scruffy Kipman presented a jaw-dropping presentation of both the immersive and reality-creating 3-D and holographic possibilities of the HoloLens.

During his talk, Kipman criticizes the way that we have become trapped by screens and describes a future world of interactive technology that is entirely immersive: "Today, we spend most of our time tapping and looking at screens." Interestingly, he then laments the social cost of this screen enslavement: "What happened to interacting with each other? I don't know about you, but I feel limited inside of this 2-D world of monitors and pixels . . . my desire to connect with people inspires me as a creator. Put simply, I want to create a new reality where technology brings us infinitely closer to each other. A reality where people—not devices—are the center of everything."

Sounds wonderful—tech that can socially connect people. The smooth-talking Kipman has the ability to sell a compelling vision of this new "human connecting" future tech. During his TED talk, the audience seems drawn into his utopian vision as, with a wave of his hand, he is able to create a 3-D ice cave, complete with hanging stalactites and growing stalagmites that seem to emerge directly out of the TED red dot on the stage.

Seeking to create what sounds like a digital Ubermensch, Kipman discusses the "infinite possibilities" of a quantum universe and the "super powers" that computers can give human beings, as he again decries the limitations of being stuck in a 2-D screen world while we can now have "digital powers" to create reality within our own world.

Later in his talk, he waves his hand and a magical garden with multicolored and oversized butterflies and 4-foot psychedelically colored mushrooms materialize, seemingly from the imagination of the Brothers Grimm—or Timothy Leary.

And as with Timothy Leary, with whom I had the opportunity to spend some time before his death—and who also, in his later years, had moved beyond psychedelic mind expansion and was talking passionately about VR mind expansion—you aren't quite sure if you're listening to a visionary or a madman—or perhaps a little bit of both.

Like a good showman, Kipman saves his best trick for last: human teleportation. As a 3-D actual representation of a Mars landscape appears on stage surrounding him, Kipman looks at the audience and says: "I invite you to experience, for the first time anywhere in the world, here on the TED stage, a real life holographic teleportation between me and my friend Dr. Jeffrey Norris from NASA's Jet Propulsion Laboratory."

And with that, a smiling, casually dressed Jeff Norris—also wearing a HoloLens, materializes on stage in the virtual Mars landscape; the effect leaves me feeling like I'm watching a Chris Angel illusion. The holographic-yet-solid-looking Norris goes on to explain that he's actually "in three places. I'm standing in a room across the street while I'm standing on the stage with you while I'm standing on Mars 100 million miles away."

Amazing as it all seems, it's important to keep in mind that, fanciful assertions aside, the biological Dr. Norris is actually in only one place: In that room across the street from the TED talk; the other two holographic Norrises are essentially CGI effects superimposed on a virtual landscape. But it's certainly an impressive feat nonetheless, awe-inspiring for the sheer technical wizardry involved.

Kipman ends his talk with a humanistic flourish: 'I dream of this future every single day. I take inspiration from our ancestors who interacted, communicated and worked together. We are all beginning to build technology that will return us to the humanity that brought us to where we are today. Technology that will let us stop living inside this 2-D world of monitors and pixels and let us start remembering what it feels like to live in our 3-D world."

It's an odd vision; using technology to "remember" what if feels like to live in our 3-D world when we actually *do* live in a 3-D world that doesn't even require Kipman's HoloLens to experience. And, ironically, it has been technology that has immersed us in the dreaded 2-D screen world that Kipman laments. We should also keep in mind that the illusion that the HoloLens creates—as technically brilliant and visually stunning as it may be—and it is all that—is still a CGI effect—a computer generated image masquerading as reality.

After watching Kipman talk, I am left wondering if I've just seen a visionary or a madman who will destroy the very essence of humanity with his VR crusade. I can't help but think again of poor Captain Pike and the Talosians; is Kipman's illusory world the one that we should all be aspiring to create and live in? Or, like the Talosians, is it the one that will decay our species? My fear is that far too many will become lost and seduced by the siren song of that VR illusion as their life in this 3-D plane of existence withers and dies.

Welcome to the Matrix. The future is now.

E-ATHLETES

It looks like a typical college pep rally: enthusiastic cheerleaders jumping up and down, leading the assembled students in a series of whoops and cheers; screaming students packed into bleachers as the various varsity teams are announced and enter the gymnasium to thunderous applause.

But this pep rally is unlike any that has ever occurred on any college campus before. This rally features one particular varsity team that is a first of its kind anywhere in the world: the first college varsity team of e-athletes— that's right, video gamers—all of whom are attending college on athletic scholarships.

Administrators at Robert Morris University, a small college in Chicago, have decided that they want to be ahead of the curve in the booming world of competitive "e-sports," a growing phenomenon in which professional e-athletes now play video games in front of thousands of adoring fans in crowded arenas like the Staples Center in Los Angeles, earning high-six-figure salaries.

Yes: there are people actually getting paid hundreds of thousands of dollars to play video games competitively.

At the Robert Morris pep rally, after the lacrosse and football teams have been announced in a frenzied auditorium and come out running and high-fiving each other, the school's e-team is announced, also to very loud applause. At this point, a motley assortment of 30 young people, who all look as if they might be auditioning for a *Revenge of the Nerds* sequel, come sheepishly and self-consciously marching out.

Kurt Melcher, Robert Morris's associate athletic director, takes the microphone and, while gesturing to the e-team, proudly boasts to the assembled student body: "We were able to recruit some very, very good players. Some of our top players are rated in the top .02 percent of all players in North America." He then walks down the line of the e-team, slapping high-fives with young men who seem uncomfortable and unaccustomed to this sports ritual.[4]

Video gaming as a competitive sport has turned into a big-money business. In 2015 SuperData Research estimated that the global e-sports industry had generated revenue of $748.8 million that year but is anticipated to reach 1.9 billion by 2018.[5] While different games hold high-purse tournaments where cash prizes can exceed $1 million, the kings of the hill are the fantasy games *League of Legends* and *DOTA* (*Defense of the Ancients*), whose teams compete against other teams in mythical strategy games.

With a rabidly loyal fan base, the *League of Legends* world championships sold out the Staples Center in 2013. At these arena tournaments, tens of thousands of screaming gaming devotees pay to watch a handful of players compete on an elevated stage while their video screens are magnified on large projector screens so that fans can watch their every move. Top players are treated like rock stars, receiving not only great sums of money but product-endorsement deals as well.

E-sports have exploded globally in the last five years, but this is not an entirely new phenomenon. We can trace its roots back to the 1990s in South Korea, where the growth of e-sports was influenced by the mass building of broadband Internet networks following the 1997 Asian financial crisis.

That financial crisis also brought about a very high unemployment rate, which caused large numbers of Koreans to look for things to do while out of work. Thus, e-sports were born. The Korean e-Sports Association, an arm of the Ministry of Culture, Sports and Tourism, was founded in 2000 to promote and regulate the controversial, fledgling sport, which was often played in mammoth cybercafes.

Then, in the second decade of the twenty-first century, e-sports experienced phenomenal global growth, in both viewership and prize money; although there had been large tournaments, the number and scope of tournaments have increased significantly since the turn of the twenty-first century, going from about ten tournaments in 2000 to about 260 in 2010.

The rise of an actual professional video gaming circuit has done several things for the lives of everyday teenage gamers. I can say that in my own experience of having worked with teenage gamers over the past decade, the industry has helped to incentivize those teens' continued and obsessive play, feeding their hopes that they too may join the elite ranks of the paid pros. Just five years ago, it would have seemed an expression of pure fantasy for a teenager to say, "I want to be a professional video gamer." Now, while unlikely, it *is* possible. So in the mind of the obsessed kid playing video games in his room for hours on end, he's now "in training."

Years ago, when I would facilitate meetings between frustrated parents and their gaming-obsessed kids, the frazzled parents would cry some version of: "What are you going to do with your future if all you do is play video games all day long while you flunk out of school!" The usual reply from the kid was either a shrug of the shoulders or, from the more ambitious, "I'm going to be a game-tester for the gaming companies!" Invariably, the parents would look down in despair.

I have found this scenario to be similar to those of kids in past generations who dreamed of becoming pro athletes, musicians or actors, however statistically unrealistic *those* dreams may or may not have been. For years, parents would often encourage their kids to dream big but keep their feet on the ground and do well in school so that they could have a plan B—just in case.

And now, just like kids who aspire to be traditional pro athletes, the video gamers have their own big-money heroes, the Michael Jordans of the e-world, whom they can tell their parents they want to emulate. Along with 'I wanna be like Mike" or "bend it like Beckham," we now have "I wanna game like Dendi" (i.e., Danil "Dendi" Ishutin, a popular 26-year-old Ukrainian player who has made over half a million dollars gaming).

Beyond competing in huge tournaments that sell out arenas, enterprising gamers now also have Twitch, the online streaming site through which gamers can have their own channels and accrue subscribers who are willing to pay $4.99 a month to watch them play.

Twitch launched in 2011 with a simple premise: that the entertainment value of—as well as the ability to monetize—video game play comes not just from playing but also from watching others play and talking about games. Twitch quickly became the top video-game-streaming site, drawing more live Internet traffic than traditional sports competitors such as ESPN, Major League Baseball and WWE.[6]

With 60 million monthly unique visitors, each spending almost two hours on the site daily, Twitch is attractive to advertisers eager to connect with its audience of mostly Generation Y males who aren't reading newspapers or watching television. Amazon.com certainly agreed—they shelled out almost $1 billion ($970 million to be exact) to buy the site in 2014.

While some gamers with channels on Twitch struggle to make enough change to buy their weekly supply of Mountain Dew, others make annual incomes in the low six figures, having achieved the video gamer's dream: sitting at home and playing video games while others pay to watch. According to my gaming clients, the key to success on Twitch is either displaying an entertaining personality while you play or being a well-known strategist from whom viewers can learn.

Still others have hit a grand slam in monetizing their gaming. Take 26-year-old Swedish gamer PewDiePie. Born Felix Arvid Ulf Kjellberg, he took a leap of faith in 2011, when he abandoned a degree in industrial economics and technology in order to focus on his burgeoning YouTube channel. His YouTube clips are what's known as "Let's Play" commentaries: entertaining walk-throughs of video games that have grown increasingly popular.

But his parents were not thrilled with this career turnaround; angry that he would give up on his academics, they cut him off financially, after which he went to work at a hot dog stand in order to fund his videos. PewDiePie soon gathered a following online, and in 2012 his channel surpassed one million subscribers. Now, with over 40 million subscribers and ten billion views, he makes an estimated $4 million a year from advertisements and endorsements.

What can parents now say when their kid says: "Mom, Dad, I want to be the next PewDiePie"? In the new, shifting media landscape of the digital age, he might have a better shot at YouTube stardom than at being, say, a book editor.

One of my obsessed video-game-playing clients, "Eric," wants to bypass college for several years so that he can train and give professional gaming his best shot. When his flummoxed father tried to talk him out of it, the young man pointed out that his dad, too, had once had a dream—playing pro baseball—and had also bypassed college in order to pursue it. The father, in fact, had played minor league ball. How is this different? Eric asked.

After that exchange, the father saw his son's situation in a different light and became more accepting of Eric's dream of playing video games professionally.

Unfortunately, the very bright Eric was failing most of his classes because of his training. And while people can become rather obsessive about sports, they don't usually develop a whole host of clinical disorders as a result of playing baseball.

Nevertheless, Eric is an articulate advocate for what the gaming experience represents for his generation. He asked me to view the documentary *Free to Play* (2014) so that I might better understand this new professional gaming culture. The very well-made film, with a guest appearance by pro basketball player and video game enthusiast Jeremy Lin, follows three top gamers as they pursue their dream of winning the *DOTA 2* championship. The compelling film paints a sympathetic and appealing picture of both gamers and the gaming culture.

But interestingly, when I looked closely at the credits, I saw that the film was made by the Valve Corporation—a video game company and the makers of *DOTA 2*.

FOURTEEN

THE SOLUTION

ESCAPING PLATO'S E-CAVE

PLATO'S CAVE

Let's talk about the so-called real world.

Plato's most famous allegory, known as "the Myth of the Cave," helps to give us a perspective about living in an illusion or living in reality.[1] Plato asks (via) Socrates to imagine a cave, in which prisoners are kept. These prisoners have been in the cave since their childhood; they are all chained so that their legs and necks are immobile, and they are forced to look at a wall in front of them. That's all that they've ever known.

Behind the prisoners is a fire, and between the fire and the prisoners is a raised walkway. The people on the walkway are carrying various objects that cast shadows on the wall in front of the prisoners. But the poor prisoners can see only the flickering images, since they can't move their heads. So they assume that the images are real, rather than just shadows of what is truly real.

Then Socrates asks: what if one of the prisoners were to break free and turn to see the fire? Sure, the bright light might hurt his eyes, since he's been used to the shadows. But then he would realize that what he thought was real wasn't real at all, but only shadows of the real items on the walkway behind him.

Then, if the prisoner were taken out of the cave and brought outside, into the sunlight, what then? The bright light would be even more blinding and disorienting than the fire. But after his eyes adjusted, he would be able to see the world as it truly is: real trees, real grass. After learning of the reality of the world, the prisoner would understand how pathetic and blind his former fellow prisoners in the cave really are. But if he returned to the cave and tried to tell them of what he had seen and discovered, they would think he was crazy; they wouldn't be able to fathom or believe that there was a reality beyond the shadows. In fact, they would probably want to stay in the illusion of the cave. But the prisoner who had escaped and seen the light—and true reality—would be free from the illusion. He would be awakened.

Put another way, the prisoner is Neo, who eats the red pill and wakes up from the illusion of the Matrix.

Whether we're talking ancient Greek philosophy or a contemporary sci-fi film, the problem is essentially the same as the solution: the protagonist has been living in an illusion and manages to escape the dream/nightmare.

In a sense, we've all been chewing on that illusion-maintaining blue pill, blurring and confusing the digital world with a fully awakened, real existence. You might say, "Of course I know that the things on my screens aren't 'real'"—and that may be true. But are your devices hypnotizing you to the point that your actual flesh-and-blood life is suffering? Rather than tools, have your screens become your cage?

Since the focus of this book is screen effects on children, I'll just leave the adult reader with this advice: if you answered yes to either of the above questions—is your personal life suffering because of your screen compulsion, or do you feel trapped by your devices—then try to imagine how a seven-year-old might struggle in a world surrounded by addicting screens and games designed by some of the smartest people on the planet to hook the poor kid.

A kid hooked by screen addiction is stuck in Plato's illusory cave—or Neo's blue-pilled Matrix. In this dehumanizing and sensory-overloading tech-filled world, millions are choosing the escape of the blue pill—they're drawn to it like a moth to the flame.

The fictional Captain Pike chose the blue pill—his reality was just too unbearable.

Unfortunately, we've lost a large number of kids and teens to the digital blue pill. They prefer the illusion of an entertaining glowing screen, oftentimes complete with archetypal myths and fantasy that let them engage in some noble quest, to the reality of their math homework or chores.

Who wouldn't? Hell, the digital blue pill has dragons and knights and excitement and camaraderie; the screen inhabitant can live a pure fantasy life and be . . . limitless.

But back in their real-life bedrooms, mom and dad are still fighting over the mortgage; that girl or boy they like just posted a humiliating taunt on Facebook. They're failing in school and don't like the way that they look. Not only is real life boring—but it just sucks!

Blue pill, please.

So what's the solution for our youngest and most vulnerable who have fallen into the Matrix? How do we pull them out?

TECH ADDICTION TREATMENT

If we look at the similarities with other addictions, we've learned some things from roughly 80 years of addiction research and treatment. As we discussed with regard to Bruce Alexander's Rat Park research, the sad irony of addiction is that a person who feels alienated, disconnected and trapped—as if in a cage—seeks an escape, but then gets trapped worse than before by the even more daunting cage of addiction.[2]

With kids and tech addiction, we can say that a kid who may feel disconnected and trapped finds a sense of connection and escape in screen life—only to get trapped in the Matrix. We get that; we can understand the escapist tendency.

So what's the solution?

Well, two things. Rat Park taught us that the happier and more fulfilled the rat's life was, the less likely it was to drink the morphine water and become addicted. So from a preventative standpoint, a kid who has healthy human connections and healthy hobbies and outlets is less likely to fall into the Matrix.

But we also know that about 10 percent of people—including kids—are predisposed toward addiction. A child among that 10 percent, even one who has the best and most loving supports, may be more vulnerable to the Matrix once they taste digital drugs like hyperarousing video games and experience their addicting dopaminergic effect.

So what to do in those instances? A kid who may not have been aware that addiction runs in the family suddenly gets hooked on a video game—or becomes an addicted texter or Facebook addict. Then what?

Breaking free of an unhealthy relationship with tech is similar to breaking free of an eating disorder; unlike drugs and alcohol, from which one can abstain, food and, it can be argued, technology are unavoidable. Except for those who have gone entirely off the grid, we all inevitably interact with tech. The key is a healthy relationship with tech through a balance with real-life experiences.

But if a person has gone too deep into the e-cave, the absolute first step is a tech fast (otherwise known as digital detox); this is necessary before a person can engage in healthy, moderate usage. We know from the field of addiction treatment that an addict—drug, digital or otherwise—needs to detox before any other kind of therapy can have any chance of being effective. That means a *full* digital detox—no computers, no smartphones, no tablets—nothing. The extreme digital detox even eliminates television. The prescribed amount of time is four to six weeks. That's the amount of time that is usually required for a hyperaroused nervous system to reset itself.

But we need to do that gradually, so we don't trigger any of the explosive behaviors that we see when addicts are detoxed cold turkey. So, for example, a kid who is online for seven hours a day needs to cut down at a rate of one hour per day. By the end of the week, he or she has been tapered to zero—abstinence. Once abstinent, the person remains screen-free for the prescribed four to six weeks.

Sometimes the child or teen, realizing the severity of the problem, is willing to do this. I've had kids begging for help in unplugging and entirely willing to ditch their screens. Others are belligerent and totally against the idea. They will throw tantrums and scream—maybe even threaten. And if there is a history of giving in to tech tantrums, rest assured you will get some more. But stay strong and be the parent. You control the plug, as we say. Negotiating a slow reduction of screen usage over a week or so should lessen the blowback.

Just as in drug detox, there will be a withdrawal period; the digitally detoxing kid—even with a gradual taper—will go through a period of increased irritability, anxiety, depression and, perhaps, even some physical symptoms like head and stomach aches. These are all natural.

In traditional drug and alcohol rehabs, like the one that I run, we also understand that it takes some time away from the triggers and the addictive behavior to learn new and healthy ways to live—new healthy habits such as going to bed and waking up at regular hours; eating healthy meals consistently; doing some chores; developing healthy outlets. All of these things help build a sense of structure and self-confidence that are often lacking.

It's also critically important that kids who are digitally detoxing not just sit around and twiddle their thumbs. They need to get busy with new, fun things to do; they absolutely have to replace the old addictive screen behavior with something new. Maybe the child reconnects with a sport he or she used to play—or a musical instrument. Maybe the child journals the entire experience or gets involved in some other creative project, like painting a mural or writing music. Perhaps the child gets involved in some volunteer work. But new hobbies must be found, or old passions need to be rekindled.

The other key is that the kids connect with other people. This is critical. Addiction is isolating; even if they were playing games with other players, that's not the same as a genuine human connection. Ideally, connecting in a support group with other recovering techies is optimal. There, they can feel a sense of understanding, empathy and connection.

And, perhaps most importantly, during this tech fast, nature immersion has been shown to be the most effective way to help people get grounded and reconnected to themselves and to reality. Engaging in actual experiences and not e-experiences can be incredibly healing.

Zen Buddhists talk of the "Zen insight" being the unfiltered and direct experience of reality. In the mental health arena, "experiential therapy" (which can include immersive wilderness programs) have been proven to be very effective in helping people suffering from disorders such as addiction, anxiety and depression. In my own practice, I've incorporated the wisdom of the Transcendentalists—Emerson, Thoreau and Whitman—in using nature to help clients shift out of neurotic patterns.

We know through the work of Edward O. Wilson at Harvard and his bio-philia movement[3] as well as from Richard Louv, who coined the term "nature deficit disorder,"[4] that human beings are hardwired toward having a genuine nature connection. According to Louv, the skyrocketing emotional and psychological problems that we are seeing with kids are all related to the erosion of children's connection with nature by their immersion in the digital world.

That's why the solution for an overstimulated kid trapped in an addictive e-world is a true Walden-like experience—and not *Walden, The Game.* Unplug. Walk in nature. Feel the sun on your skin. The two first Glow Kids I encountered in that dingy basement in Greece almost 15 years ago merely needed to unplug and walk upstairs into the sunlight—like Plato's cave dweller did—and have a direct nature experience.

I've worked with some of the most severely addicted drug users imaginable—self-destructive crystal meth and heroin addicts who seemed beyond any sort of help. One of my more challenging clients, who was not-so-slowly killing herself with her crystal meth addiction, had the most amazing and transformative experience when she took a slow, mindful beach walk and just experienced a spectacular sunset.

That's when what I like to call "the shift" can happen—the shift from the alienated, self-destructive and compulsive addict to the person who feels a deeper sense of connection with the universe and within him/herself. From these kinds of experiences, a genuine sense of purpose can emerge. Talk therapy is great, but there is something truly magical and potentially life-changing when a disconnected kid connects with the natural world.

Some programs have successfully used wilderness therapy for many years for young and troubled teens with either addiction or behavioral issues. On average those programs have had a higher success rate than traditional rehabs for young people.[5]

Nearly 17 years ago Tim Drake started Primitive Pursuits, a nonprofit nature-based program in Ithaca, New York, that has a partnership with Cornell Cooperative Extension. They teach kids—from pre-K through high school—skills related to wilderness, leadership, community living and nature. They also have an adult and seniors program in which participants learn how to make a fire, identify plant life, make a bow and arrow and generally feel comfortable in nature.

The program has even evolved into an experiential Ithaca College environmental science course called "Environmental Sentinels." Tim told me that he was amused to discover that even environmental science majors—who know all about nature academically—are still often not very comfortable *being* in nature: "I see a lot of lost souls. Even some of these environmental studies students who have chosen this career get thrown off when they get into the woods."

When I asked Tim to name the biggest benefit a kid gets from being in nature, he said: "Nature is where we come from. It brought us to where we are today. The reason we're successful as a species is because of our original relationship with nature." He adds: "Exposing a child to that touches the hardwiring of being human—they become 'activated.'"

Ironically, Tim's father was a computer programmer, but the family lived in the country, and his parents pushed him outdoors from "sunup to sunset." Tim also understands the gravitational pull of a screen on a kid, as his own son has started playing video games.

Tim believes that the key to regaining balance is building a sense of community and belonging while creating fun experiences that engage the child: "If it's just sitting at home and doing nothing while you ask a kid to not play video games—it's going to be a tough sell. I saw that with my own son. But if you can create an alternative that's appealing—that's the key." Tim talked of involving his son's friends in activities and creating outdoor adventures with them—building bonfires, hiking, canoeing, discovering new trails.

For kids stuck in the Matrix, experiencing a sense of real joy and playfulness is essential.

Kristine Mraz, author of *Purposeful Play* (2016), cites these interesting statistics about the advantages of play in a child's life:

1. MacArthur Foundation "genius grant" winners are twice as likely to win the grant if they spent more time playing.
2. NASA applications ask how you played as a child.
3. Murderers statistically have an absence of play in their childhoods; there is a reduced risk of violence in a person who spent time playing as a child.
4. Animals who play live longer.

She also cites these fascinating statistics from Upworthy.com regarding kids and "social competence," which includes traits like sharing, cooperating and helping other kids: "An increase of a single point in social competency score showed a child would be 54% more likely to earn a high school diploma, twice as likely to graduate with a college degree and 45% more likely to have a stable, full time job at age 25."

The Alliance for Childhood, a consortium of some of the top educators and mental health experts in the country, makes several recommendations to combat technology's erosion of a healthy, balanced childhood. In addition to nature exposure and time for unstructured play, they also recommend that children maintain close loving relationships with adults and have opportunities to engage in music, drama, painting and other arts. Further, they suggest that kids get involved with hands-on crafts and pursue activities that involve creative verbal expression, like poetry and storytelling.

Dr. Hilarie Cash, one of the original pioneers in tech addiction treatment, also values the role of nature and play in treating the disorder. She had been a therapist in private practice in Seattle in 1994 when she began to see clients who were clearly showing signs of Internet or gaming addiction. She decided to start a therapy group for these tech-addicted clients who were seeing their careers and marriages fall apart as a result of their compulsion.

She realized that this problem would grow as technology kept marching forward, so in 2003 she opened reSTART, the country's first rehab devoted exclusively to treating tech addiction. Thirteen years and hundreds of clients later, reSTART, with its idyllic natural setting and its motto, "Connect with Life—Not Your Device," is still helping teens and young adults overcome their tech addictions.

Dr. Cash also helps her clients develop their own technology re-entry plans. She explained that the assumption is that clients eventually have to intersect with tech and screens again. That doesn't mean, though, that the addicted video gamer goes back to playing video games a little bit less; rather, it means that the person can, over time, use the computer for healthy pursuits like researching homework. They identify "digital vegetables, or tech that can have a positive component, vs. "digital candy," tech that is only recreational and has no function other than spiking dopamine.

I've also developed an experientially based program for adolescents called Hamptons Discovery (www.hamptonsdiscovery.com), where young people struggling with tech addiction, substance and/or other emotional or behavioral problems will have the opportunity to work on their issues and engage in a variety of personal growth and therapeutic activities on an outpatient basis in an idyllic setting in the heart of the Hamptons.

Combining both traditional psychotherapy with experiential therapy like equine therapy, mindfulness meditation, martial arts, music and creative expression, our young clients also will be exposed to adventures in nature as they get to explore the hundreds of acres of pine forests, sand dunes, bays, estuaries and ocean surf. They will escape the trap of tech addiction as they discover their true selves.

Hamptons Discovery kids will also have the opportunity to participate in a new therapeutic model called Seahab (www.SeahabRecovery.com) that I've developed. On the water, with the ocean spray in their hair, the kids experience how fun real life can be while working collectively as they fish, help maintain their boat and engage in therapy. They will realize that the *World of Warcraft* is the Matrix—it's not real—as they discover that real-world experiences can be even more satisfying than digital illusion.

Recovery for Glow Kids is possible—I've seen it. The young man described in the earlier clinical snapshot—the one who chased his mother with a butcher knife—is a perfect example. He had stopped going to school and was lost deep in his video game addiction. After several weeks in a wilderness program in Vermont, with the help of therapy, he found himself again. Today his mother is happy to report that she and her husband have their son back. He uses a smartphone and watches TV, but the Xbox is gone.

He's even playing soccer again.

Health and happiness are indeed possible in a tech-saturated world; we just have to be informed and be careful about the traps that lurk in the e-cave, lest we—and our children—fall in too deep.

RAISING AWARENESS AND CREATING SOCIAL CHANGE

At the societal level, we've been asleep at the switch. Perhaps because we, as the adults, have been seduced by technology and its shiny baubles, we've been willfully blind to the serious impacts that the glowing screens have on developing little brains.

As with Plato's cave dweller or Neo in *The Matrix,* it's not just the tech-addicted kids who need to awaken. We, the sleeping adults, need to open our eyes and wake up as well. On a grassroots and mass-media level, raising awareness about the dangers of screen tech is the key. The damaging virtual epidemic is spreading due to a lack of awareness among people and the media—even among mental health professionals. As a society, we are simply unaware of the research indicating that too-early tech use and excessive screen exposure can be damaging.

The following were the recommendations by the Alliance for Children in their children-and-tech manifesto *Fool's Gold: A Critical Look at Computers in Childhood,* published way back in 2000. The Alliance for Children is an impressive organization whose National Advisory Board includes some of the most respected psychiatrists, professors, pediatricians and educators in the country; its roster reads like a Who's Who in the area of children and their well-being.[6]

These were their recommendations:

1. A refocusing in education, at home and school, on the essentials of a healthy childhood: strong bonds with caring adults; time for spontaneous, creative play; a curriculum rich in music and the other arts; reading books aloud; storytelling and poetry; rhythm and movement; cooking, building things, and other handcrafts; and gardening and other hands-on experiences of nature and the physical world.
2. A broad public dialogue on how emphasizing computers is affecting the real needs of children, especially children in low-income families.
3. A comprehensive report by the U.S. Surgeon General on the full extent of physical, emotional and other developmental hazards computers pose to children.
4. Full disclosure by information-technology companies about the physical hazards to children of using their products.

5. A halt to the commercial hyping of harmful or useless technology for children.

6. A new emphasis on ethics, responsibility, and critical thinking in teaching older students about the personal and social effects of technology.

7. An immediate moratorium on the further introduction of computers in early childhood and elementary education, except for special cases of students with disabilities. Such a time-out is necessary to create the climate for the above recommendations to take place.

We've missed the boat, folks. If we had adopted those recommendations years ago, we could have avoided an epidemic of Glow Kid clinical disorders. But I have to believe that it's not too late.

Every parent can make the decision to limit and control his or her child's screen usage. Certainly, this can be done at home, but I'd also like to help empower concerned parents to take control of their children's screen exposure at the place where they spend most of their day—school.

This can be done even at schools that have bought into the tech-is-good myth and embrace the company line of "more screens for everyone." We as parents have the right to opt out of exposing our kids to tablets. Just as in the vaccine movement, we can present our children's school with a "screen opt out waiver" (I provide a template in the Appendix and on my www. drkardaras.com Web site). I've done so at my children's public elementary school—I've asked that they not expose them to tablets. With some prodding, they've agreed.

Sadly, it's not just the schools. Even the mental health and medical communities are grossly uninformed about the research that indicates the adverse effects of screens on kids. In an effort to raise awareness, I've given talks and presentations to many educators and mental health clinicians; some are totally tuned in to the problem, while others seem totally oblivious as they nervously keep checking their smartphones. This is where raising awareness, both in the media and in educational and clinical communities, can really be helpful.

The last, and perhaps the most important, suggestion is to organize to enact legislation.

The Alliance for Children had as its fourth recommendation, "Full disclosure by information-technology companies about the physical hazards to children of using their products." We can make that happen—we *need* to make that happen.

That's why I've generated a petition on Change.org that requests that legislation be enacted so that warning labels—like those on packages of cigarettes—be put on electronic screens. The proposed language would read: "Warning: Excess usage by children can lead to clinical disorders."

I've spoken to people in the media in order to create a campaign to get this message to Washington, D.C. It may not entirely solve the problem, but as we saw after the anti-cigarette media campaign and the adoption of warning labels, the problem was greatly reduced. According to the Campaign for Tobacco-Free Kids: "The 2012 Report of the Surgeon General, *Preventing Tobacco Use Among Youth and Young Adults,* concluded specifically and unequivocally: mass media campaigns 'prevent the initiation of tobacco use and reduce its prevalence among youth.'"[7]

I would like this book to serve as a catalyst for a similar Campaign for Screen-Free Kids. For all those interested, just go to my Web sites at www .drkardaras.com or www.Glowkids.com to get more information and to sign the petition.

DOES MY CHILD HAVE A SCREEN OR TECH ADDICTION PROBLEM?

Signs to look for:

- Is your child staying up later and later to stay on the computer?
- Does your child get fidgety, anxious and/or angry if they don't have their device?
- Is their tech usage negatively impacting their schoolwork, family life or other activities or interests?
- Is your child indicating that he or she has a difficult time getting virtual imagery out of their heads?
- Is your child dreaming of virtual imagery?
- Is your child hiding their screen usage or hiding their devices from you?
- Does your child seem to be having a more difficult time regulating their emotions (also known as emotional dysregulation)?
- Does your child seem more apathetic and bored more easily?
- Does your child seem perpetually tired yet also wired ("wired and tired")?
- Are teachers complaining that your child is falling asleep in school?

Any one or combination of symptoms or behaviors from the above list could be a red flag for screen or tech addiction. Talk to your child and encourage a healthy dialogue about both their screen usage and about your concerns. I have found it effective to show kids the research about the negative clinical and neurological effects of excessive screen exposure. If things get worse, reach out for professional help with therapists trained in screen addiction (see list in Appendix on p. 248).

Before going the route of the digital detox, you might want to consider these strategies:

- If you've decided that your child needs to have a phone, then get them a flip phone instead of a "mini computer" smartphone.
- Substitute gaming time with family time; this can include cooking together, playing board games, gardening, listening to music or taking a family walk or bike ride together.
- Require your child to do a physical activity (chore, exercise, etc.) for the same amount of time that they were online. Create that expectation: i.e., one hour online is an hour of yard work.

Let your kids be bored! This is when creativity occurs, and your kids can find their talents.

TECHNOLOGY ADDICTION THERAPISTS,
TREATMENT CENTERS, AND WEBSITES FOR CHILDREN AND YOUTH

CALIFORNIA

Jason Brand, LSCW, Psychotherapy and
    Consultation
JasonBrand.com
Ages Treated: 13–17 yrs
tel.: (510) 488-3093
email: jason@jasonbrand.com
Berkeley, California

Stephanie Brown, PhD
www.stephaniebrownphd.com
Ages Treated: Families
tel.: (650) 322-0943
email: info@stephaniebrownphd.com
Menlo Park, California

Victoria Dunckley, MD
www.drdunckley.com; www.
    ResetYourChildsBrain.com
Ages Treated: 0–17 yrs
email: info@drdunckley.com
Los Angeles, California

Kim McDaniel, Thrive Professional
    Coaching
http://www.thriveprofessionalcoaching
    .com/
Ages Treated: 0–17 yrs
tel.: (425) 208-1385
email: thriveprofessionalcoaching@
    gmail.com
Newport Beach, California

Min Tan, MFT, PhD
http://www.mintanmft.com/
Ages Treated: 0–17 yrs
tel.: (415) 265-1750
email: mintan.mft@gmail.com
San Francisco, California

Lynn Telford-Sahl, Addiction
    Counseling Modesto
http://www.addictionmodesto.com/
Ages Treated: 13–17 yrs
tel. (209) 492-8745
email: lynntelfordsahl@gmail.com
Modesto, California

COLORADO

Tracy Markle, Collegiate Coaching
    Services
http://collegiatecoachingservices.com/
Ages Treated: 11–17 yrs
tel.: (303) 635-6753
email: tracy@marklesolutions.com
Boulder, Colorado

NEW YORK

Dr. Nicholas Kardaras, Hamptons
    Discovery
www.hamptonsdiscovery.com; www
    .drkardaras.com
Ages Treated: 14–19 yrs
tel.: (631) 336-2684
East Hampton, New York

PENNSYLVANIA

Kimberly Young, Net Addiction
http://netaddiction.com/
Ages Treated: 0–17 yrs
tel.: (716) 375-2076
email: netaddiction.com@gmail.com
Bradford, Pennsylvania

UTAH

Ryan Anderson, Telos
http://www.telosrtc.com/
Ages Treated: 13–17 yrs
tel.: (801) 426-8800
email: ryan@telosrtc.com
Orem, Utah

Jason Calder, Outback Therapeutic
    Expeditions
outbacktreatment.com
Ages Treated: 13–17 yrs
tel.: (800) 817-1899
email: jcalder@outbacktreatment.com
Lehi, Utah

Gail Curran, Optimal Edu Options
http://optimaleduoptions.com/
Ages Treated: 8–17 yrs
tel.: (602) 904-1282
email: gail@OptiomalEduOptions.com
Peoria, Utah

WASHINGTON

Hilarie Cash, reSTART Center for
    Digital Technology Sustainability
http://www.netaddictionrecovery.com/
Ages Treated: 15–17 yrs
tel.: (800) 682-6934
email: connect@restartlife.com
Seattle, Washington

Ann Steel, Steel Counseling PLLC
http://www.steelcounseling.com/
Ages Treated: 12–17 yrs
tel. (206) 707-1683
email: steelcounselling@gmail.com
Bellevue, Washington

CANADA

Cris Rowan, Zone'in Programs Inc.
http://www.zonein.ca/
Ages Treated: 0–17 yrs
tel.: (888) 8ZONEIN
email: crowan@zonein.ca
Vancouver, British Columbia

Ryan Spodek
Ages Treated: 12–17 yrs
tel.: (416) 318-8424
email: rspodek@hotmail.com
Toronto, Ontario

DR. KARDARAS
SEAHAB

Transformative Tech Addiction Treatment
www.drkardaras.com

Seahab was developed by Dr. Nicholas Kardaras as an experiential method where tech-addicted kids go out on a fishing boat with therapists and an experienced crew. The Seahab therapeutic experience will allow the screen-teen to forge a profound natural and spiritual healing connection via the ocean; working collaboratively as a team, the once isolated tech-addicted young person is then able to better understand not only their addiction but themselves. They will fish, work together in groups, and engage in therapy, all in the transformative beauty of the sea. Seahab experiential retreats are scheduled as either day trips or multiple-day excursions from two to fourteen days.

These intensive experiential excursions can help break the cycle of screen addiction and kick-start a new, healthier way of experiencing the world. At the end of the day, the powerful immersive experience of the screen has to be replaced by a similarly compelling real-life experience in order for the teen to be willing to shift. Seahab can offer that powerful and immersive real-life experience—the wind blowing in the young person's hair, the smell of the sea air, and the overwhelming beauty of the ocean can all make a video game or Facebook not quite so appealing.

Seahab incorporates aspects of wilderness-style programs that have proven to be particularly effective treatment interventions with young people. Also known as Outdoor Behavioral Healthcare (OBH), these types of programs have grown rapidly over the last several decades and followed the migration of the Outward Bound program from Europe to the United States in the 1950s.

According to Dr. Steve DuBois, clinical director of Second Nature, a wilderness program in Utah: "A big part of this experience is helping students experience for themselves a greater sense of self-efficacy and internal locus of control." And wilderness therapy works. According to Dr. Steve Aldana, a researcher at Brigham Young University, 91.4 percent showed significant clinical improvement and, on average, participants improved significantly from intake to six months after completing treatment.

In a 2005 study that looked at wilderness clients two years after completion, Dr. Keith Russell found that more than 80 percent of parents perceived of wilderness as effective, 83 percent of adolescents were doing better, more than 90 percent of the adolescents contacted perceived their wilderness therapy as effective, and 86 percent of the participants were in high school or college or had graduated from high school and were working.

Seahab has been designed by Dr. Kardaras to be Outdoor Behavioral Healthcare (OBH) specifically tailored for screen addiction.

THE HEALTHY TECH DIET:
DIGITAL VEGETABLES VERSUS DIGITAL CANDY

The tech addiction treatment field has identified healthier screen usage versus more problematic screen exposure. Screen exposure that is purely titillating or of the adrenaline rush variety (and thus the most dopaminergic and addicting as well as hyper-stimulating) are considered Digital Candy. This would include things like video games, internet porn, mindless YouTube videos and compulsive social media and texting.

Healthier use of screen technologies are things such as doing research online, sending emails, and engaging in face-to-face Skype sessions.

Digital Candy	Digital Vegetables
Video Games	Internet Surfing to Research a Topic
Mindless YouTube Surfing	E-mailing
Internet Porn Watching	Educational YouTube Videos
Hyper-texting	Skyping a Friend
Hyper-Social Media	Creating Music or Following a Sports Team

For those who have crossed over into tech addiction, initially, *any* screen exposure—vegetable or candy—can lead to a relapse, which is why a "tech fast" or "digital detox" of four to six weeks is encouraged. This also allows the child's adrenal and central nervous system to re-set and to no longer be in a dysregulated state of fight-or-flight hyper-arousal that oftentimes accompanies screen addiction.

This slow reintegration of digital vegetables is an individual process. After the tech fast, some can go back to using a computer in a healthy way relatively quickly. For others, they can require up to a year or more.

SCHOOL TECHNOLOGY OPT-OUT LETTER

Dear Teacher and/or School Administrator,

I would like to respectfully request that all of my child's education and educational content be presented without the use of electronic devices. This includes the use of tablets, Chromebooks, laptops or desktop computers.

We wish to help nurture and support our child's educational, social, psychological and emotional development as much as possible and have become increasingly concerned with the potential detrimental aspects of screen technologies on young children.

We understand that you, as the school, have a responsibility to present our child with state-approved educational content and curriculum. We are in full agreement with that. But it is within our right as parents to ensure that the medium by which our children's education is being presented is safe and not problematic clinically or developmentally.

There has been a plethora of research indicating the adverse effect of electronic screens on children's attentional, cognitive and social development if they are exposed at too young of an age. Please feel free to refer to the Web site www.Glowkids.com for a full list of that peer-reviewed research.

Sincerely,

The Parent(s) of: _____

NOTES

CHAPTER ONE: INVASION OF THE GLOW KIDS

1. Angelica B. Ortiz de Gortari and Mark D. Griffiths, "Altered Visual Perception in Game Transfer Phenomena: An Empirical Self-Report Study," *International Journal of Human-Computer Interaction* 30, no. 2 (2014): 95–105.
2. Kristin Leutwyler, "Tetris Dreams: How and When People See Pieces from the Computer Game in Their Sleep Tells of the Role Dreaming Plays in Learning," *Scientific American,* October 16, 2000.
3. A. Leach, "Teen Net Addicts Pee in Bottles to Stay Glued to WoW," *Register* (UK), January 19, 2012.
4. Amanda Lenhart et al., "Teens, Video Games and Civics," *Pew Research Center: Internet, Science and Tech,* September 16, 2008.
5. Carl Jung, *The Collected Works of C.G. Jung* (Princeton, NJ: Princeton University Press, 1970), 598, 28.
6. Joseph Campbell, *The Hero with a Thousand Faces* (Novato, CA: New World Library, 1949).
7. Guangheng Dong, Yanbo Hu, and Xiao Lin, "Reward/Punishment Sensitivities Among Internet Addicts: Implications for Their Addictive Behaviors," *Progress in Neuro-Psychopharmacology & Biological Psychiatry* 46 (October 2013): 139–145, doi:10.1016/j.pnpbp.2013.07.007. See also S. Kühn, et al. "The Neural Basis of Video Gaming," *Translational Psychiatry* 1 (2011): e53, doi:10.1038/tp.2011.53.
8. M. J. Koepp et al., "Evidence for Striatal Dopamine Release During a Video Game," *Nature* 393, no. 6682 (May 21, 1998): 266–268. See also Guangheng Dong, Elise E Devito, Xiaoxia Du, and Zhuoya Cui, "Impaired Inhibitory Control in 'Internet Addiction Disorder': A Functional Magnetic Resonance Imaging Study," *Psychiatry Research* 203, nos. 2–3 (September 2012): 153–158, doi:10.1016/j.pscychresns.2012.02.001.
9. Angelica B. Ortiz de Gortari and Mark D. Griffiths, "Game Transfer Phenomena and Its Associated Factors: An Explanatory Empirical Online Survey Study," *Computers in Human Behavior* 51 (2015): 195–202.
10. Angelica B. Ortiz de Gortari and Mark D. Griffiths, "Automatic Mental Processes, Automatic Actions and Behaviours in Game Transfer Phenomena: An Empirical Self-Report Study Using Online Forum Data," *International Journal of Mental Health and Addiction* 12, no. 4 (August 2014): 432–445.
11. U. Nitzan, E. Shoshan, S. Lev-Ran, and S. Fennig, "Internet-RELATED Psychosis—a Sign of the Times," *Israeli Journal of Psychiatry and Related Sciences* 48, no. 3 (2011): 207–211.

12. Joel Gold and Ian Gold, *Suspicious Minds: How Culture Shapes Madness* (New York: Free Press, 2014).

13. Tony Dokoupil, "Is the Internet Making Us Crazy? What the New Research Says," *Newsweek,* July 9, 2012.

14. H. Takeuchi et al., "Impact of Videogame Play on the Brain's Microstructural Properties: Cross-Sectional and Longitudinal Analyses," *Molecular Psychiatry,* advance online publication (January 5, 2016), http:/dx.doi.org/10.1038/mp.2015.193 (accessed February 29, 2016).

15. Perry Klass, "Fixated by Screens, but Seemingly Nothing Else," *New York Times,* May 9, 2011.

16. American Academy of Pediatrics, Council on Communications and Media, "Media Violence," *Pediatrics* 124 (November 2009): 5.

17. Andrew Careaga, "Internet Usage May Signify Depression," *Missouri University of Science & Technology,* May 22, 2012.

18. Eddie Makuch, "Minecraft Passes 100 Million Registered Users, 14.3 Million Sales on PC," *Gamespot,* February 26, 2014.

19. Mary Fischer, "Manic Nation: Dr. Peter Whybrow says We're Addicted to Stress," *Pacific Standard,* June 19, 2012.

20. Lisa Guernsey, "An 'Educational' Video Game Has Taken Over My House," *Slate,* August 6, 2012.

21. Victoria Dunckley, "Electronic Screen Syndrome: An Unrecognized Disorder?" *Psychology Today,* July 23, 2012.

22. Leslie Alderman, "Does Technology Cause ADHD?" *Everyday Health,* August 3, 2010.

23. Carlo Rotella, "No Child Left Untableted," *New York Times,* September 12, 2013.

24. Michele Molnar, "News Corp. Sells Amplify to Joel Klein, Other Executives," *Education Week,* October 7, 2015.

25. Jason Russell, "How Video Games Can Transform Education," *Washington Examiner,* April 30, 2015.

26. Richard Louv, *Last Child in the Woods* (New York: Workman Publishing, 2005).

27. Edward O. Wilson, *Biophilia* (Cambridge, MA: Harvard University Press, 1986).

28. Susan Lang, "A Room With a View Helps Rural Children Deal With Stresses, Cornell Researchers Report," *Cornell Chronicle,* April 24, 2003.

29. David Mitchell, "Nature Deficit Disorder," *Waldorf Library: Research Bulletin* 11, no. 2 (Spring 2006).

30. Ibid.

31. Lowell Monke, "Video Games: A Critical Analysis," *ENCOUNTER: Education for Meaning and Social Justice* 22, no. 3 (Autumn 2009): 1–13, www.allianceforchildhood.org/sites/allianceforchildhood.org/files/file/MONKE223.pdf.

32. NickelsandCrimes, "The Oregon Trail," YouTube video, 4:45, September 2, 2007, https://www.youtube.com/watch?v=ht8GWOwdc30.

33. Michael Kneissle, "Research into Changes in Brain Formation," Waldorf Library, http://www.waldorflibrary.org/images/stories/Journal_Articles/RB2206.pdf.

34. Tim Carmody, "'What's Wrong with Education Cannot Be Fixed by Technology'—The Other Steve Jobs," *Wired,* January, 17, 2012.

35. Amy Fleming, "Screen Time v Play Time: What Tech Leaders Won't Let Their Own Kids Do," *Guardian,* May 23, 2015.

36. Lori Woellhaf, "Do Young Children Need Computers?" *The Montessori Society,* http://www.montessorisociety.org.uk/article/do-young-children-need-computers.

37. Ibid.
38. Marcia Mikulak, *The Children of A Bambara Village*, 1991.
39. Elisabeth Grunelius et al., "The Sensible Child," *Online Waldorf Library* no. 56 (Spring/Summer 2009).
40. Ibid.

CHAPTER TWO: BRAVE NEW E-WORLD

1. Neil Postman, *Amusing Ourselves to Death* (New York: Penguin, 1985).
2. Neil Postman, *The Disappearance of Childhood* (New York: Random House, 1982).
3. Gary Cross, *Men to Boys* (New York: Columbia University Press, 2010).
4. Mark Banschick, "Our Avoidant Boys," *Psychology Today*, September 7, 2012.
5. Plato, *Phaedrus*.
6. Doug Hyun Han, Sun Mi Kim, Sujin Bae, Perry F. Renshaw, Jeffrey S. Anderson, "Brain Connectivity and Psychiatric Comorbidity in Adolescents with Internet Gaming Disorder," *Addiction Biology* (2015), doi: 10.1111/adb.12347.
7. Matthew Ebbatson, "The Loss of Manual Flying Skills in Pilots of Highly Automated Airliners," doctoral thesis, Cranfield University, 2009.
8. Katherine Woolett and Eleanor Maguire, "Aquiring 'the Knowledge' of London's Layout Drives Structural Brain Changes," *Current Biology* 21, no. 24-2 (December 20, 2011): 2109–2114.

CHAPTER THREE: DIGITAL DRUGS AND THE BRAIN

1. Hunter Hoffman et al., "Virtual Reality as an Adjunctive Non-Pharmacologic Analgesic for Acute Burn Pain During Medical Procedures," *Annals of Behavioral Medicine,* January 25, 2011, doi:10.1007/s12160-010-9248-7.
2. M. J. Koepp et al., "Evidence for Striatal Dopamine Release during a Video Game," *Nature* 393, no. 6682 (May 21, 1998): 266–268.
3. "The Genetics of Addiction," Addictions and Recovery.org, http://www.addictionsandrecovery.org/is-addiction-a-disease.htm.
4. Merriel Mandell, "Etiology of Addiction: Addiction as a Disorder of Attachment," 2011, http://etiologyofaddiction.com/attachment-theory/.
5. Howard Shaffer et al., "Toward a Syndrome Model of Addiction: Multiple Expressions, Common Etiology," *Harvard Review of Psychiatry* 12 (2004): 367–374.
6. "The Addicted Brain," Harvard Mental Health Letter, Harvard Health Publications, Harvard Medical School, June 9, 2009.
7. Daniel Goleman, "Scientists Pinpoint Brain Irregularities In Drug Addicts," *New York Times,* June 26, 1990.
8. Koepp et al., "Evidence for Striatal Dopamine Release during a Video Game."
9. James Delahunty, "Call of Duty Played for 25 Billion Hours, with 32.3 Quadrillion Shots Fired," *AfterDawn*, August 14, 2013.
10. Mark Wheeler, "In memoriam: Dr. George Bartzokis, Neuroscientist Who Developed the 'Myelin Model' of Brain Disease," *UCLA Newsroom*, September 10, 2014.
11. Anonymous, "Researchers: Does Brain 'Fat' Dictate Risky Behavior?" *Paramus Post*, March 13, 2006.
12. George Bartzokis et al., "Brain Maturation May be Arrested in Chronic Cocaine Addicts," *Biological Psychiatry* 51, no. 8 (April 15, 2002): 605–611.
13. Fuchun Lin, Yan Zhou, Yasong Du, Lindi Qin, Zhimin Zhao, Jianrong Xu, and Hao Lei, "Abnormal White Matter Integrity in Adolescents with Internet

Addiction Disorder: A Tract-Based Spatial Statistics Study," *PloS ONE* 7, no. 1 (2012): e30253, doi:10.1371/journal.pone.0030253.

14. Soon-Beom Hong, Andrew Zalesky, Luca Cocchi, Alex Fornito, Eun-Jung Choi, Ho-Hyun Kim, Jeong-Eun Suh, Chang-Dai Kim, Jae-Won Kim, and Soon-Hyung Yi, "Decreased Functional Brain Connectivity in Adolescents with Internet Addiction," *PLoS ONE* 8, no. 2 (February 25, 2013): e57831, doi:10.1371/journal.pone.0057831.

15. C. Y. Wee, Z. Zhao, P-T Yap, G. Wu, F. Shi, T. Price, Y. Du, J. Xu, Y. Zhou, "Disrupted Brain Functional Network in Internet Addiction Disorder: A Resting-State Functional Magnetic Resonance Imaging Study," *PLoS ONE* 9, no. 9 (2014): e107306, doi:10.1371/journal.pone.010730.

16. Y. Wang, T. Hummer, W. Kronenberger, K. Mosier, V. Mathews, "One Week of Violent Video Game Play Alters Prefrontal Activity," *Radiological Society of North America*, Scientific Assembly and Annual Meeting, Chicago, Illinois, November 26–December 2, 2011, http://archive.rsna.org/2011/11004116.html (accessed March 24, 2016).

17. Indiana University School of Medicine, "Violent Video Games Alter Brain Function in Young Men," *ScienceDaily*, December 1, 2011, www.sciencedaily.com /releases/2011/11/111130095251.htm.

18. Sadie Whitelocks, "Computer Games Leave Children with 'Dementia' Warns Top Neurologist," *Daily Mail*, October 14, 2011.

19. Bruce Alexander, "Addiction: The View from Rat Park," www.Brucekalexander .com, 2010, http://www.brucekalexander.com/articles-speeches/rat-park/148 -addiction-the-view-from-rat-park.

CHAPTER FOUR: INTERVIEW WITH DR. DOAN

1. Kevin Johnson, Rick Jervis, and Richard Wolf, "Aaron Alexis, Navy Yard Shooting Supsect: Who is He?" *USA Today*, September 16, 2013.

2. E. Eickhoff, K. Yung, D. L. Davis, F. Bishop, W. P. Klam, A. P. Doan, "Excessive Video Game Use, Sleep Deprivation, and Poor Work Performance Among U.S. Marines Treated in a Military Mental Health Clinic: A Case Series," *Mil Med.* 180, no. 7 (July 2015): e839-843, doi: 10.7205/MILMED-D-14-00597, PMID: 26126258. See also A. Voss, H. Cash, S. Hurdiss, F. Bishop, W. P. Klam, A. P. Doan, "Case Report: Internet Gaming Disorder Associated With Pornography Use," *Yale J Biol Med.* 88, no. 3 (September 3, 2015): 319-324, eCollection 2015.

CHAPTER FIVE: THE BIG DISCONNECT

1. Johann Hari, "Everything You Think You Know about Addiction Is Wrong," TED GlobalLondon, 14:42, June 2015, https://www.ted.com/talks/johann_hari _everything_you_think_you_know_about_addiction_is_wrong?language=en.

2. Internet Live Stats, website, www.internetlivestats.com.

3. "19 Text Messaging Stats that Will Blow You Away," www.teckst.com, https:// teckst.com/19-text-messaging-stats-that-will-blow-your-mind/.

4. Aaron Smith, "Americans and Text Messaging," *Pew Research Center*, September 19, 2011.

5. Jean M. Twenge, "Time Period and Birth Cohort Differences in Depressive Symptoms in the U.S., 1982–2013," *Social Indicators Research* 121, no. 2 (June 2014): 437–454.

6. Thalia Farchian, "Depression: Our Modern Epidemic," *Marina Times,* April 2016.

7. Holly Swartz and Bruce Rollman, "Managing the Global Burden of Depression: Lessons from the Developing World," *World Psychiatry* 2, no. 3 (October 2003): 162–163.

8. Tara Parker-Pope, "Suicide Rates Rise Sharply in U.S.," *New York Times,* May 2, 2013.

9. Michael Bond, "How Extreme Isolation Warps the Mind," *BBC Future,* May 14, 2014.

10. Michael Mechanic, "What Extreme Isolation Does to Your Mind," *Mother Jones,* October 18, 2012.

11. Andy Worthington, "BBC Torture Experiment Replicates Guantanamo and Secret Prisons: How to Lose Your Mind in 48 Hours," *Andy Worthington Blog,* January 27, 2008.

12. Boris Kozlow, "The Adoption History Project," University of Oregon, February 24, 2012, http://pages.uoregon.edu/adoption/studies/HarlowMLE.htm.

13. Saul McLeod, "Attachment Theory," *Simply Psychology,* 2009.

14. Winifred Gallagher, *New: Understanding Our Need for Novelty and Change* (New York: Penguin, 2011).

15. Mary Fischer, "Manic Nation: Dr. Peter Whybrow Says We're Addicted to Stress," *Pacific Standard,* June 19, 2012.

16. Mike Segar, "U.S. Students Suffering from Internet Addiction: Study," *Reuters,* April 23, 2010.

17. Kelly M. Lister-Landman et al., "The Role of Compulsive Texting in Adolescents' Academic Functioning," *Psychology of Popular Media Culture,* advance online publication, October 5, 2015, http://dx.doi.org/10.1037/ppm0000100 (accessed February 29, 2016).

18. Samantha Murphy Kelly, "Is Too Much Texting Giving You 'Text Neck'? *Mashable,* January 20, 2012.

19. Tracy Pederson, "Hyper-Texting Associated with Health Risks for Teens," *PsychCentral,* October 6, 2015.

20. Maria Konnikova, "The Limits of Friendship," *New Yorker,* October 7, 2014.

21. B. Gonçalves, N. Perra, and A.Vespignani, "Modeling Users' Activity on Twitter Networks: Validation of Dunbar's Number," *PLoS ONE* 6, no. 8 (2011): e22656, doi:10.1371/journal.pone.0022656.

22. Mellissa Carroll, "UH Study Links Facebook Usage to Depressive Symptoms," University of Houston, April 6, 2015, http://www.uh.edu/news-events/stories/2015/April/040415FaceookStudy.php.

23. Christina Sagliogou and Tobias Greitemeyer, "Facebook's Emotional Consequences: Why Facebook Causes a Decrease in Mood and Why People Still Use It," *Computers in Human Behavior* 35 (June 2014): 359–363.

24. Julia Hormes, Brianna Kearns, and C. Alix Timko, "Craving Facebook? Behavioral Addiction to Online Social Networking and Its Association with Emotional Regulation Deficits," *Addiction* 109, no. 12 (December 2014): 2079–2088.

25. Charlotte Blease, "Too Many 'Friends,' Too Few 'Likes'? Evolutionary Psychology and 'Facebook Depression,'" *Review of General Psychiatry* 19, no. 1 (2015): 1–13.

26. John Suler, "The Online Disinhibition Effect," *Cyber Psychology and Behavior* 7, no. 3 (2004).

27. Alex Whiting, "Tech Savvy Sex Traffickers Stay Ahead of Authorities as Lure Teens Online," *Reuters,* November 15, 2015.

28. Phil McGraw, "How a Social Media Post Led a Teen into Sex Trafficking," *Huffington Post,* May 1, 2015.

29. Louis Phillippe Beland and Richard Murphy, "Ill Communication: Technology, Distraction and Student Performance," *Center for Economic Performance, London School of Economics,* May 2015.

30. Jamie Doward, "Schools that Ban Mobile Phones See Better Academic Results," *Guardian,* May 16, 2015.

31. Greg Graham, "Cell Phones in Classrooms? No! Students Need to Pay Attention," *Mediashift,* September 21, 2011.

CHAPTER SIX: CLINICAL DISORDERS

1. Victoria Dunckley, "Electronic Screen Syndrome: An Unrecognized Disorder?" *Psychology Today,* July 23, 2012.

2. Victoria Dunckley, "Screentime is Making Kids Moody, Crazy and Lazy," *Psychology Today,* August 18, 2015.

3. Victoria Dunckley, "Video Game Rage," *Psychology Today,* December 1, 2012.

4. Amy Krain Roy, Vasco Lopes, and Rachel Klein, "Disruptive Mood Dysregulation Disorder: A New Diagnostic Approach to Chronic Irritability in Youth," *American Journal of Psychiatry* 171 (2014): 918–924.

5. Edward L. Swing, Douglas A. Gentile, Craig A. Anderson, and David A. Walsh, "Television and Video Game Exposure and the Development of Attention Problems," *Pediatrics,* published online July 5, 2010.

6. Meagen Voss, "More Screen Time Means More Attention Problems in Kids," NPR, July 7, 2010.

7. Indiana University School of Medicine, "Violent Video Games Alter Brain Function in Young Men," *ScienceDaily,* December 1, 2011, www.sciencedaily.com /releases/2011/11/111130095251.htm.

8. Margaret Rock, "A Nation of Kids with Gadgets and ADHD," *Time,* July 12, 2013.

9. John Eisenberg, "Son Aims to Make a Name for Himself," *Baltimore Sun,* April 16, 2003.

10. Marguerite Reardon, "WHO: Cell Phones May Cause Cancer," *C/NET,* May 31, 2011.

11. Danielle Dellorto, "WHO: Cell Phone Use Can Increase Possible Cancer Risk," CNN, May 31, 2011.

12. John Cole, "EMF Readings from Various Devices We Use Every Day," *Natural News,* May 26, 2008.

13. Josh Harkinson, "Scores of Scientists Raise Alarm about the Long Term Effects of Cell Phones," *Mother Jones,* May 11, 2015.

14. "Damaging Effects of EMF Exposure on a Cell," *Cancer, EMF Protection and Safety,* February 27, 2016.

CHAPTER SEVEN: MONKEY SEE, MONKEY DO

1. Goerge Comstock and Haejung Paik, "The Effects of Television Violence on Antisocial Behavior: A Meta-Analysis," *Communication Research* 21, no. 4 (August 1994): 516–46.

2. Kevin Browne and Catherine Hamilton-Giachritsis, "The Influence of Violent Media on Children and Adolescents: A Public-Health Approach," *Lancet* 365, no. 9460 (February 19, 2005): 702–710.

3. American Academy of Pediatrics, American Academy of Child and Adolescent Psychiatry, American Psychological Association, American Medical Association, American Academy of Family Physicians, American Psychiatric Association, "Joint Statement on the Impact of Entertainment Violence on Children: Congressional Public Health Summit—July 26, 2000," www.aap.org/advocacy/releases/jstmtevc.htm (accessed February 29, 2016).

4. M. E. O'Toole, *The School Shooter: A Threat Assessment Perspective* (Quantico, VA: Federal Bureau of Investigation, U.S. Department of Justice; 2000).

5. C. Anderson et al., "The Influence of Media Violence on Youth," *Psychological Science in the Public Interest* 4, no. 3 (2003): 81–110.

6. Federal Communications Commission, "In the Matter of Violent Television Programming and Its Impact on Children: Statement of Commissioner Deborah Taylor Tate,"MB docket No. 04–261, April 25, 2007, http://hraunfoss.fcc.gov/edocs_public/attachmatch/FCC-07-50A1.pdf (accessed February 29, 2016).

7. American Academy of Pediatrics, Council on Communications and Media, "Media Violence," *Pediatrics* 124 (November 2009): 5.

8. C. Barlett, R. Harris, and R. Baldassaro, "Longer You Play, The More Hostile You Feel: Examination of First Person Shooter Video Games and Aggression during Video Game Play," *Aggressive Behavior* 33, no. 6 (June 27, 2007): 486–497.

9. Joseph Dominick, "Videogames, Television Violence, and Aggression in Teenagers," *Journal of Communication* 34, no. 2 (1984): 136–147.

CHAPTER EIGHT: VIDEO GAMES AND AGGRESSION

1. Craig Anderson et al., "Longitudinal Effects of Violent Video Games on Aggression in Japan and the United States," *Pediatrics* 122, no. 5 (November 2008).

2. Jack Hollingdale and Tobias Greitemeyer, "The Effect of Online Violent Video Games on Levels of Aggression," *PLoS ONE* 9, no. 11 (2014): e111790, doi:10.1371/journal.pone.0111790.

3. C. Barlett, R. Harris, and R. Baldassaro, "Longer You Play, The More Hostile You Feel: Examination of First Person Shooter Video Games and Aggression During Video Game Play," *Aggressive Behavior* 33, no. 6 (June 27, 2007): 486–497.

4. M. E. Ballard and J. R. Wiest, "Mortal Kombat: The Effect of Violent Videogame Play on Males' Hostility and Cardiovascular Responding," *Journal of Applied Social Psychology* 26, no. 8 (April 1996): 717–730, doi: 10.1111/j.1559-1816.1996.tb02740.x.

5. Tobias Greitemeyer and Neil McLatchie, "Denying Humanness to Others: A Newly Discovered Mechanism by Which Violent Video Games Increase Aggressive Behavior," *Psychological Science* 22, no. 5 (May 2011): 659–665.

6. Jack Hollingdale and Tobias Greitemeyer, "The Changing Face of Aggression: The Effect of Personalized Avatars in a Violent Video Game on Levels of Aggressive Behavior," *Journal of Applied Social Psychology* 43, no. 9 (September 2013): 1862–1868.

7. Indiana University School of Medicine, "Violent Video Games Alter Brain Function in Young Men," *ScienceDaily* December 1, 2011, www.sciencedaily.com/releases/2011/11/111130095251.htm.

8. Craig Anderson, Akiko Shibuya, Nobuko Ihori, Edward Swing, Brad Bushman, Akira Sakamoto, Hannah Rothstein, and Muniba Saleem, "Violent Video Game Effects on Aggression, Empathy, and Prosocial Behavior in Eastern and Western Countries: A Meta-Analytic Review," *Psychological Bulletin* 136, no. 2 (March 2010): 151–173.

9. Chris Ferguson, "Does Media Violence Predict Societal Violence? It Depends on What You Look At and When," *Journal of Communication* 65 (2014): e1–e22, doi: 10.1111/jcom.12129.

10. Jason Ryan, "Gangs Blamed for 80% of U.S. Crimes," *ABC News*, January 30, 2009.

11. Tracy Miller, "Video Game Addiction and Other Internet Compulsive Disorders Mask Depresssion, Anxiety, Learning Disabilities," *New York Daily News*, March 25, 2013.

CHAPTER NINE: RIPPED FROM THE HEADLINES

1. "Daniel Petric Killed Mother, Shot Father Because They Took Halo 3 Video Game, Prosecutors Say," *Cleveland Plain Dealer*, December 15, 2008, http://blog .cleveland.com/metro/2008/12/boy_killed_mom_and_shot_dad_ov.html.

2. Meredith Bennett-Smith, "Nathon Brooks, Teen Who Allegedly Shot Parents Over Video Games, Charged With Attempted Murder," *Huffington Post*, March 13, 2013, http://www.huffingtonpost.com/2013/03/13/nathon-brooks-teen-shot -parents-video-games_n_2868805.html.

3. Tony Smith, "'Grand Theft Auto' Cop Killer Found Guilty," *Register* (UK), August 11, 2005, http://www.theregister.co.uk/2005/08/11/gta_not_guilty/.

4. Martha Irvine, "A Troubled Gaming Addict Takes His Life," Associated Press, May 25, 2002, http://www.freerepublic.com/focus/news/689637/posts.

5. Lauren Russell, "Police: 8-Year-Old Shoots, Kills Elderly Caregiver after Playing Video Game," CNN Monday, August 26, 2013, http://www.cnn.com /2013/08/25/us/louisiana-boy-kills-grandmother/.

6. Abigail Jones, "The Girls Who Tried to Kill for Slender Man," *Newsweek*, August 13, 2014, http://www.newsweek.com/2014/08/22/girls-who-tried-kill-slender -man-264218.html.

CHAPTER TEN: THE NEWTOWN MASSACRE

1. Tom McCarthy, "Shooting in Newtown, Connecticut School Leaves 28 Dead," *Guardian*, December 14, 2012, http://www.theguardian.com/world /us-news-blog/2012/dec/14/newtown-connecticut-school-shooting-live; Daniel Bates and Helen Pow, "Lanza's Descent to Madness and Murder: Sandy Hook Shooter Notched Up 83,000 Online Kills Including 22,000 'Head Shots' Using Violent Games to Train Himself for His Massacre," *Daily Mail*, December 1, 2013, http://www.dailymail.co.uk/news/article-2516427/Sandy-Hook-shooter -Adam-Lanza-83k-online-kills-massacre.html.

2. Matthew Lysiak, *Newtown: An American Tragedy* (New York: Gallery, 2013).

3. Office of the Child Advocate, State of Connecticut, "Shooting at Sandy Hook Elementary School," Report of the Office of the Child Advocate, November 21, 2014, http://www.ct.gov/oca/lib/oca/sandyhook11212014.pdf.

4. Office of the State's Attorney Judicial District of Danbury, "Report of the State's Attorney for the Judicial District of Danbury on the Shootings at Sandy Hook Elementary School and 36 Yogananda Street, Newtown, Connecticut," December 14, 2012, http://www.ct.gov/csao/lib/csao/Sandy_Hook_Final_Report.pdf.

5. Mike Lupica, "Morbid Find Suggests Murder-Obsessed Gunman Adam Lanza Plotted Newtown, Conn.'s Sandy Hook Massacre for Years," *New York Daily News*, March 25, 2013.

CHAPTER ELEVEN:
ETAN PATZ AND THE END OF INNOCENCE—AND OUTDOOR PLAY

1. Project Jason: Guidance for Families of the Missing, http://projectjason.org /forums/topic/126-missing-children-issues-general-news/.
2. Hanna Rosin, "The Overprotected Kid," *Atlantic Monthly*, April 2014.
3. Michael Wilson, "The Legacy of Etan Patz: Wary Children Who Became Watchful Parents," *New York Times*, May 8, 2015.
4. Lenore Skenazy, *Free Range Kids: How to Raise Safe, Self-Reliant Children* (New York: Jossey-Bass, 2010).

CHAPTER TWELVE: FOLLOW THE MONEY

1. "Education Technology Worth 59.9 Billion by 2018," Wattpad, January 31, 2014, https://www.wattpad.com/story/12102629-education-technology-ed-tech -market-worth-59-90.
2. Richard Rothstein, "Joel Klein's Misleading Autobiography," *American Prospect*, October 11, 2012.
3. Diane Ravitch, "*New York Post* Reveals Another Part of the 'Bloomberg-Klein' Failure Factory Legacy," *Diane Ravitch's Blog: A Site to Discuss Better Education For All*, February 23, 2014.
4. Bob Herbert, "The Plot Against Public Education: How Millionaires and Billionaires are Ruining Our Schools," *Politico*, October 6, 2014.
5. Georg Szalai, "Former NYC School Chancellor to Earn $2 Million a Year as News Corp. Exec," *Hollywood Reporter*, January 4, 2011.
6. "The Impact of Digital Technology on Learning: A Summary for the Education Endowment Foundation," Durham University, November 2012, https:// v1.educationendowmentfoundation.org.uk/uploads/pdf/The_Impact_of_Digi tal_Technologies_on_Learning_(2012).pdf.
7. Richard Clark, "Reconsidering Research on Learning from Media," *Review of Educational Research* 53(1983): 445–459.
8. Jason Rogers, Alex Usher, and Edyta Kaznowska, *The State of e-Learning in Canadian Universities, 2011: If Students are Digital Natives, Why Don't They Like e-Learning?* (Toronto, ON: Higher Education Strategy Associates, 2011), higheredstrategy .com/wp-content/uploads/2011/09/InsightBrief42.pdf.
9. Michele Molnar, "News Corp. Sells Amplify to Joel Klein, Other Executives," *Education Week*, October 7, 2015.
10. Howard Blume, "Federal Grand Jury Subpoenaed Documents from L.A. Unified," *Los Angeles Times*, December 2, 2014.
11. Annie Gilbertson, "The LA School iPad Scandal: What You Need to Know," NPR/Ed, August 27, 2014.
12. "Another Publishing Exec Caught Dishing Dirt on Common Core," ProjectVeritas.com, January 13, 2016.
13. Natasha Bita, "Computers in Class a 'Scandalous Waste': Sydney Grammar Head," *Australian*, March 26, 2016.
14. Ann Mangen et al., "Reading Linear Texts on Paper versus Computer Screen: Effects on Reading Comprehension," *International Journal of Educational Research* 58 (2013): 61–68.
15. Ferris Jabr, "The Reading Brain in the Digital Age: The Science of Paper vs. Screens," *Scientific American*, April 11, 2013.

16. Colleen Cordes and Edward Miller, *Fool's Gold: A Critical Look at Computers in Childhood* (New York: Alliance for Childhood, 2000).

17. Carlo Rotella, "No Child Left Untableted," *New York Times,* September 12, 2013.

18. Chris Mercogliano and Kim Debus, "An Interview with Joseph Chilton Pearce," *Journal of Family Life* 5, no. 1 (1999).

19. Mona Mohammad and Heyam Mohammad, "Computer Integration into the Early Childhood Curriculum," *Education* 133, no. 1 (Fall 2012).

CHAPTER THIRTEEN: IT'S AN E-WORLD

1. David Rose, *Enchanted Objects* (New York: Scribner, 2015).

2. Abhijit, "Microsoft Hologram' This is the Future of Computing. Mind blowing Combination of Virtual reality and Augmented reality," *Infomatic Cool Stuff,* April 30, 2015.

3. Alex Kipman, "A Futuristic Vision of the Age of Holograms," TED Talk, 19:05, Vancouver, February 2016, https://www.ted.com/talks/alex_kipman _the_dawn_of_the_age_of_holograms?language=en.

4. Jerry Bonner, "Esports Phenomenon to Be Examined Further on HBO's 'Real Sports with Bryant Gumbel," *HNGN: Headline & Global News,* October 19, 2014.

5. Jeff Grubb, "e-Sports Already Worth $748M but It Will Reach 1.9 B by 2018," *Venture Beat,* October 28, 2015.

6. Cecillia Kang, "He Wants to Make It Playing Video Games on Twitch. But Will People Pay to Watch?" *Washington Post,* December 31, 2014.

CHAPTER 14: THE SOLUTION

1. Plato, *The Republic.*

2. Bruce Alexander, "Addiction: The View from Rat Park," www. Brucekalexander .com, 2010, http://www.brucekalexander.com/articles-speeches/rat-park/148 -addiction-the-view-from-rat-park.

3. Edward O. Wilson, *Biophilia* (Cambridge, MA: Harvard University Press, 1986).

4. Richard Louv, *Last Child in the Woods* (New York: Workman Publishing, 2005).

5. Tori DeAngelis, "Therapy Gone Wild," *American Psychological Association* 44, no. 8 (September 2013): 48.

6. Colleen Cordes and Edward Miller, *Fool's Gold: A Critical Look at Computers in Childhood* (New York: Alliance for Childhood, 2000).

7. Campaign for Tobacco-Free Kids, website, http://www.tobaccofreekids.org/.

REFERENCES

Alderman, Leslie. "Does Technology Cause ADHD?" *Everyday Health,* August 3, 2010.

Alexander, Bruce. "Addiction: The View from Rat Park." www.Brucekalexander.com, 2010.

American Academy of Pediatrics, American Academy of Child and Adolescent Psychiatry, American Psychological Association, American Medical Association, American Academy of Family Physicians, and American Psychiatric Association. "Joint Statement on the Impact of Entertainment Violence on Children: Congressional Public Health Summit—July 26, 2000."

American Academy of Pediatrics, Council on Communications and Media. "Media Violence." *Pediatrics* 124 (November 2009): 5.

Anderson, C., L. Berkowitz, E. Donnerstein, et al. "The Influence of Media Violence on Youth." *Psychological Science in the Public Interest* 4, no. 3 (2003): 81–110.

Anderson, Craig et al. "Longitudinal Effects of Violent Video Games on Aggression in Japan and the United States." *Pediatrics* 122, no. 5 (November 2008).

Anderson, Craig, Akiko Shibuya, Nobuko Ihori, Edward Swing, Brad Bushman, Akira Sakamoto, Hannah Rothstein, and Muniba Saleem. "Violent Video Game Effects on Aggression, Empathy, and Prosocial Behavior in Eastern and Western Countries: A Meta-Analytic Review." *Psychological Bulletin* 136, no. 2 (March 2010): 151–173.

Ballard, M. E., and J. R. Wiest. "Mortal Kombat: The Effect of Violent Videogame Play on Males' Hostility and Cardiovascular Responding." *Journal of Applied Social Psychology* 26, no. 8 (April 1996): 717–730.

Banschick, Mark. "Our Avoidant Boys." *Psychology Today,* September 7, 2012.

Barlett, C., R. Harris, and R. Baldassaro. "Longer You Play, The More Hostile You Feel: Examination of First Person Shooter Video Games and Aggression during Video Game Play." *Aggressive Behavior* 33, no. 6 (June 27, 2007): 486–497.

Bartzokis, George, et al. "Brain Maturation May be Arrested in Chronic Cocaine Addicts." *Biological Psychiatry* 51, no. 8 (April 15, 2002): 605–611.

Beland, Louis Phillippe, and Richard Murphy. "Ill Communication: Technology, Distraction and Student Performance." *Center for Economic Performance, London School of Economics* (May 2015).

Bita, Natasha. "Computers in Class a 'Scandalous Waste': Sydney Grammar Head." *Australian,* March 26, 2016.

Blease, Charlotte. "Too Many 'Friends,' Too Few 'Likes'? Evolutionary Psychology and 'Facebook Depression.'" *Review of General Psychiatry* 19, no. 1 (2015): 1–13.

Bond, Michael. "How Extreme Isolation Warps the Mind." *BBC Future,* May 14, 2014.

Bonner, Jerry. "E-sports Phenomenon to Be Examined Further on HBO's 'Real Sports with Bryant Gumbel." *HNGN: Headline & Global News,* October 19, 2014.

Browne, Kevin, and Catherine Hamilton-Giachritsis. "The Influence of Violent Media on Children and Adolescents: A Public-Health Approach." *Lancet* 365, no. 9460 (February 19, 2005): 702–710.

Campbell, Joseph. *The Hero with a Thousand Faces* (Novato, CA: New World Library, 1949).

Careaga, Andrew. "Internet Usage May Signify Depression." Missouri University of Science and Technology, May 22, 2012.

Carmody, Tim. "'What's Wrong with Education Cannot Be Fixed by Technology'— The Other Steve Jobs." *Wired,* January, 17, 2012.

Carroll, Mellissa. "UH Study Links Facebook Usage to Depressive Symptoms." University of Houston, April 6, 2015.

Clark, Richard. "Reconsidering Research on Learning from Media." *Review of Educational Research* 53(1983): 445–459.

Cole, John. "EMF Readings from Various Devices We Use Every Day." *Natural News,* May 26, 2008.

Comstock, George, and Haejung Paik. "The Effects of Television Violence on Antisocial Behavior: A Meta-Analysis." *Communication Research* 21, no. 4 (August 1994): 516–46.

Cordes, Colleen, and Edward Miller. *Fool's Gold: A Critical Look at Computers in Childhood* (New York: Alliance for Childhood, 2000).

Cross, Gary. *Men to Boys* (New York: Columbia University Press, 2010).

DeAngelis, Tori. "Therapy Gone Wild." *American Psychological Association* 44, no. 8 (September 2013): 48.

de Gortari, Angelica B. Ortiz, and Mark D. Griffiths. "Game Transfer Phenomena and Its Associated Factors: An Explanatory Empirical Online Survey Study." *Computers in Human Behavior* 51 (2015): 195–202.

———. "Altered Visual Perception in Game Transfer Phenomena: An Empirical Self-Report Study." *International Journal of Human-Computer Interaction* 30, no. 2 (2014): 95–105.

———. "Automatic Mental Processes, Automatic Actions and Behaviours in Game Transfer Phenomena: An Empirical Self-Report Study Using Online Forum Data." *International Journal of Mental Health and Addiction* 12, no. 4 (August 2014): 432–45.

Dellorto, Danielle. "WHO: Cell Phone Use Can Increase Possible Cancer Risk." CNN, May 31, 2011.

Dokoupil, Tony. "Is the Internet making us Crazy? What the New Research Says." *Newsweek,* July 9, 2012.

Dominick, Joseph. "Videogames, Television Violence, and Aggression in Teenagers." *Journal of Communication* 34, no. 2 (1984): 136–147.

Dong, Guangheng, Yanbo Hu, and Xiao Lin. "Reward/Punishment Sensitivities among Internet Addicts: Implications for Their Addictive Behaviors." *Progress in Neuro-Psychopharmacology & Biological Psychiatry* 46 (October 2013): 139–145.

Dong, Guangheng, Elise E. Devito, Xiaoxia Du, and Zhuoya Cui. "Impaired Inhibitory Control in 'Internet Addiction Disorder': A Functional Magnetic Resonance Imaging Study." *Psychiatry Research* 203, nos. 2–3 (September 2012): 153–158.

Doward, Jamie. "Schools that Ban Mobile Phones See Better Academic Results." *Guardian,* May 16, 2015.

Duncan, D., A. Hoekstra, and B. Wilcox. "Digital Devices, Distraction, and Student Performance: Does In-Class Cell Phone Use Reduce Learning?" *Astronomy Education Review* 11 (2012).

Dunckley, Victoria. "Screentime Is Making Kids Moody, Crazy and Lazy." *Psychology Today*, August 18, 2015.

———. "Video Game Rage." *Psychology Today*, December 1, 2012.

———. "Electronic Screen Syndrome: An Unrecognized Disorder?" *Psychology Today*, July 23, 2012.

Ebbatson, Matthew. "The Loss of Manual Flying Skills in Pilots of Highly Automated Airliners." Doctoral thesis, Cranfield University, 2009.

Farchian, Thalia. "Depression: Our Modern Epidemic." *Marina Times*, April 2016.

Federal Communications Commission. "In the Matter of Violent Television Programming and Its Impact on Children: Statement of Commissioner Deborah Taylor Tate," MB docket No. 04–261, April 25, 2007.

Ferguson, Chris. "Does Media Violence Predict Societal Violence? It Depends on What You Look At and When." *Journal of Communication* 65 (2014): e1–e22.

Fischer, Mary. "Manic Nation: Dr. Peter Whybrow Says We're Addicted to Stress." *Pacific Standard*, June 19, 2012.

Fleming, Amy. "Screen Time v Play Time: What Tech Leaders Won't Let Their Own Kids Do." *Guardian*, May 23, 2015.

Gallagher, Winifred. *New: Understanding Our Need for Novelty and Change* (New York: Penguin, 2011).

Gold, Joel, and Ian Gold. *Suspicious Minds: How Culture Shapes Madness* (New York: Free Press, 2014).

Goleman, Daniel. "Scientists Pinpoint Brain Irregularities In Drug Addicts." *New York Times*, June 26, 1990.

Gonçalves, B., N. Perra, and A. Vespignani. "Modeling Users' Activity on Twitter Networks: Validation of Dunbar's Number." *PLoS ONE* 6, no. 8 (2011): e22656.

Graham, Greg. "Cell Phones in Classrooms? No! Students Need to Pay Attention." *Mediashift*, September 21, 2011.

Greitemeyer, Tobias, and Neil McLatchie. "Denying Humanness to Others: A Newly Discovered Mechanism by Which Violent Video Games Increase Aggressive Behavior." *Psychological Science* 22, no. 5 (May 2011): 659–665.

Grunelius, Elisabeth, et al. "The Sensible Child." *Online Waldorf Library* 56 (Spring/ Summer 2009).

Haifeng Hou, Shaowe Jia, Shu Hu, Rong Fan, Wen Sun, Taotao Sun, and Hong Zhang. "Reduced Striatal Dopamine Transporters in People with Internet Addiction Disorder." *Journal of Biomedicine & Biotechnology* (2012): 854524.

Han, Doug Hyun, Sun Mi Kim, Sujin Bae, Perry F. Renshaw, and Jeffrey S. Anderson. "Brain Connectivity and Psychiatric Comorbidity in Adolescents with Internet Gaming Disorder." *Addiction Biology* (2015).

Han, Doug Hyun, Nicolas Bolo, Melissa A. Daniels, Lynn Arenella, In Kyoon Lyoo, and Perry F. Renshaw. "Brain Activity and Desire for Internet Video Game Play." *Comprehensive Psychiatry* 52, no. 1 (January 2011): 88–95.

Harkinson, Josh. "Scores of Scientists Raise Alarm about the Long Term Effects of Cell Phones." *Mother Jones*, May 11, 2015.

Herbert, Bob. "The Plot against Public Education: How Millionaires and Billionaires are Ruining Our Schools." *Politico*, October 6, 2014.

Hoffman, Hunter, et al. "Virtual Reality as an Adjunctive Non-Pharmacologic Analgesic for Acute Burn Pain during Medical Procedures." *Annals of Behavioral Medicine*, January 25, 2011.

Hollingdale, Jack, and Tobias Greitemeyer. "The Effect of Online Violent Video Games on Levels of Aggression." *PLoS ONE* 9, no. 11 (2014): e111790.

———. "The Changing Face of Aggression: The Effect of Personalized Avatars in a Violent Video Game on Levels of Aggressive Behavior." *Journal of Applied Social Psychology* 43, no. 9 (September 2013): 1862–1868.

Hong, Soon-Beom, Jae-Won Kim, Eun-Jung Choi, Ho-Hyun Kim, Jeong-Eun Suh, Chang-Dai Kim, Paul Klauser, et al. "Reduced Orbitofrontal Cortical Thickness in Male Adolescents with Internet Addiction." *Behavioral and Brain Functions* 9, no. 1 (2013): 11.

Hong, Soon-Beom, Andrew Zalesky, Luca Cocchi, Alex Fornito, Eun-Jung Choi, Ho-Hyun Kim, Jeong-Eun Suh, Chang-Dai Kim, Jae-Won Kim, and Soon-Hyung Yi. "Decreased Functional Brain Connectivity in Adolescents with Internet Addiction." *PLoS ONE* 8, no. 2 (February 25, 2013): e57831.

Hormes, Julia, Brianna Kearns, and C. Alix Timko. "Craving Facebook? Behavioral Addiction to Online Social Networking and Its Association with Emotional Regulation Deficits." *Addiction* 109, no. 12 (December 2014): 2079–2088.

"The Impact of Digital Technology on Learning: A Summary for the Education Endowment Foundation." Durham University, November 2012.

Indiana University School of Medicine. "Violent Video Games Alter Brain Function in Young Men." *ScienceDaily*, December 1, 2011.

Jabr, Ferris. "The Reading Brain in the Digital Age: The Science of Paper vs. Screens." *Scientific American*, April 11, 2013.

Jung, Carl. *The Collected Works of C.G. Jung* (Princeton, NJ: Princeton University Press, 1970), 598, 28.

Kang, Cecillia. "He Wants to Make It Playing Video Games on Twitch. But Will People Pay to Watch?" *Washington Post*, December 31, 2014.

Kelly, Samantha Murphy. "Is Too Much Texting Giving You 'Text Neck?'" *Mashable*, January 20, 2012.

Kim, Sang Hee, Sang-Hyun Baik, Chang Soo Park, Su Jin Kim, Sung Won Choi, and Sang Eun Kim. "Reduced Striatal Dopamine D2 Receptors in People with Internet Addiction." *Neuroreport* 22, no. 8 (June 11, 2011): 407–411.

Kipman, Alex. "A Futuristic Vision of the Age of Holograms." TED Talk, 19:05, Vancouver, February 2016.

Klass, Perry. "Fixated by Screens, but Seemingly Nothing Else." *New York Times*, May 9, 2011.

Kneissle, Michael. "Research into Changes in Brain Formation." Waldorf Library. http://www.waldorflibrary.org/images/stories/Journal_Articles/RB2206.pdf.

Ko, Chih-Hung, Gin-Chung Liu, Sigmund Hsiao, Ju-Yu Yen, Ming-Jen Yang, Wei-Chen Lin, Cheng-Fang Yen, and Cheng-Sheng Chen. "Brain Activities Associated with Gaming Urge of Online Gaming Addiction." *Journal of Psychiatric Research* 43, no. 7 (April 2009): 739–747.

Koepp, M. J., et al. "Evidence for Striatal Dopamine Release during a Video Game." *Nature* 393, no. 6682 (May 21, 1998): 266–268.

Konnikova, Maria. "The Limits of Friendship." *New Yorker*, October 7, 2014.

Kühn, S., et al. "The Neural Basis of Video Gaming." *Translational Psychiatry* 1 (2011): e53.

Lang, Susan. "A Room with a View Helps Rural Children Deal with Stresses, Cornell Researchers Report." *Cornell Chronicle*, April 24, 2003.

Lenhart, Amanda, et al. "Teens, Video Games and Civics." *Pew Research Center: Internet, Science and Tech*, September 16, 2008.

Leutwyler, Kristin. "Tetris Dreams: How and When People See Pieces from the Computer Game in Their Sleep Tells of the Role Dreaming Plays in Learning." *Scientific American,* October 16, 2000.

Lin, Fuchun, Yan Zhou, Yasong Du, Lindi Qin, Zhimin Zhao, Jianrong Xu, and Hao Lei. "Abnormal White Matter Integrity in Adolescents with Internet Addiction Disorder: A Tract-Based Spatial Statistics Study." *PloS ONE* 7, no. 1 (2012): e30253.

Lister-Landman, Kelly M., et al. "The Role of Compulsive Texting in Adolescents' Academic Functioning." *Psychology of Popular Media Culture.* Advance online publication, October 5, 2015.

Louv, Richard. *Last Child in the Woods* (New York: Workman Publishing, 2005).

Lupica, Mike. "Morbid Find Suggests Murder-Obsessed Gunman Adam Lanza Plotted Newtown, Conn.'s Sandy Hook Massacre for Years." *New York Daily News,* March 25 2013.

Lysiak, Matthew. *Newtown: An American Tragedy* (New York: Gallery, 2013).

Mandell, Merriel. "Etiology of Addiction: Addiction as a Disorder of Attachment." 2011.

Mangen, Ann, et al. "Reading Linear Texts on Paper versus Computer Screen: Effects on Reading Comprehension." *International Journal of Educational Research* 58 (2013): 61–68.

Mechanic, Michael. "What Extreme Isolation Does to Your Mind." *Mother Jones,* October 18, 2012.

Mercogliano, Chris, and Kim Debus. "An Interview with Joseph Chilton Pearce." *Journal of Family Life* 5, no. 1 (1999).

Mitchell, David. "Nature Deficit Disorder." *Waldorf Library: Research Bulletin* 11, no. 2 (Spring 2006).

Mikulak, Marcia. *The Children of A Bambara Village,* 1991.

Mohammad, Mona, and Heyam Mohammad. "Computer Integration into the Early Childhood Curriculum." *Education* 133, no. 1 (Fall 2012).

Monke, Lowell. "Video Games: A Critical Analysis." *ENCOUNTER: Education for Meaning and Social Justice* 22, no. 3 (Autumn 2009): 1–13.

Nitzan, U., E. Shoshan, S. Lev-Ran, and S. Fennig. "Internet-Related Psychosis—A Sign of the Times." *Israeli Journal of Psychiatry and Related Sciences* 48, no. 3 (2011): 207–11.

Office of the Child Advocate, State of Connecticut. "Shooting at Sandy Hook Elementary School." Report of the Office of the Child Advocate, November 21, 2014.

Office of the State's Attorney Judicial District of Danbury. "Report of the State's Attorney for the Judicial District of Danbury on the Shootings at Sandy Hook Elementary School and 36 Yogananda Street, Newtown, Connecticut." December 14, 2012.

O'Toole, M. E. *The School Shooter: A Threat Assessment Perspective* (Quantico, VA: Federal Bureau of Investigation, U.S. Department of Justice; 2000).

Pederson, Tracy. "Hyper-Texting Associated with Health Risks for Teens." *PsychCentral,* October 6, 2015.

Postman, Neil. *Amusing Ourselves to Death* (New York: Penguin, 1985).

———. *The Disappearance of Childhood* (New York: Random House, 1982).

Ravitch, Diane. "New York Post Reveals another Part of the 'Bloomberg-Klein' Failure Factory Legacy." *Diane Ravitch's Blog: A Site to Discuss Better Education for All,* February 23, 2014.

Reardon, Marguerite. "WHO: Cell Phones May Cause Cancer." *C/NET,* May 31, 2011.

Rideout, Victoria J., Ulla G. Foehr, and Donald F. Roberts. "Generation M2: Media in the Lives of 8- to 18-Year Olds." Kaiser Family Foundation Study. 2010.

Rock, Margaret. "A Nation of Kids with Gadgets and ADHD." *Time*, July 12, 2013.

Rogers, Jason, Alex Usher and Edyta Kaznowska. *The State of e-Learning in Canadian Universities, 2011: If Students are Digital Natives, Why Don't They Like e-Learning?* (Toronto, ON: Higher Education Strategy Associates, 2011).

Rose, David. *Enchanted Objects* (New York: Scribner, 2015).

Rosin, Hanna. "The Overprotected Kid." *Atlantic Monthly,* April 2014.

Rotella, Carlo. "No Child Left Untableted." *New York Times,* September 12, 2013.

Rothstein, Richard. "Joel Klein's Misleading Autobiography." *American Prospect,* October 11, 2012.

Roy, Amy Krain, Vasco Lopes, and Rachel Klein. "Disruptive Mood Dysregulation Disorder: A New Diagnostic Approach to Chronic Irritability in Youth." *American Journal of Psychiatry* 171 (2014): 918–924.

Russell, Jason, "How Video Games Can Transform Education." *Washington Examiner,* April 30, 2015.

Sagliogou, Christina, and Tobias Greitemeyer. "Facebook's Emotional Consequences: Why Facebook Causes a Decrease in Mood and Why People Still Use It." *Computers in Human Behavior* 35 (June 2014): 359–363.

Segar, Mike. "U.S. Students Suffering from Internet Addiction: Study." *Reuters,* April 23, 2010.

Shaffer, Howard, et al. "Toward a Syndrome Model of Addiction: Multiple Expressions, Common Etiology." *Harvard Review of Psychiatry* 12 (2004): 367–374.

Skenazy, Lenore. *Free Range Kids: How to Raise Safe, Self-Reliant Children* (New York: Jossey-Bass, 2010).

Suler, John. "The Online Disinhibition Effect." *Cyber Psychology and Behavior* 7, no. 3 (2004).

Swartz, Holly, and Bruce Rollman. "Managing the Global Burden of Depression: Lessons from the Developing World." *World Psychiatry* 2, no. 3 (October 2003): 162–163.

Swing, Edward L., Douglas A. Gentile, Craig A. Anderson, and David A. Walsh. "Television and Video Game Exposure and the Development of Attention Problems." *Pediatrics,* published online July 5, 2010.

Takeuchi, H., et al. "Impact of Videogame Play on the Brain's Microstructural Properties: Cross-Sectional and Longitudinal Analyses." *Molecular Psychiatry,* advance online publication January 5, 2016.

Tindell, D., and R. Bohlander. "The Use and Abuse of Cell Phones and Text Messaging in the Classroom: A Survey of College Students." *College Teaching* 60 (2011): 1–9.

Twenge, Jean M. "Time Period and Birth Cohort Differences in Depressive Symptoms in the U.S., 1982–2013." *Social Indicators Research* 121, no. 2 (June 2014): 437–454.

Voss, Meagen. "More Screen Time Means More Attention Problems in Kids." NPR, July 7, 2010.

Wee, C-Y, Z. Zhao, P-T Yap, G. Wu, F. Shi, T. Price, et al. "Disrupted Brain Functional Network in Internet Addiction Disorder: A Resting-State Functional Magnetic Resonance Imaging Study." *PLoS ONE* 9, no. 9 (2014) : e107306.

Wang, Y., T. Hummer, W. Kronenberger, K. Mosier, V. Mathews. "One Week of Violent Video Game Play Alters Prefrontal Activity." Radiological Society of North America, Scientific Assembly and Annual Meeting, Chicago, Illinois, November 26–December 2, 2011.

Weng, Chuan-Bo, Ruo-Bing Qian, Xian-Ming Fu, Bin Lin, Xiao-Peng Han, Chao-Shi Niu, and Ye-Han Wang. "Gray Matter and White Matter Abnormalities in Online Game Addiction." *European Journal of Radiology* 82, no. 8 (August 2013): 1308–1312. doi:10.1016/j.ejrad.2013.01.031.

Whitelocks, Sadie. "Computer Games Leave Children With 'Dementia' Warns Top Neurologist." *Daily Mail,* October 14, 2011.

Whiting, Alex. "Tech Savvy Sex Traffickers Stay Ahead of Authorities as Lure Teens Online." *Reuters,* November 15, 2015.

Wilson, Edward O. *Biophilia* (Cambridge, MA: Harvard University Press, 1986).

Wilson, Michael. "The Legacy of Etan Patz: Wary Children Who Became Watchful Parents." *New York Times,* May 8, 2015.

Woellhaf, Lori. "Do Young Children Need Computers?" *Montessori Society.* http://www.montessorisociety.org.uk/article/do-young-children-need-computers.

Woolett, Katherine, and Eleanor Maguire. "Acquiring 'the Knowledge' of London's Layout Drives Structural Brain Changes." *Current Biology* 21, no. 24–2 (December 20, 2011): 2109–2114.

Yuan, Kai, Wei Qin, Guihong Wang, Fang Zeng, Liyan Zhao, Xuejuan Yang, Peng Liu, et al. "Microstructure Abnormalities in Adolescents with Internet Addiction Disorder." *PLoS ONE* 6, no. 6 (June 3, 2011): e20708.

Yuan, Kai, Chenwang Jin, Ping Cheng, Xuejuan Yang, Tao Dong, Yanzhi Bi, Lihong Xing, et al. "Amplitude of Low Frequency Fluctuation Abnormalities in Adolescents with Online Gaming Addiction." *PLoS ONE* 8, no. 11 (November 4, 2013): e78708.

Yuan, Kai, Ping Cheng, Tao Dong, Yanzhi Bi, Lihong Xing, Dahua Yu, Limei Zhao, et al. "Cortical Thickness Abnormalities in Late Adolescence with Online Gaming Addiction." *PLoS ONE* 8, no. 1 (January 9, 2013): e53055.

Zhou, Yan, Fu-Chun Lin, Ya-Song Du, Ling-di Qin, Zhi-Min Zhao, Jian-Rong Xu, and Hao Lei. "Gray Matter Abnormalities in Internet Addiction: A Voxel-Based Morphometry Study." *European Journal of Radiology* 79, no. 1 (July 2011): 92–95.

INDEX